To

Mike & Sta...

with Love

[signature]

[signature]

ITCHY FEET

An overland Journey From Covent Garden To Sri Lanka

- GARY MOBSBY -

FAR AFIELD BOOKS

ITCHY FEET
An Overland Journey From
Covent Garden To Colombo

Published by: FAR AFIELD BOOKS

Copyright © Gary Mobsby 2011

Printed and bound in the UK by CPI Antony Rowe, Chippenham.

Cover design and maps by Gary Mobsby and Tom Barnard

Cover photos by Gary Mobsby

All correspondence and comments to
'gary@farafieldtravel.co.uk'

This book is dedicated to my dad, Roy 'Cogger' Mobsby and, of course, to my dear sister Candice.

CONTENT

ACKNOWLEDGEMENTS

Yes, you may well have gathered by now that this book has been a long time coming! In fact it's the true story of my overland trip that ended up in Sri Lanka -though most of the time was spent in India- and which took place during the long winter of 82/83. It was originally drafted shortly after that time -painstakingly in longhand- twice, but left to gather dust for the best part of a generation. It was later rewritten and edited over three beautifully warm winters whilst sitting under a lemon tree in southern Spain.

My exceedingly grateful thanks have to go out to my dear long suffering wife for all her patience during this period; also for her hard work in originally typing all of this up, her re-readings, and for sharing with me all the arduous editing.
My thanks also have to go out to Liz Fels for her invaluable efforts at proof reading, authors: Richard I'Anson, Graeme Chesters, Paul Gordon and Stella Whitelaw for their literary support and to Jamie Home and Mike McCreery for their technical/computer support.

And lastly...my thanks to John Denner for his friendship and unwavering humour; who was forced to put up with my readings whilst being a captive audience. John suffered from multiple sclerosis and sadly passed away this very year...without ever hearing the end!

INTRODUCTION

"You're lucky I came back" I said, pouting like a small child; and she was you know. I'd made up my mind that I'd never ever return, but it's tough out there in the leafy wilds of Dragons Green; all too easy to get hopelessly lost.

You see, I'd left home after a disagreement with my mum and had hit the open road, striding out purposefully, fully equipped with wigwam, a dog called Poppins and a hastily wrapped cheese sandwich. A mile and a half later though and I was already having second thoughts. Was I really doing the right thing? Was this really it; the time to break free; to finally leave the comfort of home? But how would my mum manage without me? My mind was abuzz, in turmoil, filled with indecision. Yes, life can be traumatic when you're seven!

I suppose this was my very first lone adventure really. Hardly an epic journey I know, but a sign perhaps, of what was to come.

But where does this lust for adventure come from? Is it something within you or simply a desire brought about by outside influences? Is it natural; part of some dormant travel gene; awakened, triggered by gathered information, or a gradually acquired craving? Maybe in my case it comes from having a granddad who'd twice circumnavigated the globe in a wooden boat and who'd regaled us with accounts of his experiences…almost daily: tales of the very much expected!

This particular journey of mine though took place during the winter of 82/83. I'd left home a young man, with two weeks wages in my pocket and with the vague notion of trying to hitch-hike as far around the world as possible. It was my first time out of Europe and my mum, bless her, had organised a surprise party as a send-off, which only added to the anxiety I already felt. "Just how far would I get" I thought, "how long would I have to be away to avoid the inevitable ridicule from my friends? How could I face the laughter as I returned from Eastern Europe, Switzerland or, heaven forbid, Calais even?"

This is the story of that journey. It may have been originally written nearly a generation ago but it's as relevant today as it's always been. Many things change in life but life itself seldom does. How people act and how they interact with each other is not only consistent but, paradoxically, consistently unpredictable; a constant source of interest and amazement.

It may or may not be a particularly exciting or gripping account of a journey, it is, nevertheless, extremely honest; a quality, I've since discovered, all too rare within so called 'non-fiction' books. But why exaggerate, fib or lie; why gild the lily in what is already an extraordinarily weird and wonderful world.

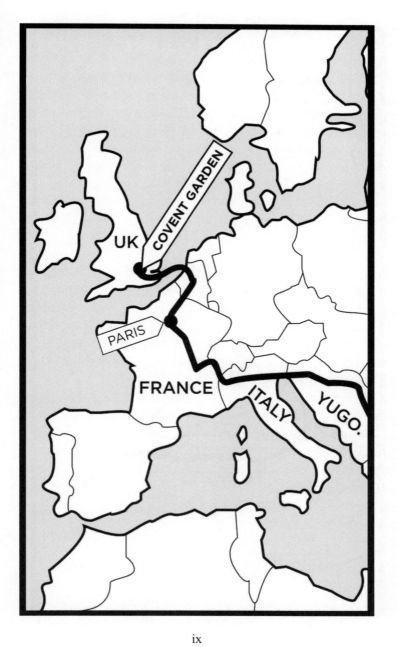

ISTANBUL

TURKEY

GR.

IRAN

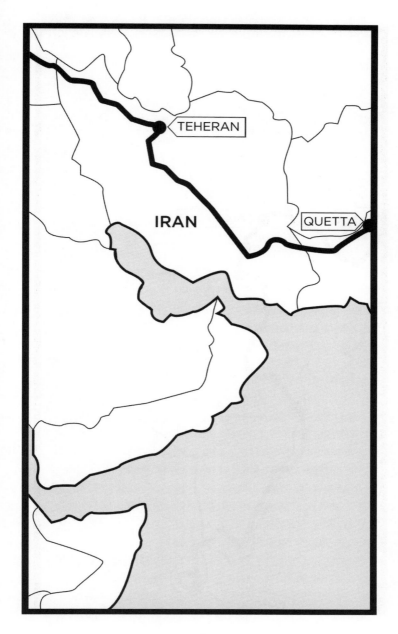

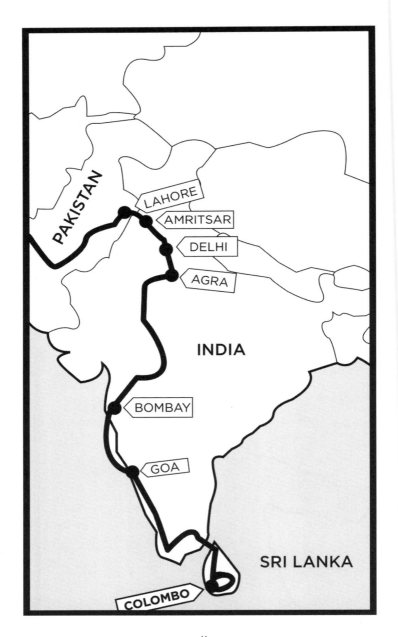

PAKISTAN

LAHORE

AMRITSAR

DELHI

AGRA

INDIA

BOMBAY

GOA

SRI LANKA

COLOMBO

CHAPTER 1

- STARTING OUT -

From London to the Sea

On reflection, perhaps tearing down the beach with a dolphin under my arm wasn't one of my better ideas, and especially when hotly pursued by thirty rather drunk and disgruntled fishermen. But then, you know, hindsight's a wonderful thing!

Not that this was my only regret of course. But you're bound to make the odd faux pas if you happen to be landed with that 'give it a go' adventurous type gene. Just a shame really, that on this particular adventure, common sense didn't prevail a little more often. But then, as a wise African once said to me, "One of the most uncommon things is common sense." And this surely applies to the young and naïve, let alone the young, naïve and, it has been said, slightly extrovert, like myself.

Still, nobody ever sat back in a squidgy armchair and looked back fondly remembering a mundane or average day, did they! Life's memories are made up of highs and lows so, I figured, why not go out and try to fill them with as many highs as possible. That said, this particular journey could hardly have started more inauspiciously...

Not altogether surprisingly it was another cold and drizzly November night when I found myself alone in the middle of Covent Garden market. The place looked rather sad and bleak at this time of night; a great swathe of tarmac and

1

concrete; rows of empty parking bays waiting to be filled; misty flood-lights peering through the drizzle awaiting the first trucks of the day.

I dumped my over-laden rucksack up against a dry wall, just beyond reach of the slanting rain, and wandered off in search of some form of life. Away from the protection of the loading bays the chill of the winter breeze flushed my cheeks and watered my eyes. I squinted through the darkness half stooped under the hood of a 'roll up and stick in your pocket' type Mac. Out here in the open the rain appeared to be gathering momentum. I looked back at the desolate looking buildings to see needle-like shafts of water darting obliquely through the beams of the lights before disappearing into the ground.

It may have seemed a rather depressing start to a journey but I knew that, before long, Covent Garden would magically spring to life again as trucks from the Continent would roll up from out of the darkness heavily laden with box loads of fruit and veg. You see I'd started journeys like this before, from the very same place and, despite the rain, couldn't help but feel a twinge of excitement at the prospect of setting out on another little adventure. Okay, so on previous occasions, my lifts from here were merely a prerequisite to a bit of 'bumming' around Western Europe but, perhaps somewhat perversely, this huge slab of concrete still seemed to me a bit like an old friend. In any case, this time round, I did hope to get rather further.

Thankfully I didn't have long to wait. Before I'd even squelched my second lap round the depot I spotted a couple of trucks parked up on the outskirts. They were over by the neat little stacks of used pallets, the two of them huddled up alongside one another, their drivers slumped over steering wheels in dimly lit cabs; tyres still steaming in the rain. A third truck slowly trundled in from somewhere behind me and hissed to a halt at the far end of the market. Then another appeared from behind the row of loading bays, then another and another and another. Quickly I tried to make out the trucks' origins as each passed beneath the light, hoping to spot something just a little foreign looking printed on the side, a possible destination perhaps; but it was still too dark to see anything properly.

Within an hour though, and still well before first light, little hunched Lowry figures started appearing from all over the place and before I knew it metal shutters were being rolled up all around me. Trucks started to jockey for position from every angle; porters were portering, unloaders were unloading and everywhere, men clanked and clonked trolleys and doors, whistling, singing and shouting as they went as if in some giant communal bathtub.

I darted around like a very damp and demented truck anorak, trying to get in close, eagerly eyeing the side of every truck that came into view. Liverpool, Birmingham, Cardiff...they were all there; Manchester, Bristol, Southampton; just incredible! There were lorries well...by the lorry load. They were all over the place: a jamboree of multi-sized, multi-shaped and multi-coloured vehicles representing every corner of the country. Amongst all this surely there must be just the odd one from over the water...mustn't there?

An hour passed and, by now, every trucker and his dog seemed to be here but not one name that sounded even remotely French. Two hours passed; still more trucks poured in; still the rain tinselled down all around and not so much as a sniff of 'un camion'. I stepped up the search, running this way and that, twizzling my head in every direction like an over-amorous owl; my clothes were getting wetter and wetter by the second, not from the deluge of rain but from the warm flood of condensation running down everywhere 'within' my rubberoid jacket and trousers. (Fat lot of good they are!)

I talked to porters who pointed, shrugged and frowned and just occasionally made encouraging noises, but still no blasted lift. By the time the third hour had passed my optimism was beginning to show signs of wear, quite simply because there were no 'signs of where' my lift out of here was going to come from! "Christ," I thought; "I could have bloody walked to France by now"!

Feeling a little dejected I trudged just one more lap of the lorry park and then, with a heavy sigh of resignation, hauled on my sodden pack -perhaps it wasn't up against such a dry wall after all- and then, a little ungratefully perhaps, accepted a lift all the way, or about three millimetres on my world map, to a café halfway down the M2

It was a great relief to be on the move at last but alas, it seemed my discarded waterproofs had barely the time to leave a small puddle on the rubber mat before I was donning them once again and being unceremoniously deposited on the roadside. Still, who was I to complain; after all I was hardly in a position to be picky. I jumped down from the warmth of the cab, tried my absolute bestest to look grateful and plunged straight into an ankle deep torrent. (I was sorely tempted at this point to say that it was raining cats and dogs and that I jumped down into a poodle but....I'll resist that one!) Anyway, as I waved goodbye, the lorry driver murmured something indecipherable and nodded towards the roadside café. Then, he checked I'd shut his door properly, graunched into gear and sped off into the distance, creating the wake and spray of a large but exceedingly blunt speedboat -my little puddle on his mat no doubt a welcome souvenir for his trouble. I turned and ran through what was now a torrential downpour, off toward the lonely café and hurled myself through the door for a well earned mug of motorway tea.

The place was pretty quiet when I arrived. It was still early morning; that lull; that rare time of the empty hours somewhere between nightclub kick-out and sadistic cockerel. I sat alone cradling my mug, nose squashed up against the café window, peering out into the damp and darkness, wondering where my next lift was going to come from. It was already clear that my new walking boots were indeed waterproof, as promised, because there didn't appear to be so much as a single drop escaping from within them. This as a result of running around Covent Garden and their being nicely filled to the brim by the run-off from my equally waterproof but woefully short trousers. Consequently, whilst sitting in the café dripping rhythmically from the ankle up, the bit of floor just under the table remained surprisingly dry; or dry that is until I wrung my socks out. Well, it was that sort of place.

Over the next few hours I seemed to do an awful lot of mug cradling. Occasionally my hopes would be raised as a darts-player sized lorry driver would waddle in with his Sun newspaper for a small trough of bacon and eggs; but then, they would be quickly dashed again as each in turn would reply to my pleas for a lift with a variety of negative grunts - usually something about going on to

Covent Garden.

Yet three more hours drifted by before, with light fast approaching, at long last I was once again back on the road, courtesy of a middle-aged French couple returning from their annual holidays in England.

"Lovely weather for the time of year," I said pitifully.

Two rather round, Gallic faces turned in unison and smiled sympathetically. A short while later though and the rain had at last stopped. We pulled up at the port of Dover; I uncorked my bulging rucksack from the boot, thanked the couple for their generosity and made my way past the growing columns of cars, vans and lorries toward the dock.

I had, by this time, grown rather weary from what little progress I'd made on the journey thus far and so, after receiving just one too many rebukes from a lengthy queue of rather restless and tetchy drivers waiting to board the ferry, I decided to bite the bullet and actually pay for a ticket to cross the Channel to Calais.

NB. On previous occasions I'd managed to cross over for free, riding in a cab as a second driver. Apparently, for truckers of the time, a cross-channel ticket would allow for both a vehicle and two drivers, and as there was almost invariably just the one driver, this left an opening for a lucky hitchhiker-cum-second driver. Though sadly, I fear this is no longer the case because, as with most things in the modern world, this too has been tied up in the never-ending straggly string of bureaucratic knots and insurance restrictions.

By now it was a rather more civilised time of the morning and so I decided to give my Mum a call.

"Hello darling," she said in a 'just got out of bed' sort of voice, "How are you getting on?"

"Oh fine," I said, "good line isn't it!"

"Yes very," she replied full of surprise, "Where are you?"

"Oh umm, just west of Geneva...Dover actually!" I gave her a brief synopsis of my progress so far and assured her that I was still in high spirits and just as determined as ever to reach my goal. Though in truth my spirits were severely diluted by the lack of sleep and, as for a goal well, I'd never really had one in the first place...other than trying to get as far from home as possible. Still, it was nice to speak to her all the same. We had a quick chat about next to nothing, said our goodbyes and I promised to write just as soon as I had enough news to warrant a letter. Then off I trotted to board the next ferry heading east to Calais.

On reaching one of the many lounging areas around the boat I settled into a quiet corner and promptly...lounged, one limb always in contact with my rucksack. I then, even more promptly, fell into a deep, deep sleep.

It was a good hour later when a raucous shout from somewhere in the distance rocked me from my short but well-earned slumber; and as I gazed around decidedly piggy-eyed, it occurred to me that the boat didn't seem terribly busy. I thought little of this really but then, as I peered through the nearby window, I became absolutely horrified -I kid you not- to see that the boat, the very boat in which I sat, was being hotly pursued by a humongous two hundred foot high tidal wave! Why, it was immense and bearing down on us not a gnat's whisker away. "Jesus Christ" I thought, "What the...!" I was immediately jolted into the full consciousness of panic; It was terrifying, absolutely terrifying!…Well, terrifying that is for a full three seconds before I spotted the give-away green trim on top of the wave and realised that we hadn't actually left the white cliffs of Dover yet. Well…how was I to know! I slouched off down the corridor of the totally deserted lounge area feeling more than a little stupid and eventually managed to find somebody in uniform.

"Excuse me, but do you know what's going on here?"

"Yeah mate" said the uniform, "there's some sort of strike over there," he gestured vaguely in the direction of France, "we're not goin' now!"

"Was somebody trying to tell me something" I thought; was I never meant to leave these shores? I heaved on my bundle again and trooped the eighty metres or so back to England, hiking boots gaily swinging to and fro from their moorings on top of the rucksack. (At rest I'd decided to slip into something both a little more comfortable and a lot drier, namely, the only other footwear I possessed: a pair of £4.50 black canvas bumper boots.)

Back on terra firma again, the very same people seemed to be sitting in the very same queues. I didn't much care now where I was going just as long as I got back on a boat again; any boat in fact, provided it was actually going somewhere. And so I simply followed a small crowd along the dock under the shadow of the great Dover tidal wave and sleepwalked onto the first ferry I came to. One that, as it turned out, was bound for Zeebrugge in Belgium.

CHAPTER 2

-DRUNKEN PARISIANS AND MAD GREEKS-

Belgium to Istanbul

As exhausted as I was, it was simply impossible to sleep through the revelries of the stag party from Manchester; but, at the same time, I'd neither the energy nor the inclination to move from my spot. Eventually though, after what seemed an interminably long four and a half hours at sea, the ferry did pull into Zeebrugge harbour where the drunken Mancunian horde staggered off in a happy alcoholic haze to disturb somebody else's sleep.

In Belgium the sky was as equally a dull grey as the one I'd just left and every passenger, as is the norm, clambered around the doorway as if Harrods had just announced a 'ninety percent off everything', closing down sale. You know I can never quite fathom why such a large proportion of the human race seem so determined to swarm together and jostle each other forward, barely an inch at a time, to arrive at a destination ten minutes ahead of those of us who nonchalantly lie back and wait for the crowd to disperse. It really beats me!

Anyway, I digress; having at last set foot onto continental Europe, there was yet another four hour wait in Belgium before I found myself being whisked off down the motorway by a local truck bound for 'gay Paris' and the hitching hub of Europe…Garanor.

9

Now Garanor is probably not a place familiar to those possessing a vehicle with anything less than a dozen wheels, but happens to be one of several absolutely gi-normous lorry parks dotted around the outskirts of Paris and must surely be, to my mind, one of the very best places in the world to cadge a lift to well…just about anywhere. The strange thing is that in all the times I've found myself there -three actually- I've rarely spotted as much as another single hitchhiker. Somewhat surprising, as in my view, wandering around casually looking for your chosen destination on a cab door is infinitely more preferable to standing on a roadside, thumb erect, in God knows where waiting for God knows what!

It was 1.30 the next morning by the time I walked into Garanor. I looked around bleary-eyed at the vast arena of concrete; a never ending chicken-wire type fence separated the depot from the motorway and its perpetual traffic. I was far enough away here for the roar of vehicles to merge into the background, but still the thin night air was filled with a constant hum and every bare surface around reverberated with the bass tones of passing trucks. I headed over toward one of the few small lights that dimly lit the corners of this place. It was still far too early for any activity now and so I found a 'cosy' concrete step on which to see out the rest of the night. Then, I pulled out and unfurled my trusty sleeping bag and settled down to make myself as comfortable as possible to await the bewitching hour of 8am when all around would explode into action.

It was pretty hopeless trying to sleep of course; Paris was in the grips of winter, the temperature barely above

10

freezing and I could never quite mould my body to suit the concrete steps. Consequently, I lay there frustratingly awake all night fidgeting and shuffling about in my sleeping bag like an oversized pupae with scabies; hour after hour gormlessly counting spots of dirt on the concrete wall; watching my breath freeze into the air and wondering what on earth went through the minds of all those Kamikaze moths as yet another one would head-butt the light bulb with a sharp 'ting' and bounce off only to return again and again for another go. Clearly I was desperate for distraction, any sort of entertainment, and it wouldn't have been quite so bad had it been a one night only performance but well, sadly, some two and a half days later, that very same concrete step was still my bedroom; not somewhere I'd be quick to recommend, I might add. ("Umm...what shall I have from the mini-bar? I know, a nice glug of ice cold water from that army type water bottle; and the film tonight?...Blow me if it isn't 'Return of the Kamikaze Moths' again!")

Now, to spend nearly three days in a lorry park may, to some, seem somewhat masochistic, but there were moments during this time when I could have accepted many a lift to places all over Europe. Unfortunately, most trucks were either not heading my way or not heading far enough my way. I realise that this may sound a little greedy or over-optimistic perhaps but I knew darned well that it was only a matter of timing -and perhaps, a smidgen of luck- before the right lift would come along. And there were indeed numerous glimmers of hope. For example, the one very memorable evening spent downing large vodkas with a small gaggle of Russians, none of whom spoke a word of English but, at the time, it just didn't really seem to matter. The entertainment for this particular evening came in the form of a tall, thin, wavy-haired Frenchman who, completely and utterly Smirnoffed, had proceeded to dance the whole night away amongst the cabs accompanied by the incomprehensible, crackly local radio station emanating from the bowels of his vehicle. Apparently the Frenchman's mother was Russian and this seemed reason enough for him to lighten the rather sombre Russian drivers of most of their vodka. Not that they minded; quite the reverse. In fact these quiet and reserved men were clearly being entertained as much by the mad Frenchman as I was. That is to say, until his particular blend of Franco-Russian had slurred passed the point of comprehension -though personally I never understood a word of it in the first place- and his back-slapping and hugging became just that bit too amorous for the Russians' liking and they all retired to their cabs for the night. Thankfully though, this had signalled a natural end to the evening as, even after a few vodkas, I too wasn't quite up to a smooch with a half-paralytic Frenchman. So, noticing he'd lost his party mates, he soon snaked off to his cab and I back to my concrete step. Still, it had been an interesting 'cultural' night out!

Then, of course, there was the other memorable evening in the company of a gang of Greeks awaiting return loads from somewhere in Northern Europe back to Athens. They'd happily agreed to take me with them but, only on the understanding that we wouldn't be leaving Paris until the call came through regarding their return loads. In the meantime, of course, we all did our fair share of chatting, oh, and eh...drinking; and by late evening I ended up sprawled fast asleep in the back of a Greek cab. (No I wasn't paying for my passage; many cabs do, in fact, come with twin bunks!) Now, this was a splendid result on two counts; firstly, it meant that if that all important call came through during the night, I wasn't going to miss my lift to Greece but, perhaps even more importantly at that particular moment, it meant that I'd be able to have just one heavenly night without the constant pinging of Kamikaze moths in my ears and my spine being tri-sected by a concrete stairway.

Well, as things transpired, the night wasn't quite as heavenly as hoped for. True, the bunk was comfortable enough but sometime during the early hours of morning, my peace was totally shattered; I was awoken by a sudden jolt and found myself being thrown rapidly and violently about my bed; it was unbelievable! Here I was just enjoying my first night of real comfort on the trip and now I found myself being bumped, banged and tossed around like a lost slipper in a washing machine. I grappled to right myself and on peering between the front seats soon realised what had happened; these lunatic Greeks had unhitched their trailers and were racing each other around and around the centre of Paris. And every time our cab would overtake one of his mates, my cheery and stubbly-faced driver would give a great blast on his horn and throw back his head in uncontrollable laughter. It was total madness, but what could I do! I lay back down and put my head beneath the pillow, not so much to deaden the loud and raucous laughter but to at least give myself a little protection as I was pin-balled around between the front seat and back of the cab. Christ, what a night. Just when I thought I was in for a bit of 'R.and R.'! Yes, don't get me wrong, I was glad of the company and the chance of a lift alright but somehow, well, it felt like I'd been offered a

13

bag of sweets and then been clobbered round the head with a cricket bat for taking one!

Amongst all this though, somehow and somewhere along the line, I must have actually dropped off -or perhaps was knocked unconscious- who knows. In any case, the next thing I know I was waking up back at Garanor with Zorba snoring away like a blissfully contented warthog just three feet above me.

Later that morning the all important call came; the one that I'd been waiting for. Yes, hurrah! There was to be a return load from Paris to Athens…in three days' time. I left Zorba and his crazy cronies to it and went to try my luck elsewhere.

That afternoon, feeling a little sorry for myself, I decided to take a break from the lorry park and head into Paris to look up an old friend called Samuel who lived near the Bastille. I'd met him a couple of years previously when he'd kindly agreed to take my girlfriend and I with him from the south of France up to Paris. Now, Samuel was a kind man but of such comical appearance that it was hard not to smile. He stood barely five feet tall, had a great shiny dome of a head, little curranty dark eyes and an absolute beaute of a hooked nose that, when coupled with the round National Health type specs that perched upon it, looked remarkably like he'd been the inspiration for the false nose and glasses sets that you might find in a joke shop.

Anyway, Samuel was on his way back from his annual naturist holiday on the Med -though goodness knows what he'd have looked like starkers- and had pulled up in his full to the gunnels 2CV, next to some fellow hitchers at the entrance to the motorway at Avignon. My girlfriend and I had arrived there a little late in the morning to find that several couples had beaten us to the prime spot and so, of course, as hitching protocol dictates, we were obliged to move on down the line a little. Well, when this little Citroen pulled up, I could see from my position down the road that a great deal of gesticulating was going on between a bespectacled gnome in a 2CV and the couple on the roadside and I gleaned, from all the arm waving, that the driver simply didn't have the space for two extra people. So, the next thing I know, he'd shut the door and was speeding off up the road and gathering pace past the queue of hitchers towards us. Well, even pre-lorry park days I really didn't relish the idea of roadside hitching so, before you could say 'L'Escargot', I was off after him and banging on his window. Do you know, it took quite a few minutes to convince Samuel that, in fact, he did actually have enough room for two passengers and that, moreover, my girlfriend would be, "Only too pleased to ride all the way to Paris on top of his luggage". (This isn't something I'm at all proud of and I'm sure there was a very good reason why I didn't do the gentlemanly thing but well, it escapes me right now!)

Anyway, the long and short of it was that we got our lift and took off up the motorway leaving a lot of young studenty furrowed brows and open-mouths behind us. Then, we proceeded to drive all the way to the capital through perpetual and torrential rain with not so much as a single cat's-eye to guide the way. (Apparently, the French are pretty hot on nuclear physics but not quite so hot on putting little glass balls in tarmac...possibly due to the fact that the idea came from an Englishman perhaps!) Then, to cap it all, at journey's end, my girlfriend and I ended up being extremely grateful guests at Samuel's very own flat in Paris.

He'd been such a kind and friendly man, old Samuel; but you know whatever else, my over-riding memory will forever be of this bald Frenchman hunched over a steering wheel, squinting through the rain, hour after hour with that generously proportioned hooter squashed to the screen.

Anyway, meanwhile back in the present…I spent a nice evening full of reminiscences with Samuel. We chatted happily over a bottle of wine at a local restaurant and so, in the morning, I felt sufficiently refreshed to tackle Garanor again.

When I arrived, the place was as busy as ever with all its comings and goings but, as exciting as this may have been, right now all I wanted was just one lift; one preferably that was going to take me all the way to Turkey perhaps or even beyond. This wasn't simply a wild, fanciful dream. You see, I'd learnt that occasionally, just occasionally, trucks go from here to as far away as Iran or even to Pakistan. It was all down to timing; I just desperately needed that little slice of luck.

Well, in the end, sad to say, my lift to Asia never did materialise. Having endured a whole three days at Garanor truck park, having laughed and drunk vodka with Russians, raced around Paris with Greek nutters and chewed the cud for hours with numerous other nationalities, I happily accepted a lift with a Frenchman all the way to …well, just east of Lyon.

This may seem rather pathetic after all the possible alternatives but, as things turned out, it could hardly have been a better move; for this one short hop was to lead to far greater things. The moment I climbed aboard the shiny new cab I was enthusiastically greeted by Martin, the driver. Now Martin was an extraordinarily cheery Frenchman in his early thirties who wore jeans, open necked shirt -complete with Bee-Gee style gold medallion- ultra cool shades and a marvellously infectious grin. He was so instantly likeable and thankfully spoke very passable English -which was just as well for me as my grasp of French was very much of the school boy variety. Martin seemed to have an enviable existence, spending all his winters up in the French Alps as a ski instructor and the summers running all over the country in his little lorry, radio blaring and keeping in constant touch with all around him via his CB radio. (For those not in the know, CB -or Citizen Band- radio was a big thing at this time in the Western world and was used for tuning in to any other personal radio user who cared to air his or her views in public, or just for generally spending an awful lot of time talking about next to nothing...rather in the way that e-mail is used today!)

Anyway, as we trundled south down the motorway to Mâcon and turned off eastwards towards Geneva, for the first time I felt that I was really making progress, at long last truly on my way. Martin was a great companion and sang to himself almost constantly, every so often gabbling away in French over his personal radio, trying to arrange my next onward lift for me. Time passed quickly in this jovial atmosphere and, shortly before dusk, we'd already reached the Alps and then slowly began our ascent into the mountains. Then, as darkness fell, so we began to climb higher and higher; and the higher we went so more and more snow covered the ground all around us. French accordion music wafted from the radio filling the cab and we started swaying to and fro round ever tightening hair pin bends, snaking this way and that, climbing and climbing. I smiled to myself; everything seemed perfect, just perfect.

Much later, somewhere up amongst the mountain tops, we neared a small log café. Martin turned to me and, with a beam that stretched from sideburn to sideburn said,
"Okay, you wait 'ere; Italy driver comes 'ere in one hour and 'ee weel tek you to Mont Blanc. From zere, zometime tomorrow, weel come a Frrrench convoy goin' to Iraq".
It all sounded too good to be true; could it really be so easy! We slowed to a halt and, as the airbrakes let out a hiss of relief, I stepped down into the roadside sludge, thanked Martin profusely, said my fond farewells and hurried over to the café.

It was the early hours of the morning by now and the café was deserted save for a lone figure behind the counter. I ordered an extremely welcome cup of coffee and, after a quick chat with the quiet and mellow café owner, sat at a little round pine table with one eye on the falling snow outside and the other on the small wooden clock that 'tocked' by above the counter. (Rather like a far grander clock in a Gentleman's club in London perhaps, there was a noticeable absence of ticks!) There was absolutely no other sound in the room; just the pretentiously sedate clock on the wall and the shrill whistle of wind around the windows.

I sat alone in the café caressing my cup and catching up on the diary. Then I sat back in my chair and gazed up at the ceiling chewing a biro, gently mulling over the past few days. In seemingly no time at all I noticed that across the room the little clock had just tocked by a full one hour. I peered outside again half expectantly, but could see nothing. But, just then, just when I'd returned to my diary, the door to the café flew open. The wind howled through the opening and a squat bearded figure bundled in, encased in an old oversized lumberjack-type jacket and turned up trousers. He fought to close the door but before he had the chance, a great waft of snowflakes whistled in behind him, each and every flake swooping around the door edge, fighting to fill the turn-ups of his trousers. He clunked the door shut and peace was magically restored.

By now the café owner had disappeared around the back somewhere and, as I was his only customer, when the newcomer gazed around the room it was easy to catch his eye.

"Erm, are you going to Italy?" I said hopefully.

He nodded, releasing a forelock of frozen dandruff which spiralled to the floor. Then he allowed himself the subtlest of smiles before turning and, without a single word, heading back to the door. I quickly gathered my things together, got back into my damp water-but-not-condensation-proof jacket, and chased after him, rucksack slung from one shoulder.

I followed him to his waiting truck, piled in through the cab door, flung my bag over the back and we set off together to drive the comparatively short distance through the snowy night and then right on through to the other side of the Mont Blanc tunnel. En route I made several attempts at communicating with my new travel mate in both English and schoolboy French, but he either didn't understand a word I was jabbering on about in either language or he was simply quite content to trundle along in his own little world; music-less, CB-less and totally speechless. All the same, I was glad to be with him.

By the time we'd roared the seven odd miles through the Mont Blanc tunnel and pulled up at the Italian customs post, dawn was already breaking through, mistily and mysteriously filling the valley deep below. I stepped down from yet another cab, waved off my chatty truck mate and took my first big gulp of fresh Italian mountain air. Behind me the sun climbed quickly through the surrounding peaks burning off the early morning haze and, before long, I was surrounded by impossibly white, snowy-cloaked mountains jutting up into a clear blue sky. I looked down into the evermore greening valley far below me then closed my eyes for a moment, absorbing the heavenly quiet and the tingling sensation given by the sun's first rays. I stood there for a while in contemplation, oozing utter contentment, bathed in warmth and freshness. "How lucky we are," I thought, "how lucky that something so wonderful, so precious, can cost us nothing, absolutely nothing."

The early morning drifted lazily by as I sat in the café up above the customs station. It was the perfect place to keep an eye on the cars and lorries as they came and went, each pausing briefly at the barrier before being waved on down the valley. Just then though, lo and behold, exactly as Martin -the CB radio junkie- had promised, two identical French trucks pulled up at the barrier. I quickly downed my coffee and sped down the stairway and out across the snow to the first truck. Then, I peered up through a misty window to see the outline of a small straggly-haired young Frenchman busily shuffling through an assortment of papers. When eventually I tapped on the cab door, a pale piggy eyed face that looked like it had just been driven non-stop for twenty-four hours looked down at me through the opened window.

"Oui", it said.

"Eh...are you to going to Iraq?"

"Oui", it said again.

"Um....can I come with you"? I asked, in extremely broken French (my French might have been 'merde' but I gesticulated quite fluently.)

"No problem", came the reply.

So that was it; within half an hour, papers in order, me and Jacques Le Grand, the distant relation -he assured me- of the ever-so-slightly famous pianist Michael Le Grand, were off.

Down the valley we snaked on the start of what was to prove not only an unexpectedly long and interesting journey but an equally interesting relationship: me practising my schoolboy French and Jacques practising his nodding, smiling and replying, "No problem". (As things turned out these were the only two words of English he knew...which, to someone wanting a lift, could actually be a lot worse!)

But, do you know, for all the communication problems we got along quite famously, me and Jacques; and indeed he turned out to be an excellent host. In fact we hadn't wound our way more than three miles down into the valley before pulling into the first available parking place. Then, before you could say Fanny Craddock, Jacques had whipped out his little primus and two large slabs of fillet steak and four eggs were sizzling away in a pan between the front seats. Then, as if it were the most natural thing in the world, from somewhere amongst the tangle of bedding of his top bunk, a bottle of red wine was produced and we were tucking into a truly sumptuous meal on a couple of camping chairs beside the truck. Well, this wasn't quite what I'd come to expect from life on the road, but I was forced to admit that when it came to roughing it, old Jacques certainly knew a thing or two. Also, as things turned out, this gourmet treat was not only very much appreciated but was to be the first of many. The fact is, for Jacques and his pals in the other lorries, there simply didn't seem to be any rush to get anywhere at any time, and so this one lift, for me, ended up a full six day epic, all the way from the French border to Istanbul.

Now naturally, on such a journey, there were the odd bouts of boredom, particularly when Jacques only had the two words of English, 'no' and 'problem', but even so, this would turn out to be pretty much a hitch without a hitch. Actually, having said that, I confess that long evenings spent with a whole herd of non-English speaking French truckers can be extremely lonely. The trouble is that several of them would meet up every night and indulge in a banquet lasting from around six in the evening until getting on for midnight, which was all very fine for them but, as I hardly understood a word that was being said, I often longed for the evenings to pass quickly so that I could retire to my bunk again, then wake up in the morning and get back on the road; a road of ever changing scenery as we ploughed on first through Italy then Yugoslavia and then Greece.

By the way, another thing about being part of a French convoy: it wasn't only occasionally a tad lonely but also proved to be a rather costly experience. For though Jacques cooked up some fabulous meals by day, I found it well nigh impossible not to join in with the extraordinary amount of eating and drinking that went on in the restaurants every evening when the French truckers got together. Still, I guess that was my problem; the inevitable price to pay for a temporarily weakened will!

The long, long days of travelling between France and Istanbul, though interesting to experience, hardly warrant talking about here as ninety percent of the time they were spent either in a cab, on a bunk...or at a restaurant table. Nevertheless, I enjoyed most of the journey most of the time, and passed with great interest all manner of sights and sites from traditional Italian boat-builders and Yugoslav farmers caught in a Bronze Age time warp, to small but stately Greek funeral processions in busy streets. Interesting, certainly, but on this occasion alas, that's all I did...pass them.

Jacques' truck was one of several at this time supplying machinery to Iraq and Saudi Arabia and, as such, I could easily have joined Jacques and his mates all the way to Baghdad. However, as Iran and Iraq were currently at war with one another and I already had an Iranian visa stamped in my passport, it seemed prudent to call it a day once we'd arrived in Istanbul. (Thankfully I'd had the forethought to get an Iranian visa in London before I left, that being the only one I needed anywhere between Horsham and Delhi; this, just in case I should ever get that far!)

NB. With the aid of an interpreter I was informed by more than one French trucker that, at this time, I could just as easily have been part of a French convoy supplying arms to both the Iranian and Iraqi war efforts...such are the morals of politicians and businessmen; but thankfully, seldom those of us ordinary folk.

CHAPTER 3

-WEST SIDE STORY AND OTHER TURKISH DELIGHTS -

In Istanbul

It was late evening when we pulled into the lorry park just above Istanbul and I felt a strange mixture of sadness and relief as I bade farewell to Jacques and walked down the hill into the city. As I walked along I reflected on the past couple of weeks and then smiled to myself remembering my hesitant thoughts about embarking on the whole thing back in England.

I'd now reached perhaps my first major goal on the trip, but far from having thoughts of returning now had only one thing on my mind; to continue eastward; to forge on right across my freshly opened Bartholomew's map of Central Asia. I was now in unchartered territory, the realm of the independent traveller. My quest, to boldly go where no 'wet behind the ears' inter-railer had gone before.

That evening, on the night of my arrival in the big city, my intention had been to simply find a quiet and non-moving bed for the night and move off first thing in the morning, but...things were about to change. You see, nothing had quite prepared me for the pull of chaotic and exotic Istanbul.

After a short walk through the streets it wasn't long before I discovered a hostel right next to the Aya Sofia mosque. Then, I checked in and, eager to get my money's worth, promptly fell asleep in my dorm bed totally oblivious to the cacophony of snoring and farting around me. It was gone 8am when I woke, and as soon as I felt halfway coherent, the usual ritual of introductions and exchanges of travel tips was observed with my new found room mates.

The dorm was surprisingly small by hostelling standards, containing just four beds; nevertheless there was still a variety of characters from a variety of places. These were -apart from myself of course- a goldy-locked Pete Townsend look-a-like student from Berlin, a lanky guitar-strumming American high school graduate, and Mark, a rather chunky Canadian real estate speculator, who at twenty eight was very much the father figure amongst us. Well, barely an hour had passed by before the four of us had struck up quite a friendship and we soon realized that we all shared something other than a passion for travel, namely, a remarkably similar and slightly warped sense of humour; that is, of course, apart from the American, who would wear the same blank expression for a full five seconds after every joke was told before bursting into raptures of manufactured laughter.

We were a happy bunch though and it felt so good, not only to be amongst like minded souls, but to be able to converse in my own native language again. (After six days with Jacques and his mates you'd have thought my French would've come on in leaps and bounds. Sadly it remained very much broken French - broken that is, in that it didn't work anymore!) But, not only was it great to be amongst English speakers again, I also found Istanbul to be so wonderful, so exotic, that it was an extremely hard place to leave. Consequently, I was stopped in my tracks for a full week. Hardly moving in I know, but a significant stop nonetheless.

Of the days there, well, most of them I spent alone, excitedly exploring the nooks and crannies of my new surroundings. But virtually all of the nights were spent in the same way...reunited with my new gang of dorm-dwellers, sampling far too much Turkish beer and then roaming the streets at night singing our very own rendition of 'West Side Story'. This, I enjoyed immensely, though unfortunately, the bar loads of domino slamming, coffee swilling Turks we came across didn't always appear to share our enthusiasm for Bernstein's work, or not our particular version of it anyway. Still there's no accounting for taste is there.

NB. Just a note on Turkey for even greener and younger explorers than myself: No! The Midnight Express experience doesn't befall every young Westerner venturing east of the Bosphorus; and though the film did for Turkish tourism what Adolf did for world peace, I found very little to dislike about Turkey.   In fact I feel forced to agree with that worn down to the bone cliché that Turkey really is 'where East meets West'. Not only geographically which, of course, it is; but culturally, religiously -Islam for beginners- and cuisine-ingly; where good cheap beer and fast food rub shoulders with all manner of rich, sticky cakes and a host of unidentifiable exotic dishes.

Now, I realise of course, that this one brief visit to the city hardly qualifies me to comment but, I found most of the people whom I met in Istanbul to be both reasonably content with their lot and remarkably charming -though, it must be said, I much prefer to judge individuals on their own merits and not by the countries from which they come. I fear it's far too easy to generalise about human characteristics somehow relating to their particular country of origin. This isn't a sermon by the way and I'm sure that in the past I've also been guilty of gross generalisation at times but, incidentally, while we're on the subject...No! The Second World War wasn't started by 'The Germans', but rather by a handful of nutters -led by one almighty nutter- who just happened to come from that part of the world! Of course, common sense -that all too often uncommon trait of the human psyche- should tell us that the majority of people are generally good and therefore against such vastly radical ideas. And this, of course, would apply to the people of Germany as well as the rest of the world's populous. Sadly though, this is seldom appreciated and when tribalism raises its ugly head, far too many of our species seem to become devoid of sense...common or otherwise!

You know, there was just so much to do and see in Istanbul; from marvelling at all the multi-minaretted mosques and exploring bustling back streets to aimlessly wandering the 'stuffed to the gunnels' bizarre bazaars. At the weekend, men and boys pondered over chess games in every square and shady corner, and everywhere exotic smells wafted from a thousand food stalls.

For light relief from the hustle and bustle of the busy city, one of the more pleasant ways to spend a day was to walk down to the river and board a boat for a leisurely trip down the Bosphorus, gently 'putt-putting' along the shoreline and gazing back at Istanbul from a whole new and calming perspective. Then perhaps the boat would pull in and I'd hop off and visit one of the many vendors down by the waterside, and sit in the shade with a cool beer and a fish sandwich; the fish so fresh that it can hardly have been hooked before hitting the grill and being slapped between two halves of heavily buttered French baguette. Hot, fresh, simple and...absolute heaven!

As a place to stay, the Aya Sofya Hostel turned out to be a great find. Being so centrally located it was obviously a little on the noisy side but, as luck would have it, was run by a handful of Turkish students who were not only good English speakers, but all of whom I found to be totally trustworthy; the latter, being no small a consideration in a major city like this, unless you happen to have masochistic tendencies and enjoy sightseeing everyday with your worldly possessions on your back.

It was tough leaving the hostel and Istanbul, but after a week I felt it was time to move on again. It was to be the end of the short but close acquaintance between myself and my three new found friends, but one which would leave me with happy and juvenile memories.

Before long we were all going our separate ways; the German was flying back to Berlin; the American, bussing down to Southern Turkey before flying off home somewhere in the States, and Mark, the Canadian, said he had to get back to his real estate job in Canada. It was sad to see them all go having forged such close friendships in such a short time, but then...travel is like that isn't it; it provides the same highs and lows that you experience in normal everyday life but, with such amazing intensity.

So, one by one during that day, I gradually saw them all off on their respective ways and the following morning found myself sitting in a café, alone once again, but happily soaking up the local atmosphere over a cup of Turkish coffee.

Now the taste of Turkish coffee could, I suppose, best be described as 'acquired', which I, for one…certainly haven't. However, as with most things, I felt compelled to try it -indeed several times- in the belief that so many people just can't be wrong; for, well, how can I describe it, it's erm?…sort of reminiscent perhaps -though I have no personal experience of this- of drinking a very small cup of warm and powdery tar. Not that I'm necessarily a connoisseur in these sort of things, I guess it just so happens that it isn't my um…cup of tar. In any case, whatever my own personal view, it's undoubtedly popular enough with the locals, and if nothing else, this stuff is absolutely guaranteed to give you a 'morning fix' that'll keep you looking Marty Feldman-like for the rest of the day and well into the evening. In fact, after spending a little time here, I'd assumed that the old Turkish one-eyed squint was just a reaction to the sun coming from a particular direction, but I now realise that this is totally wrong; all the people around here would be doing the same common or garden double eyed squint, were it not simply for the coffee forcing the other eye to stay open!

Anyway, where was I? Oh yes! Whilst still in the early stages of whiling away the morning in the café, a tall, lean and well tanned chap sauntered in and gestured to the fat waiter for his daily tar fix. He then had a quick look around the room, wandered over and sat down at my table. Like so many other men in Istanbul, his dress was more European than Turkish. He wore cheap looking Eastern-Bloc type jeans - i.e. flared all over and at least two sizes

29

too big- an open necked, checked shirt and a dusty pair of comfortable shoes. Of course, I didn't mind at all that he happened to choose my table (aren't we possessive with things, it wasn't actually 'my' table at all) I assumed he'd just popped into his local before the daily grind of work. But once the coffee had arrived and we'd exchanged a few pleasantries, it transpired that he wasn't local but a German lorry driver; in fact, a German lorry driver who was about to leave that very evening for Eastern Turkey. Well, this seemed to me too good an opportunity to miss and when I popped the obvious question, to my great delight he replied that "Yes of course," he'd be "only too happy to take me along with him".

So, consequently, as a result of that one 'chance' encounter, we ended up spending all day together and getting on like a mosque on fire. And when, much later, back in that same café, he asked for £5 -or the equivalent- to get me my special permit to visit Eastern Turkey, I saw no reason on earth to be suspicious, especially as this man appeared to be so well-known in the café and that by now we'd spent so much time together. Now, call me gullible but well, some three hours later that evening, I was still sat in the same seat in that same café eagerly awaiting his return; -well, eagerly for the first hour anyway. Then, as the room emptied of customers and the fat waiter began stacking his plastic chairs on his plastic tables, with a nauseatingly dull thud, the penny finally dropped. I'd been had, conned, hoodwinked…bugger! Still, I knew there was nothing for it; after all what could I do! I shrugged and slinked back disappointedly to the hostel, yet to fully appreciate the little lesson I'd just learnt.

After a surprisingly good night's sleep I awoke still with a sense of disappointment at having had my trust betrayed, but the moment had gone now and, good or bad, it would just have to go down as another 'experience'.

As it happens, a couple of days earlier, on advice from the students at the hostel, I'd visited a local travel agent and managed to obtain prices for long haul buses heading east from Istanbul. And so I now decided that, being that it was so incredibly cheap in this part of the world to travel by public transport, it probably wasn't really worth the aggravation of trying to hitch a lift any further -especially after my meeting with the non-German, non-lorry driver. So, on eventually finding the right ticket office, I splashed out on a bus ticket -for the grand sum of fourteen pounds- that would take me all the way across Turkey and Iran to Pakistan...or so I thought!

NB. It would be a great shame, of course, to rush through Iran, but as previously mentioned, both they and the Iraqis were currently at war with one another and so I was more than a little concerned at having to spend too much time in the area.

So, later that day, with rucksack stashed in the hold, map in hand and my mind firmly back in travel mode, I boarded the luxury bus for Pakistan.

The reason it was the luxury bus wasn't really all that clear except for the fact that it had 'luxury' emblazoned on the front of it. Still, it seemed reasonably comfortable and, most important of all, was heading off in the direction I wanted to go. Well, before long the bus had been stacked up with an array of bags and boxes, the remaining passengers waiting outside had slowly filed on and, as we pulled slowly away, I was afforded a last long look at old

Istanbul's centre; a slowly passing slice of Turkish life; row after row after row of poor but semi-exotic, semi-monochrome scenes framed neatly by my window; a non-stop trailer for a 1920's movie epic. I sat back and relaxed, ready and prepared for the long journey ahead.

It wasn't until much later, during an all too common bout of day dreaming, I realised that in all the time I'd spent in Istanbul, I'd experienced neither Turkish wrestling, a Turkish bath nor even so much as a single mouthful of Turkish Delight! Oh well, I suppose there's always another day!

CHAPTER 4

-AFGHANS, PERSIANS AND THE BUXOM BLONDE -

Turkey to Iran

The bus was completely full at the start of the journey, of what I can only assume were Turks. Most of these were middle-aged couples and single men, or crinkly old women dozing under crocheted headscarves surrounded by bulging carrier bags from the big city. But then on closer inspection, I noticed that amongst the rows of tanned and leathery faces there were also a few younger people on board; two of them a pair of rather peaky and pasty looking young girls who were sat up near the back. I couldn't help staring of course, but after only a few seconds was caught in the act. Not that I was exactly leering in any way -for they were hardly leering material- it's just that they looked a little well, different; a little less exotic say than the other passengers. (I later learnt that they came from Ramsgate.) Somewhat oddly, they were making their way from their home in Kent, right around a quarter of the globe to Delhi...by bus.

They looked quite an ordinary couple of girls these two; ones that, at home, you'd pass in the street without looking back. Here in Asia though, they stood out like two very pale and sore thumbs. In fact, the only other Westerner on the whole bus -bar me- was an exceedingly quiet and balding Frenchman in his late twenties who was partway through a round-the-world bike ride. He, like myself, had had slight reservations about travel in Iran at this time, and so had also resorted to using public transport for this part of his journey.

The girls seemed a most unlikely pair to bump into on a bus bound for Delhi. Admittedly I was hardly a travel guru myself, but these two looked like they'd never set foot out of the British Isles...or even Ramsgate for that matter; more your sort of shopping, pub and club type than avid culture vultures. They were also remarkably different, not just from everyone else on the bus but from one another. One: slightly built and with short-cropped, razored-up-the-back dark hair, had quite thin and shrew-like features, whilst her clearly more domineering travel companion was a whole lot more robust all over; with a round, open face and a mop of unruly blonde hair that mirrored her character perfectly. She also wore a small, gold stud in one side of her nose -still unusual at this time back in England- and a white cotton shirt opened halfway to her navel revealing a cleavage significantly bigger than a builder's bum. This last feature, of course, was blatantly obvious to all who happened to glance in her direction, and had she still been in Kent, her more than ample bosom would certainly have drawn plenty of lingering looks from liberalised but more accustomed Western men. Here though, further east, where females tend to come better wrapped than an O.C.D. sufferer's pass the parcel package, well surely I thought, it would provoke a free for all!

It became quite obvious that neither one of this slightly odd couple had any experience whatsoever of customs and cultures outside of Europe, or indeed....any experience of culture. Their marathon excursion had quite simply come about because Sue -her of the voluminous chest- had gone to the social services in floods of tears, claiming that unemployment had led her to depression and that she was in desperate need of a holiday for which, of course, she had no money. And so the social services, in their infinite wisdom, had agreed to pay for her to go to India, but on the proviso that she went by the cheapest means available, namely...by bus. Now this in itself may sound ludicrous enough, however, it didn't end there; for this would have meant her going on holiday all alone. And so Sue managed to persuade the authorities that, not only should they pay 'her' fare all the way to India and back, but that they should also pay for a friend to accompany her; a friend who, incidentally, was fully employed in work at the time. Now that seems fair, doesn't it!

I shared my seat on the bus with a wizened old man whose small leathery face had been concertina-ed into pencil pleats by years of one-eyed squinting. And whilst it was nice to be on the move once again, it was even more exciting to be on a journey surrounded by such a sea of dark and mysterious faces, each and every one of them simply oozing character. In fact, I was enjoying it so much, I confess to having felt a little cheated at having to share my bus full of locals with three other Europeans. Still, I suppose that somewhere deep in the recesses of my mind I may have taken just a little comfort in knowing that I could at least communicate with somebody in my own language...should the need arise.

Anyway, complete with this bus load of assorted characters, we wriggled through the streets of Istanbul and slowly made our way out of the busy city centre, through the ramshackle suburbs and out into open country.

Contrary to what I'd expected, it turned out the bus was more luxurious than at first thought. The most surprising thing of all is that it actually boasted a heating system, and for me, this alone warranted the luxury label. In fact this single attribute was soon to become something very, very much appreciated.

The road leading out from Istanbul took us, all through the day and night, right across central Turkey passing vast and tired looking expanses of farmland and tiny deserted looking villages. Then gradually, as we forged ever eastward, winter became ever more wintry and the landscape more and more desolate, until eventually we reached the high and bleak terrain to the north of Lake Van.

After numerous stop-offs at unpronounceable places we arrived and stopped at a small and equally unpronounceable place just east of 'Dogubayazit' up near the Iranian border. The village itself seemed to have little to recommend it but I decided to get out and take a walk around all the same -if only for a stretch and a breath of fresh air. But after only five minutes I'm rather glad I did, for on closer inspection, do you know what: this small village…still had little to recommend it! However, I just couldn't help but feel affection for its rustic simplicity. Nothing much appeared to go on here. Chickens pecked away half-heartedly at the hard bare earth scratching a meagre and short existence; dark featured men ambled about equally unenthusiastically hunched in drab, colourless clothing seemingly fashioned from discarded blankets; and a bored looking donkey 'ee-ored' away between mouthfuls of root vegetable tops, tethered to a paint-less and one hinged door.

It was difficult to imagine what anyone did here for entertainment or even what they did to survive. Maybe though, the answer lies not in the village itself but in its position; for not only is this place directly on one of the few routes through to Iran, it also does have one quite unique claim to fame. For, as far as I could make out, this small community is about the nearest there is to the snow-capped peak that rises up from the plains to the north. Its name....Mount Ararat! Yes, supposedly the very peak where a chap called Noah -and his boat full of animals-came to rest after the receding of the waters from a particularly nasty downpour. It would have been rather nice to pay Ararat a visit of course, but alas, it wasn't to be. Unfortunately, being as this was just another 'stretch your legs and toilet stop', Noah's docking place would have to be yet another thing for the future.

When we finally reached the Iranian border it was the dead of night. The bus slowed to a halt and a bored thug of a border guard with fuzzy-felt moustache and eyebrows leapt aboard and sternly ordered us all off. Now remember, I'd just been travelling in a luxury bus whose heating was perhaps a little too luxurious for my liking i.e. stuck on maximum. Consequently, at this time, I was wearing nothing but T-shirt, trousers and my £4.50 baseball boots. I soon realised, on leaving the bus, that outside it was a whole lot different. In fact, at this particular place and at this particular time, it was a rather chilly minus 20 degrees centigrade. Unfortunately for me, none of the green uniformed officials waiting outside looked terribly friendly or charitable, and the way they were ushering my fellow passengers around with dictatorial jerks of their hip held rifles, I must say, I felt a little reluctant to ask permission to grab a jumper from out of my rucksack. Luckily though -and I never thought I'd say this- the guards wanted to search through all of our luggage. This gave me the opportunity to open up my pack and, under the ever watchful eye of the attentive guard, take out and don almost my entire wardrobe -that is to say...both my other two T-shirts, my one semi-smart border post shirt and a jumper. This, as it turned out, was just as well, for we were left to stand in the cold night air for a full two hours whilst visas and belongings were thoroughly scrutinised. Mind you, as a Westerner, I admit to having got off rather more lightly than the locals did; maybe my apparent eagerness to 'rifle' through my own rucksack and turf out all the contents made the guards less enthusiastic to do the same. Sort of removing sadistic power through playing the masochist perhaps!

The Asians on the bus however faired rather less well, and by the way these poor people were hassled, bullied, interrogated and searched, you'd have thought the guards had had a water-tight tip-off into a major 20th century drugs haul. Okay, so the guards had a job to do -and amongst any group of people in uniform there's always going to be the odd one or two who are a touch over zealous- but, judging by their actions, I'm quite sure these men were simply underpaid, bloody cold and totally and utterly bored stiff. All the same this wasn't the best welcome to Iran, and when every single coat, shirt, pair of trousers, shoe and item of underwear had been thoroughly gone through (in fact, particularly the underwear) I have to say that I've never ever been happier to be back on a bus.

The road east wound its way through a far rockier

landscape now and everywhere great drifts and fluffy mounds of snow were picked out in the bus's headlights. A sizeable mountain river that would have once run alongside us in gushing torrents was now paralysed by ice. All across Turkey the women passengers on the bus had gradually become fewer and fewer in number as each had disembarked with armfuls of shopping and then melted away toward distant villages.

Eastern Turkey had been an altogether much wilder place than I was used to and by the time we'd entered Iran, every one of the passengers bar the Ramsgate duo were men. Around the border area various people had got on and off the bus and by now all the non-Western passengers were made up solely of a mixture of local Turks, Afghan refugees and Iranian soldiers.

Miss Cleavage was naturally attracting a great deal of attention, and after a brief and feisty stand, was eventually persuaded to cover up a little more of her whiter than white protruding flesh. This persuasion, curiously, came from some of the more boggle-eyed and dribbling men folk; perhaps in order to, 'lead themselves not into temptation'! But clearly, a couple of fastened buttons was never going to be enough for them; for then -as is Islamic custom- both girls were also strongly advised by a host of other passengers to cover their heads. This they did - albeit somewhat reluctantly- but unfortunately, as neither of the girls possessed anything remotely resembling a hat, they then proceeded to spend the entire journey through the rest of Iran with pairs of trousers laid across their heads and neatly buttoned up around their faces. Well, this sort of did the trick I suppose, but it left the two of them with a pair of rather long, limp legs dangling down their backs so that they looked remarkably like a couple of giant, disgruntled angora rabbits. So, whilst this did go some way to hiding their femininity from a whole shed load of hot-blooded Muslim males, it didn't exactly make them blend in with things. Granted, they could hardly have done more to make themselves less sexually appealing, but it still didn't stop the majority of the Iranian men from showing an enormous amount of interest in the two of them. "Perhaps I'd got it all wrong," I thought; "perhaps it was me who was the odd one out here, and that -in the Muslim world- this new, fetching contemporary headgear only served to enhance a girl's beauty!" Whatever the reasons, as a consequence of travelling through Iran with these two Western girls -covered or not- I was to get involved in an awful lot of very persistent conversation with any local man who could string more than two words of English together, and indeed, many who couldn't. Every time we stopped anywhere, for some reason it was assumed by all concerned that these girls 'belonged' to me - presumably because it was a little unusual to see two young white women travelling alone. And so, on numerous occasions, I'd be approached by some local chap who wondered by chance, "if I might not be needing one of my girls for the night?" Now, had I been just a little more entrepreneurial, I'm quite sure I could have done rather well out of this financially, but alas, my morals -and the anticipated wrath of two young Kentish women- would always win the day and I'd manage to persuade the men that I wasn't currently 'open for business'!

Gazing out of the bus window as the great expanse of rural Iran passed by, there was little to break the tedium of the journey, and although I knew that back at home there would be concern for my safety in this part of the world, I saw very little evidence of the war that was currently taking place with neighbouring Iraq. Sure, there were plenty of untidy corrugated iron shanty towns along the route, but for all I knew, this could easily be attributed to more modern methods of bottom rung housing as to the consequences of war. (A rather sad indicator of housing standards isn't it, when you don't know if people have been temporarily displaced or not.)

Sometime during the following day we reached the Iranian capital of Teheran, where all the passengers were let off for what I assumed would be yet another short but much needed break. As things turned out though, it was to be a rather longer break than anticipated, for shortly after coming to a halt and getting down from the bus, to my horror, it started to pull away again. Well, quickly I tore across the road, lunged for the still open doorway and staggered aboard to confront the driver.
"What's happening" I spluttered, "where are you going? We're supposed to be going to Pakistan!"
"No", replied the driver casually, "this is end, I go back now".
   I fumbled around in my trousers and quickly presented him with the ticket which I'd safely wedged into the bottom of my pocket with an over-sized polka-dot hanky. He took the ticket and thumbed through the three little sheets to the back page where, as clear as day, the word 'Teheran' was written across it. Then he handed back my ticket and, with an exceedingly nonchalant, single, raised eyebrow, gave me a "Well, so what do you expect me to do?" sort of look. My sudden anxiety turned to a dull and despairing resignation. I suppose the fact that our bags had

been unloaded and now lay in a heap on the roadside should have been a clue to what was happening, but for whatever reason, it clearly wasn't clue enough. Back in Istanbul I'd seen what was written on the ticket but was assured by the bus company that this was merely written in as the major stopover en route to India. Why would I have any reason to disbelieve them; they seemed a nice enough bunch. Still, there was nothing much that I could do about it. It would just have to be jotted down in the notebook of life as yet another bloody, bloody, bloody annoying learning experience -or at least...an experience!

Do you know, I took little comfort from the fact that two giant angora rabbits and a bald, mute Frenchman stood equally open-mouthed beside me; resigned, as they were, to the same fate. Within seconds, what had been our home for the past three days, returned down the road from whence it came and disappeared in a billowing cloud of white dust. We stood there limply amongst an assortment of baggage, staring after the bus, feeling disgruntled and cheated but maybe, just maybe a little wiser.

Meanwhile, a youngish Iranian chap and fellow passenger, who'd witnessed these goings on, beckoned us to follow him. So with nothing to lose, we gathered our collective composure, slung our bags on our backs and picked our way through the throng of bodies and into the bus terminal building.

Inside, Teheran Central bus station sweated and heaved with the hustle and bustle of heavily bearded men. The whole place was choc-a-bloc with near identical tall, cloaked, biblical looking figures as if we'd entered an enormous waiting room for extras auditioning for 'Carry on up the Khyber'. Each man there was jostling for position, shoulder to shoulder, trying to scan the huge timetables above for his desired destination. I looked up myself, hopelessly trying to decipher the columns and columns of Alphabeti-Spaghetti that somebody had thrown up randomly on the blackboard, but it was quite pointless; it might as well have been written in a language I'd never set eyes on -which actually...it was. At that moment I felt our immediate fate lay very much in the hands of our new found guide and acquaintance. To his credit though, he clearly sensed our feeling of vulnerability and gestured calmly for us to stay put. He then promptly disappeared into an ocean of woolly beards to find news of an onward bus.

Shortly, our new best friend returned through the crowd and managed, in broken English, to inform us that we'd have to spend the night in Teheran, as the next long haul bus going east wasn't due to leave until the following morning. By this time though it came as no surprise, so we gladly took his advice and joined him on the next local bus into down-town Teheran to spend the night.

Now, near the city centre, by a lucky coincidence, our 'friend' just happened to know a friend who owned a cheap hostel. This may or may not have been our travel-mate's plan in the first place but, for now, under the circumstances, I felt only too happy to go along with proceedings. Besides, at this very moment in time, I was surrounded by people with whom there was no way of communicating -save by hand signals- and all I wanted was a bed for the night; a place where I could see out the remainder of the day and look forward to a new one that I hoped would bring rather better fortune.

When we reached the hostel we went straight to bed and the following morning all rose early to be enthusiastically greeted by our Iranian friend-cum-hotel guide. I still didn't really know if the befriending and hotel thing was a bit of a scam -were we being taken in by being 'taken in'? - but whatever the case, I decided that I quite liked this chap. For someone who could speak so little of our language he somehow managed to convey an incredible love of life, an almost tangible brightness that contrasted so amazingly sharply with the drab clothing which both he and all his fellow countrymen spent their entire lives dressed in.

I once more hauled on my heavy load and followed our Iranian down the hostel staircase and out into a hazy sun; then we hopped onto the first available local bus back to the central station. Shortly, we were saying our thanks and goodbyes and were once again on our way; back on our staccato tour across Asia. It was such a terrible shame not to have seen anything of Teheran -bar a bed and bus station. Still, I'd made the decision to go and anyway, the sun was shining now, seeping its way into the cold and bleakness of the Iranian winter; and so with renewed vigour I once more looked forward to whatever it was that lay ahead.

The road running south-east out of Teheran ran right across the huge and rocky expanses of central Iran via the cities of Qom, Yadz and Kerman. The scenery here changed very little and so my attention was turned more to what -or who- was inside the bus rather than outside it. Apart from us four young Westerners the passengers were all now either Iranians or Afghans. But though these people may have been geographical neighbours they were alike as chalk and a banana (visually, I never really understood the cheese analogy); the short and clean cut Iranians were all neatly turned out in khaki uniform ready to take on the Iraqis whilst, scattered amongst them, the tall bearded Afghans sat proudly in their drab but somehow elegant tribal gear, temporarily displaced, as they were, from their homeland by invading Russian troops. Yet, though they were different, like people everywhere, they were still both united by that one simple and ultimate goal...to live a normal, happy and peaceful existence.

I cursed the fact that I was unable to converse with my fellow passengers; they may have seemed quite a dowdily dressed bunch to us Europeans but all of them, especially the Afghans, had such incredibly interesting, tanned and chiselled faces. I felt somehow drawn in, almost mesmerised by these people and I couldn't help but eye each of them up and down, wondering what on earth they did in their lives and how they fitted into their world. What stories, I wondered, lay hidden behind such faces.

After some time had passed by, one especially tall and upright Afghan sitting directly opposite my seat caught my curious stare. But before I'd had the chance to look away he smiled warmly, lent forward and offered me, what I assumed to be, a small brown paper bag full of nuts. I smiled back appreciatively, reached for a small handful and popped them into my mouth. Well, instantly the Afghan's face lit up like a child's; then I detected a slight watering around the eyes and, within seconds, I could see that behind this quiet, kind and polite smile was a man

45

convulsing with fits of laughter. Obviously something wasn't quite right here. I immediately spat the tiny and exceedingly crunchy nuts back into my hand. My neighbour, seeing this, kindly gestured to me that "perhaps they may taste a little better with the shells removed." Well naturally I could do little but see the funny side to this and had to agree, on cracking open one of the nuts with my front teeth, that they did indeed taste rather better shell-less. Mind you, if you ask me, having to crack open such a tiddly little shell to get at a nut no bigger than a grain of Uncle Ben's rice well, the work hardly warrants the reward, does it. In fact, the opening of them appears to me to be more a form of long-haul traveller occupational therapy than to access a snack. Still I could hardly hand them back could I, especially with their shiny new coat of spittle! So the only thing for it, if I wasn't going to eat them, was to 'lose' them on the floor somewhere amongst the deep-pile carpet of shucks...on the blind side of my Afghan friend.

This however, wasn't the end of the in-flight entertainment for, no sooner had calm been restored, than the very same chap went on to offer me a rather large, red, rounded, shiny and appetising looking fruit. This, of course, I also accepted equally graciously and promptly went to take a large bite out of it. God! Strooooth! Well, I kid you not; I very nearly lost all my front teeth. It was like trying to take a chunk out of an over-baked house brick. I reeled back clasping my poor wounded gums; my nut naivety may have been one thing but this was quite another. The next thing I know my Afghan friend could contain himself no longer; he desperately tried to look away but it was just too late; like a once dormant volcano, his shoulders began to shake uncontrollably, his cheeks billowed out with pressure, his lips gave way and a whole mouthful of non-crunchy nut puree cascaded all over the chap in front. Then, he collapsed violently back in his seat clutching his ribs, eyes brimming with water and he was simply overcome by fits of loud and raucous laughter, reduced totally to a gibbering, hysterical wreck; and this, along with every other person within earshot -namely just about everyone on the entire bus!

Of course, since that day I've seen many a pomegranate, but well...it's just that this happened to be my first. Fortunately, I found the incident just as comical as everyone else did and, although the lack of a common language still remained a barrier between us, we proceeded to pass the whole of the rest of the journey like two naughty schoolboys; periodically tittering at one another and exchanging mischievous grins.

As usual, on a long haul bus ride, we made regular stops every three or four hours to eat, drink, get rid of drink or just to have a stretch. Most of these intermissions, of course, though very welcome, were fairly uneventful. However, there was one such occasion which left me with an image that has stayed with me ever since. You see the whole contents of the bus had emptied into a roadside café and we'd all sat down at the rows of wooden tables to consume whatever each of us had bought from the very basic buffet-style counter. I was one of the first to be seated as tiredness had left me quite unable to stomach anything on offer. Shortly though, I was joined by a short and stocky Iranian soldier, probably in his early thirties, who'd collected his plated meal and sat down at my table facing me. There then followed a remarkable conversation

47

between the two of us without as much as a single word being uttered by either. Granted, most of this consisted simply of him offering me a variety of food and drink and me trying, but failing miserably, to refuse it -much to his satisfaction; but you know, there was more to it than that. For though this interlude to the journey was a brief one, it provided well...a special moment; a moment where there was no audible interaction, none at all. We simply looked at one another across a table, both knowing that deep down we really weren't that different; that, like the rest of humanity, we shared a certain something; the same dreams perhaps, the same hopes for a happy and peaceful life. Sure, we were worlds apart in many respects -this man's life was in total turmoil due to a war over which he had no control. As for myself, I was merely passing through. But for now, for one brief moment, the difference seemed quite insignificant.

I enjoyed my encounter with Iran -albeit a desperately short one- and I was shown nothing but kindness by those who made any attempt to communicate. That said, this would certainly have been a rather sensitive time to visit had I been an American citizen. Not unusually, the Americans weren't exactly flavour of the month here at this time, and on several occasions I found myself staring up at a full colour poster of Ronald Reagan -or was it Ronald McDonald- with his throat being slit by a soldier. One day though, I thought, I really must return and see just a little of the beauty that old Persia has to offer.

CHAPTER 5

-THE SAND BORDER-

Into Pakistan

After a long and exhausting five days we finally arrived at the small eastern Iranian town of Zahedan and transferred to a local bus for the last 40 miles to the Pakistani border. The climate was noticeably warmer now and the air thick and body hugging. In fact it was so hot that it would have been nice to dispense with clothing completely; but as this didn't seem the most sensible option, I once again donned the only half respectable lightweight shirt in my possession -my only shirt, in fact- in readiness for the border post. (I usually made at least some attempt to look a little less unkempt at borders, as so many countries seemed to have an aversion to anyone even remotely resembling a hippy!)

We were now passing between two great Muslim countries. How odd then, I thought, that whilst we were being processed through the customs building of an alcohol free country, there should be little else for sale here but row upon row of ultra-cheap whisky. In fact, at the equivalent of just £2 a bottle, the cheapest I've ever seen anywhere. Perhaps though, the whisky wasn't available to be drunk by the locals, I don't know. Come to think of it, at that price, perhaps it wasn't meant to be drunk at all. More a single malt shed preservative than actual Scotch.

Anyway, all went fairly smoothly, if somewhat slowly, on the Iranian side of the border; then we were herded onto yet another bus to be ferried over the no-man's land to Pakistani customs. The surrounding country here was distinctly flat and arid, but just to the north - within a dromedary's spitting distance- I could see the bare jagged peaks thrusting skyward from the plains, forming the frontier that leads tantalisingly into Afghanistan. It would have been so very tempting to scale these mountains and take a peak inside, but right now Afghanistan was off limits to outsiders. It was a country whose people were currently in a desperate struggle to rid themselves of the might of the Soviet Union. Freedom, of course, would eventually come for them...but at what price!

Over the next couple of hours at the border post, Pakistani officials, like their Iranian counterparts, rummaged through every single item of our luggage whilst we stood around patiently surveying our new surroundings. Not that I minded all that much or indeed had any choice in the matter. At least the officials were more laid back about the whole thing than they'd been when we entered Iran. And in any case, it was a far more desirable climate for waiting around. (Which is why, I suppose, the officials were more laid back in the first place!)

Then, after some time, when all the rummaging had almost come to an end and everything appeared to be in order, I was just thinking about getting back on the bus when a cry rang out from behind me. I spun round toward the source only to see one deliriously happy guard produce two bottles of beer from the bottom of somebody's rucksack....yep, mine. "Bugger!" Now, let me explain, you see, I'd been carrying these two bottles all the way from

England and, having come this far, thought how nice it would be to save them for a Christmas treat in well, wherever I might happen to be at that particular time. "Fat chance now", I thought. But for some bizarre reason the customs guard appeared totally elated by his discovery and now gleefully held the bottles aloft like an apprentice magician pulling his very first rabbit from a hat. It was futile trying to deny that they were mine of course; the beers were clearly English and clearly in my rucksack.

Well, the little official looked across at me, then to his colleagues and then back at me again; and by the way he was both grinning and shaking his head disapprovingly I thought, "There's only one person who's going to be drinking these beers and it ain't gonna be me"! I was just beginning to realise the truth about living in an alcohol free country; it wasn't a case of having to abstain at all, it simply meant that -for some people at least- you didn't have to pay for the stuff!

Anyway, I said nothing but climbed back on board the bus with the others and took my seat, feeling just a little peeved. After all, I'd just humped these two bottles of bitter right the way across Europe and halfway across Asia and well, I wouldn't have minded so much but, I'd put off so many occasions when I could have savoured my little treat. Now, here I was on the edge of the Baluchistan desert being thwarted at the eleventh hour by an exceedingly dark and hairy Paul Daniels. How bloody annoying. You know, Christmas dinner just wouldn't be the same! Still, what could I do except resign myself to the situation; after all I suppose it was a 'fair cop'...though obviously not by a fair cop!

Shortly, the bus started up, the engine was revved into action and we went to pull away. But...before we'd hardly moved an inch, there was a rap at the door and, lo and behold, that very same little customs officer -the one who'd 'stolen' my beers- leapt aboard. Then, he took a quick look around the bus and started striding confidently down the aisle toward me -I had no idea what to expect of course. He stopped next to my seat, his dark eyes fixed on mine; his sweat stained uniform pressed tight against the edge of my seat. And then, standing right there beside me, suddenly he gave a wink and a grin and thrust his two hands out from behind his back; and in them…two bottles of good old English bitter. "What a surprise; what a kind and faith restoring gesture" I thought. I gratefully accepted them, put them back in my bag, then the very nice customs man merrily hopped off the bus and we took off up the desert road into Pakistan.

Unfortunately this was one lesson I was destined not to learn. For further on into Pakistan, rather than drink the things whilst the going was good, we were later stopped at a police checkpoint and my exceedingly well-travelled Christmas treat was confiscated by another not so charitable official.

CHAPTER 6

-DESERT BUSES AND GLITZY TRUCKS-

Southern Pakistan

We were now in Pakistan on the edge of the vast expanse of desert that makes up the western part of Baluchistan. Of course, modern day boundaries seldom bear any relationship to those recognised by local tribal people, but here at least -by coincidence perhaps- somebody seemed to have got it right. Everything in this area appeared so incredibly different from where I'd just left: so distinct, as if I'd walked through an invisible door and stepped onto, what was now, a totally different film set. One where every single extra wandered the scene dressed in loose matching cotton trousers and shirts, or 'shalwar kameez' as they're collectively known here, and topped off by a multitude of multi-coloured pill-box hats (the latter, an item of clothing that achieved almost cult status when it became sort of symbolic of all the Western hippies passing through in the Sixties.)

But, surely the most remarkable single feature of this desert landscape, this entire region of Asia, is not actually what adorns the people, but that which adorns the incredibly glitzy and personalised trucks and buses that can be seen everywhere. The trucks, especially, can only be described as absolutely stunning -in a very garish sort of way- and appear as if decorated by a flock of totally mad and wildly eccentric bower birds. Every one of them with brilliantly shining metal canopies, spangled with mirrors and multi-coloured glass inlays; littered with ribbons and banks of horns. Whilst inside, bright plastic flowers, yet more mirrors and gaudy religious personal shrines bedeck every single facia, canopy and dashboard. I decided to join one such bus for the gruelling twenty three hour drive across the desert to Quetta; a daunting prospect you may think, but a journey which was to prove one of the most memorable of this entire trip.

Our driver -bless his cotton souks- didn't appear to have a schedule as such, so when he'd eventually finished chewing the fat outside with a few of his colleagues - which was some considerable time later- he clambered aboard.

Meanwhile, I'd taken up my position down near the front of the bus, teetering on one of the metal frameworks that presumably, in some former life, had actually been a well padded seat. Then, I turned my head to see who was joining me on this journey and was puzzled to notice that all of my fellow passengers were sat about the bus like loosely bound mummies, only their dark eyes peering out from their swaddling bandages. This seemed a little odd at first...until we pulled away, that is. For, within seconds, the reason for their state of dress became glaringly obvious, as the whole of the Baluchistan desert began billowing in between the ill-fitting blue and orange plastic window panes. Quickly we gathered pace and soon we were hurtling at breakneck speed across the compacted desert sand; Arabic music shrieking and wailing in one ear whilst I was sand blasted in the other. I struggled to close my half open window but to no avail; more and more dust and sand tornado-ed in. I swivelled my head once again to gauge the reaction of the other passengers to all this but it

54

was too late…they'd already disappeared into a hazy assortment of shapes and bundles; a collage of bodies cowering behind a thick beige shower curtain. It was extraordinary. In fact it was so unbelievably bad, so chokingly dense, I swear that had my own mother been sitting on the rear seat I wouldn't have recognised her through the wildly swirling opaque cloud that now filled the bus. Just incredible!

The funny thing is though, however perverse this may seem, that after a couple of hours of squatting on my tubular steel bar and pursing every orifice against this internal sand storm, I found that I was actually enjoying myself. I don't know, it just felt so exhilarating, so exciting to be racing across the desert being rocked and rolled, buffeted and bashed in this thick, thick atmosphere. Sure, I might have felt like a small chunk of meat being vigorously shaken in a bag of flour but well…it was great!

We drove on and on through most of the night and I somehow managed to grab odd snatches of sleep as we bumped along our way. Don't ask me how this was possible. Perhaps after several hours my senses had become numbed or just accustomed to it all, or maybe the cloud of dust had abated a little due to the stillness of the night. Whatever the case, it never once seemed to bother our driver one iota. In fact, as the hours passed by, I began to have greater and greater admiration for drivers such as him, for not only did he appear to totally shun tiredness - perhaps they exist solely on Turkish coffee- but his only navigational aid across a flat and almost featureless desert were the red and white painted oil drums that dotted the route every few miles, all the way from the border to Quetta. Quite remarkable!

Sometime during the early morning, as the sun rose over a rocky outcrop, we stopped for something to eat. There was little around here but a cluster of baked mud -or adobe- buildings. A single line of pale grey hunched figures slowly filed out of the bus and onto the hot sand, stretching and yawning in the fresh, still air; spitting grit from dry mouths; white eyes peering through mud-coloured faces. There was a wonderful peace. The last few hours had felt like I'd just taken part in a pogo-stick marathon in a wind tunnel and it was strange to get my land legs again. This was the first time I'd ever experienced a real desert and, after being subjected to non-stop engine noise and hour upon hour of screeching and screaming from the Arab pop diva from hell, the quietness and tranquillity of this vast place was extraordinary and beautiful.

A handful of local men stood outside the four mud walls that were their home, and as we left the bus we were greeted by warm and friendly smiles. For the majority of passengers food was only their second priority, for now they fanned out from the bus in every direction as if in readiness for a humungous maypole dance. Then, each and every one of them turned out from the centre of the circle to perform their daily ablutions in what privacy the desert could afford -namely none. They simply shielded themselves using nothing but their own clothed bodies, men and women alike, squatting down on the ground to hide their modesty. This complete, they all returned to the shade of the bus and went about producing carefully concealed picnics whilst the four of us Westerners and the driver were enthusiastically beckoned inside one of the adobe buildings for a hearty breakfast.

After the glaring brilliance of the light outside, the little room into which we stepped was as dark as a Munchkin's coal hole. But then, as my eyes gradually became accustomed to the gloom, all around at crotch level, I could just about make out a circle of eyes and then, within the centre of that circle, the huge shallow bowl of glutinous rice that was drawing their attention. Thankfully, my eyes adjusted just in time to prevent me from stepping into their breakfast. Then, one happily beaming chap shuffled up a little to one side and beckoned me with his sticky brown hand to sit down beside him. So, I sat down cross-legged on the dirt floor and, within seconds, was heartily tucking in, along with all the others.

You know, there's definitely a kind of knack to eating sticky rice with thumb and fingers without plastering the stuff all over your cheeks and chin and halfway up your nostrils; but after such a gruelling journey I was far too hungry to worry about such things. Besides, I was rather more concerned as to whether or not I was using the correct hand than anything else, being as traditionally, I was told, Muslims only ever eat with the right hand - reserving the left for rather more personal matters i.e. dealing with the rice after it's been digested.

It soon became obvious that a fondness for rice in this part of the world was going to be something of an asset. This is because a typical meal here, such as this, generally consists of nothing more than a mound of the stuff the size of Mont Blanc topped with a teaspoonful of near-lethal fiery, curry sauce. Nevertheless, though it may not have been quite what I was used to, this meal did prove an unforgettable occasion. After all, here was I, a young carpenter from Horsham, sitting in a mud hut amongst a small circle of robed desert men, watching them alternatively scoop double fingerfuls of sticky rice from the communal mound, shovelling it down their gullets and then throwing their arms about wildly in incomprehensible conversation. Quite wonderful! Actually, come to think of it, I feel particularly pleased the rice was of the sticky variety otherwise, due to the many extremely animated exchanges of view, I'd no doubt have been wearing most of it!

Now, not being able to communicate with local people in their own language is surely the biggest bane in the lives of any keen traveller. Having said that, there are undoubtedly certain times when it's simply nice to sit and observe and to soak up the atmosphere around you rather than be involved. That first meal in the desert was just one such time. And, although often a little heated, the indecipherable chatter between all of these men was nothing but music to my ears; a noisy but authentic, companionable accompaniment whilst I happily tucked into handfuls of dust coated rice and licked it from my sticky chops. Perfect!

Shortly, we were all hailed back to the bus to resume our journey and each and every one of the passengers re-planted themselves back into the same perfect, dust free images that their bodies had left behind. I pulled back my orange plastic window -which, unlike the blue one, did actually move a little- and took one more look at the quiet and serene desert before the spell was again broken. Then, just there, there over a small dune I spotted it; something I'd never yet witnessed but had heard so much about from books and TV back home....Yes, a camel train; a genuine load lugging, dune plodding camel train. Fantastic! Well okay, maybe not so much a train as a box-car perhaps -for the line of camels didn't exactly taper off into the distance- but you know what I mean. In fact, if I'm really honest, this particular train consisted of just two camels and four boys, varying in age and size from about eleven to eighteen; but hey, it was exciting to me!

Anyway, I quickly grabbed my camera, hopped off my metal perch, held up an open palm to the bus driver - hoping he'd understand my signal to wait- and ran out across the dune. You know, there were barely 300 metres between me and those camels but, as I ran, the soft golden sand quickly sapped the strength from my legs. Soon I was wading shin deep; I began waving and shouting frantically at the boys to stop as if in a deliberately hammed up am-dram version of Lawrence of Arabia. Thankfully this did the trick; the boys stopped immediately and, on seeing my camera, all turned completely in unison and posed proudly next to their beasts of burden. Well, I was pleased they'd stopped of course but umm...this wasn't quite the image I was after. And, in fact, it was with considerable difficulty that I managed to cajole them into walking on again in order to get my 'authentic looking' camel-train picture. Still, they did eventually get the idea and me? I got my authentic photo...more or less. Then, that done, the camels plodded moodily on their way and, with the young cameleers still grinning over one shoulder, I thanked them, waved them off and raced back to rejoin the bus.

Hours later and we'd finally reached our destination, the old and famous frontier town of Quetta; that bustling hub of a market town where people from desert and mountain -

and even from the distant Indus valley to the east-converge, as they have done for generations, to do business.

Quetta teemed with life after the desert quiet; a mélange of sights and sounds where snow-capped mountains formed a glistening and spectacular backdrop along the sky line and colour filled the streets. There were flower bedecked donkeys everywhere you looked; mounds and mounds of multi-coloured fruit, vegetables and spices and myriad glitzy, be-jangled lorries honking, clanking, clattering and kicking up the dirt roads that criss-crossed the town. The day was hot and crusty; the sky a hazy blue; and every corner of shade fostered small heaps of irregular-shaped bodies in grey or brown robes, waiting out the merciless midday sun.

We left the bus, spat out the last remnants of the Baluchistan desert and quickly -or as quickly as the heat allowed- sought sanctuary in a nearby hostel.

It was a very plain and basic sort of place, this hostel. A low modern-ish white-washed bungalow but with the bonus, at least, that it came complete with electricity and running water -occasionally. It was also surrounded by a walled garden containing real grass (both the grass and running water something of a luxury in a dry old place such as this.) The four of us had no difficulty whatsoever finding rooms available, of course, as there'd been little tourist traffic between Turkey, Iran and Pakistan over the past two years. This was largely due to the typically pessimistic and inevitably exaggerated reports about the general state of things given out by the Western media regarding the Iran-Iraq War. Not that Pakistan was lacking visitors at this time...just paying ones! In fact, there was an absolute abundance of non-paying guests here. The reason being that, currently, the then Soviet forces had occupied Afghanistan and, by now, some three million Afghans were reported to have fled their country, most of whom were holed up here in Pakistan. In fact, it seemed that a good many of them had actually been given refuge within the walled garden of our hostel. Not that they had many sensible options mind; for most Afghans who'd fled the war raging in their country, there was little choice but to accept any temporary residence in any town that could afford them space to eat and sleep. This they did in their droves ...reluctantly certainly, but always with grace and gratitude.

Once again I cursed my not being able to communicate with these people properly, for they seemed so proud and generous spirited and I wanted so much to know more about their way of life and about the plight that they now found themselves in. It was obvious that most longed to return to their homes and, even during this war many, I learnt, would go back and forth through the mountains, dodging the Soviet military en route and doing whatever they could to try to help their fellow countrymen. How strange and how tragic to think that just across those mountains there were innocent people by the hundreds and thousands caught up in a conflict through no fault of their own, their younger countrymen fighting for their lives; fighting to regain some sort of normal existence.

To this day I still harbour deep regrets at not accepting one of the many offers that I received to accompany these men on their forays into Afghanistan. The temptation to go was almost unbearable. Though I can't deny feeling more than a little concerned about becoming another casualty of war; just one more small but sad statistic.

NB It must also be said that, although I cannot vouch personally for how the Afghan refugees were treated long term, the Pakistani people were good enough at this time to give temporary residence to a staggering proportion of the Afghan population, and this in a country with more than a fair share of its own problems.

I enjoyed immensely the hustley and bustley atmosphere of Quetta, and it left me with incredibly vivid memories; most of them good, others not so; but...memories all the same.

I suppose, one of the things that Westerners find the most hard to bear in so called 'under developed' countries, is the apparent lack of hygiene. For me, this surely reached an all time low (or is it 'high') in this very town, when I witnessed my first roadside public toilet -and I do mean roadside! Briefly, it consisted of nothing but a five foot high, three sided concrete block enclosure -shielded from the road but totally open on the pavement side- and well, what can I say but, without beating about the bush, this particular public convenience was piled up so high with heaps of human excrement that, had I even contemplated adding to it, I'd have had to have been...a good foot taller! Thankfully I was never quite desperate enough to put it to the test. Still, in their defence, you can hardly accuse them of failing on trades description can you; why, I have never in my life seen a toilet so public or so convenient ...provided you're at least a seven footer!

Public toilets aside, there was really very little in Quetta to dislike...apart perhaps, from the intense heat, the dust, the mosquitoes and the totally erratic plumbing and electrics and umm? No, but seriously, in truth, I really did genuinely like it here. And for those of us who long to sample the delights of other cultures, these things are all just part of 'the experience'. All in all, you just have to be able to take the rough with the smooth and just hope to God that there's not too much rough!

By and large nearly everybody I came across in Quetta greeted me with enthusiastically smiling faces and seemed keen that I should leave their country with nothing but fond memories. Memories perhaps, like the evening when I was invited to the one cinema in town. Playing there was an American war film which -lacking any subtitles- must surely have gone over the heads of nearly all of those who sat before the giant screen. However, my host, who seemed to have adopted me for the night, didn't appear terribly bothered by the film anyway. It didn't take long to realise that it was far more important to him that I was seen to be enjoying myself than it was for him to be doing the same. In fact so much so, that he spent almost the entire film staring at me and trying to gauge my reaction to whatever was going on, rather than watching the film himself. It occurred to me what a strange picture we must have made; a young European sitting in the darkness amid rows and rows of brilliant white robes and teeth, watching an American war film on the edge of an Asian desert. (The majority of locals in the cinema, by the way, were almost certainly not from the lower echelons of society and were, every one of them, dressed up in their all white Sunday best.)

But if all this seemed a little strange, it was nothing compared with what was to come; for when the film was halted for halftime refreshment, there was no mass evacuation to the foyer for gargantuan amounts of coca-cola or chocolate bars, nor the phoneboothed-sized buckets of popcorn that we're accustomed to seeing in the West. Why, there wasn't even so much as a single ear-twisting rustle of sweet papers from the back row, or the sudden appearance of the plump and bored looking middle-aged hostess with her floodlit tray of overpriced ice-creams. Indeed, nobody even left their seats. Instead, the only action during the interval came from a solitary young man -unsurprisingly dressed in white- who slowly came down the steps from behind and then stopped at the end of our row. Now, by this time the lights had come up fully and the whole auditorium was bathed in light (or more accurately 'dribbled' with light, as the light source was very much of the economic variety and about as much use as a painfully shy glow worm.) So, because of this, it was a little hard to make out exactly what this chap at the end of the row was doing at first. All that I could make out was that he was stooped over slightly and, by his actions, appeared to be umm…pouring tea from a teapot. "Don't be daft" I thought to myself, "pouring out tea in the middle of a Pakistani cinema?" But well, that was indeed exactly what he was doing: pouring hot and fresh tea into real china cups; all of which were carefully handed down the row until each of us had one. Then, that done, this was closely followed by another handing along the line; but no...not of an accompanying Rich Tea biscuit or a thin slice of Victoria sponge, but by a hard boiled egg and a Rizla-sized piece of newspaper containing a pinch of both salt and pepper. My local cinema back home would never seem the same again!

I whiled away the next couple of days moseying around

the markets and passing the time chatting to fruit and veg. and spice and linen sellers. There were many in Quetta who spoke at least a little English -a legacy of the former British occupation here- and they were only too pleased to practise what they knew. In fact I soon learnt that, unlike most countries that I'd visited so far, where to find an English speaker it was necessary to look for someone still young enough to be studying; here, the opposite was true; and the best bet, invariably, was to approach anyone who looked 'old' enough to have been around when the Brits were still here. This was fine in theory of course, and I have to say that I did have several very interesting conversations. In practice however, the main problem was that it was quite hard to find someone old enough, but who still also had enough teeth left that you could understand what they were saying.

Being in the desert there was little colour to the outlying surroundings apart from yellowy-brown, browny-yellow, yellow, brown or…grey. But there was always something around every corner to add a splash of contrast. Mostly this was provided by the glitzy trucks, the flowery donkeys or the bright little pyramids of spices in the market place; but around the side of the old fort in Quetta the colours on display there were quite extraordinary. It was almost as if the locals here had long been preparing for some sort of festival; as if a huge three dimensional rainbow had been graffiti-ed along the base of the wall. On closer inspection this turned out to be nothing more than mile upon mile of freshly dyed wool that had been left out to dry in the sun. All around the fort, taut woollen strands of every conceivable colour ran between posts that had probably stood there for a whole herd of donkey's years; every one of the strands barely a gnat's whisker apart from one another and running in long straight lines from ankle level up to a full wool-dyer's reach. It all made for such a stunning contrast against the mud coloured walls of the great fort; so much so in fact, it seemed the long lines of brilliantly coloured wool had been literally lit up; magically enhanced somehow into a surreal technicolour swathe of light; as if the multi-coloured headlights of rush hour traffic had been smeared across a photo by an ultra-slow shutter speed. Of course, I dare say all this wool dyeing and drying could have been done almost anywhere in town had the posts been put in that particular location. But I couldn't help wondering if it hadn't always been done right here, here in this the most central of places for the very purpose of cheering things up a little; adding a giant splash of colour to an otherwise monotonous scene.

Before leaving Quetta I was back outside my room again, idly chatting away the morning with Terry, the bald, bicycling Frenchman. We'd been discussing our possible travel options from here on in when we were interrupted by the arrival of one of his fellow countrymen. He was a young and fresh-faced chap, this Frenchman; probably in his early twenties at most, with a gangly body and even ganglier hair that sprouted from beneath a bright but well worn yellow fez. (That is to say, it was well worn rather than worn well.) He also wore matching baggy cotton shirt and trousers, Jesus type sandals and an exceedingly garish hand-embroidered waistcoat; in fact just about all the traditional hall marks that a young born-again hippy could ever wish for. I suppose I should have anticipated the answer to my first question but I asked it anyway,

"So, how long have you been on the road?"

"How long? Man, I live on the road"! He thought himself so totally cool and laid back it made me smile for, quite unbeknown to him, he blended into the local community here like a nun at a rugby club. Of course, as he was travelling west it was inevitable that we were going to have to listen to his 'great tales' of India; but from the very start, it was equally obvious that, despite his well practised super-coolness, he too would gain a terrific buzz from relaying his experiences.

Still, I have to confess that, despite trying to listen as nonchalantly as possible, all the tales he conveyed did appear rather colourful and exciting. He seemed to have all manner of travel stories from scores of far flung places and, though secretly envious of his exploits, with every story, I was at last able to fill in just one more missing piece of the exotic jigsaw which I'd already begun to create in my mind. It was so exhilarating, so mouth-watering listening to him. In fact by the time this young Frenchman had finished his story telling, regardless of how much of it was actually true, I couldn't wait to get out there and see things for myself.

Within ten minutes I'd packed up my stuff and, bidding the hippy Frenchman a bon voyage, I went to leave for Quetta railway station. However, before I'd even left the room, he called me back. He then produced from his designer waistcoat pocket, a cellophane wrapped package about the size of a pack of cards. This, he carefully unwrapped and, with a cheap and rusty penknife, sliced off a great chunk of something that looked remarkably like a large sweaty Oxo cube. Next, he gestured for me to take

67

it as casually as if it were a boiled sweet. Well, it was an exceedingly generous offer of course, but as it seemed unlikely to be a large sweaty Oxo cube -even I had a fair idea what it really was- I thanked him and declined the offer. This was one experience that I didn't feel quite ready for...yet! So, with that, I said goodbye and off I headed down the road leaving 'le hippy' on the end of the bed casually rolling a joint and with a lump of hash stashed in his pocket that would have fetched a fortnight's wages back in Europe.

Down towards the train station, under a dazzling midday sun, it was business as usual in Quetta. I passed by the market and stall holders waved and smiled from behind their spicy pyramids. Linen sellers, buried amid piles and piles of neatly folded, brightly coloured cloth, beckoned with their chubby brown fingers. Despite the sun, everything everywhere was still illuminated by dangling fluorescent tubes. On the dirt roads, lorries honked and spat up dust, and squat, wizened old mountain men led heavily laden donkeys in all directions, every single animal adorned with bright pink and yellow tassels running down their foreheads and dancing about their eyes as they walked. (The tassels, whilst undeniably colourful, weren't there purely as decoration of course, but to help keep the pesky flies at bay. Though, whether or not the donkeys consider the tassels preferable to the flies...I shall probably never know!)

CHAPTER 7

-BOOZE, BETELNUT AND THE RANDY PROPRIETOR-

Up the Indus to Lahore

It was a long but exciting train journey across the barren and rocky southern half of Pakistan. I was heading east again but only as far as the junction at Sukkur when, for the first time on this trip, I would turn to the north and follow the mighty Indus river valley all the way up to Lahore.

As in many countries which have had the good fortune of encompassing a great river, there was plenty of evidence to suggest that at one time this river had seen grander times. Not that the Indus isn't still grand, it is; but stately and serene as it may be, any river that has had to sweat its way across hundreds and hundreds of miles of flat and sun-baked desert to reach the sea, has to lose a little something. Still, even if a shadow of its former self, the Indus River continues to be a vital artery, the jugular of Pakistan, for it gives the people who make their homes in its valley a means of life through the millions of acres of fertile land that spread from its banks.

But, the trees and crops lining the valley here not only provide a living for a good many people but also for a host of other life forms, and in particular a multitude of water birds. Egrets and herons in particular, are everywhere, standing motionless in muddy fields with their pointy bills and pipe-cleaner necks; their feathers unruffled and their concentration undisturbed by the passing train. I continually observed their calm but predatory rituals through my carriage window or, more often, from my pole position standing at the open doorway. Occasionally, as we passed by, I'd see one jab its head forward, thrusting its oversized bill into the water; then it would juggle a frog into position before swallowing the hapless creature whole. Above the fields, meanwhile, colourful kingfishers and small birds of prey took full advantage of the telegraph poles and cables that marked our route, whilst large raptors soared in lazy circles overhead.

I began to spend more and more of the journey standing up at the open carriage door, chugging rhythmically along, immersed in the thick and humid eastern atmosphere, grateful for what breeze the train created but totally spellbound by my surroundings. Everyone we passed seemed so friendly, young and old alike, smiling and waving enthusiastically as if greeting a loved one back from a long crusade. Men and women everywhere worked the fields; runny nosed, bare-bottomed children drew in the dust with sticks and oxen looked on whilst chewing the cud: wet nosed, twitchy eared and with that same bored yet somehow contented expression as if to say, "Yeah, okay, so life's not a bed of roses but you won't find me losing any sleep over unpaid bills."

The train rattled on ever northward, through the paddy fields and scrub, stopping at numerous little villages consisting of little more than a half dozen mud-brick houses. Either side of the villages, dirt tracks would taper off into the distance and, at the trackside, bicycles and oxcarts waited patiently in the heat for the last carriage to trundle by before they could continue on their way.

At every stop we made, farmers would either leave or join the train and children would offer their wares to the passengers aboard, holding aloft baskets and bags full of unknown things; strange fruits and alien looking vegetables, thrust up at the windows. And at every single stop, a smiling face would appear and beam at me through my open carriage window then, in an enthusiastic and questioning voice, would inquire, "whether or not I would like a curry or perhaps, a cup of tea?" These people seemed remarkable; they were just so unbelievably friendly and generous. I tried to pay every person who appeared at my window for their various offerings but they refused every single rupee offered; In fact, they were most insistent that I didn't pay. It was staggering! I thought to myself, here am I, a comparatively wealthy Westerner, being unequivocally humbled by the sheer generosity of the people of the Indus valley. It took me several stops to realise that all the smiling faces that kept appearing at my window actually belonged to the same man and not someone who happened to have an extremely close cousin in every village. Yes, okay, granted, this may seem like gross stupidity on my part but well, I was a little tired; and besides....this part of the world does have rather more than its fair share of well-tanned, moustached young men!

It was shortly after this revelation that I twigged, (I guess I must have been on a branch line) this chap wasn't a good Samaritan at all but a railway employee who was riding the train; seemingly with the sole purpose of looking after my personal needs. But, you know, having at last worked out that he actually worked on the train, it still came as a bit of a shock, on finally reaching Lahore, to be confronted by a relatively large bill to cover all the

71

catering for the entire journey. The truth is, I suppose I felt a bit miffed and disappointed really at having to pay, when all along I'd thought it nothing more than a great show of kindness. Still, although there was perhaps a brief twinge of disappointment, I could hardly feel any animosity toward my happy catering attendant could I. After all, he'd simply been going about his business, and the whole thing had been very much a misunderstanding on my part. I put the incident down to yet another mild bout of naivety.

After the quiet and the wide open expanses of the Indus valley, the busy urban bustle of Lahore was both a vivid and sobering contrast. People and traffic were absolutely everywhere. And it was here that I first discovered that, whatever other religion or religions reign in this part of the world, surely the most dominant of them all is cricket! Absolutely everyone and everything, all over Lahore is used as part of the game. Boys and young men alike, cavorting between traffic four and five lanes across in hot pursuit of a little round ball; dodging auto-rickshaws, taxis, buses and carts and hurling the ball back to a homemade wicket of orange boxes over the heads of shoppers, traders and businessmen; all of them clearly resigned to being just another obstacle in the 'great game'.

All over the city, every single time I spoke to anyone, I constantly faced the one same question; not an enquiry into my beliefs, my culture or my politics but a question that to the people of Lahore, was far, far more important; "So who do you think is best: Imran Khan, Kapil Dev or Ian Botham?" Cricket wasn't simply a sport here, it was a way of life! I was left in no doubt whatsoever that this undying passion, virtually from the moment every male leaves the womb, has had a great deal to do with the Pakistani's many successes at international level. It's simply in their blood! It made me think back fondly to the days when I was a child, when almost every English street was occupied by a handful of boys and a football; when jumpers were goalposts and the game only ever ended when it was tea time. Sadly those days are now a distant memory and it's hard to imagine them returning; certainly not to the fanatical extent as cricketing in Pakistan, or indeed India or Sri Lanka for that matter. Still, at least there's a little more 'footballing' interest at home again at grass roots level which, I'm convinced, can only be a positive thing; not necessarily to promote competitiveness but to encourage team bonding and good sportsmanship.

Having spent the best part of the morning wandering the streets of Lahore, I thought it time to rid myself of my heavy load and so, with the Ramsgate duo still in tow, I checked into a slightly seedy but friendly looking hotel near the centre of town. There were a number of travellers already staying at the hotel -presumably because of its twin assets of being both cheap and central- and they appeared to come from all four corners of the globe (though, despite numerous journeys since, I have yet to find an edge to the globe, yet alone a corner.) I then enjoyed a nice long afternoon with an equally nice long drink, sitting around out of the heat and catching up on a bit of global gossip.

The proprietor of the hotel, who'd obviously done rather well out of his business, was not only well dressed but, amongst a somewhat lean nation, looked extremely well fed. This to such an extent that, though almost certainly already in his late forties, it was difficult to gauge due to the chubbiness of his whole little rotund body ironing out any sign of wrinkles. Why, even his face was totally wrinkle free and this, coupled with an exceedingly shiny bald head and a pair of very large forward pointing nostrils, well, I couldn't help thinking that had he been down the local bowling alley he'd have been in imminent danger of taking a rather greater part in the game than he'd have wanted.

Like so many people I'd met on this trip before him, the hotel owner came across as being an amazingly jolly and friendly chap, but it soon became all too obvious that my friendship wasn't the first of this proprietor's priorities. For as we chatted together, with the two girls sitting close beside me, I began to realise that I was rapidly losing his attention as his eyes started switching more and more from mine to theirs. Then, before long, midway through a sentence I must have become completely invisible; for now this man, the man who'd been chatting away to me like a long lost friend, was totally transfixed by these two young white females. Very soon he was directing all of his conversation towards the girls, and as he did, so his dark piggy eyes lit up like a pair of highly polished conkers and globules of saliva all but dribbled from the corners of his mouth. Well, this blatant lusting was a little annoying at first and I couldn't help but take the ignoring personally; however his obvious 'fondness' for the girls did turn out to have its advantages because, very shortly, the three of us were treated to a brief tour of the city in his own private car, and then the tour was rounded off by an extremely nice meal at his favourite restaurant.

Now, most of the evening, of course, I might as well have been just another one of the many cheese-plants in the corner of the room, as Abdullah played an exceedingly 'hammy' host (somewhat ironic in a Muslim country) to his new female audience; but well, despite feeling decidedly gooseberry-like, it was a good night out all the same. At least I got to learn a few things about Pakistan, even if the information was very much directed toward our Ramsgate contingent. (Maybe he wasn't being rude but just happened to have two very wonky eyes! Though at least it couldn't be quite as embarrassing as my first ever conversation with a man with a so called, lazy eye; where I kept looking over my shoulder to see who the poor chap was talking to!)

One of the things I learnt on that evening, and something that had had me a little perplexed ever since I first arrived here, was why people chew betel nut; or more correctly, 'store' betel nut -as it's actually left in the mouth for some considerable time and gives the user the appearance of a very large hamster on hard times. It seems to me a pretty ghastly habit but appears every bit as popular here as smoking cigarettes was back in post war Britain. The difference being though, that whilst dog-ends hardly enhance the beauty of our towns and countryside back home in England, they are at least easily removable. By contrast, the result of betel nut chewing in Pakistan, or rather the discarding of it afterwards, is not only a damned sight more obvious, but nobody seems in the least bit interested in removing the evidence. In fact everywhere you look, great red blotches and splodges haphazardly decorate walls, pavements, roads and houses, as if some vast plague of extremely well nourished mosquitoes had just hit town and committed mass suicide. Of course, if this rather strange ritual were fashionable in 'any' part of the world it would have been bad enough, but against a background of buildings made up largely of off-white and white, the bright red splattering positively shone. And it seems that here in Lahore, just about everything within 'spitting distance' is a bona fide target; that is, everything that doesn't move…but come to think of it, even some that do. Either that or they've got some rather strange looking Dalmatians around here.

Now betel nut, I'm reliably informed, is a mild stimulant and is taken on a regular basis by a good proportion of the local population here; not least the elderly who, no doubt keen to improve their dwindling sex appeal, sit around in every available doorway smiling happily at passers-by through three or four well spaced and red-stained teeth. Not that it's the sole preserve of the elderly -there doesn't appear to be an age of consent for betel nut- but it's with the elderly that the results are that much more obvious. This is perhaps for two reasons; for not only do the elderly tend to engage more in the national pastime of doorway squatting -having already retired from cricket- but they typically make no apology for their betel nut habit; nor indeed do they try to hide it. So much so, in fact, that were it not for the broad gappy grins everywhere you look, you could easily be forgiven for thinking that each and every one of them frequented the same madly sadistic dentist.

You know, I've always been keen to try anything new that comes my way -with the obvious exceptions of bestiality and ironing shirts- and here in Lahore seemed the ideal time and place to give betel nut a go. Well, back at the hotel the opportunity duly came along, and it was the fat hotel proprietor who talked me through the preparation of the betel nut package whilst I carefully took note and copied his every move. So, this is how it goes:

Firstly, you get yourself a vine leaf. Then secondly, you place your nut in the middle of the leaf and spray some sort of concoction of chemicals over it -though I haven't a clue what these chemicals are, or if it's normal practice to do so. Thirdly, you roll the leaf and all its contents up in a tight bundle and pop the whole thing into your mouth. And well....that's about it! Of course, I'd been following the hotel owner's every move up till now, and when we got to the "pop the whole thing in your mouth" stage, the next and last move I thought, seemed like stating bleedin' obvious; and so, in one go, I swallowed the lot...whole! Well, what can I say but, within less than ten seconds, and much to the amusement of all around, I sat down on the chair with a heavy 'thud' and felt so violently ill that I just couldn't move. I clutched at my stomach feeling horribly, horribly sick and the others, yes...they clutched at theirs in fits of hysterical laughter. In fact, whilst I was sitting there close to dying, all the others were falling about so much that it was a good five minutes before the laughter had completely subsided. Then, when the proprietor felt composed enough to speak, he informed me that, in all his days, he'd never actually seen betel nut taken in that way. He then went on to explain that 'normally' the package is simply placed in the side of the mouth and lodged against the gum so that the bloody cocktail can ooze out over a considerable period; this provides perhaps, a slightly numbed lip but, more importantly, "a nice tingling sensation". Well, a nice tingling sensation most definitely wasn't what I was feeling. My stomach felt more like I'd just swallowed a large lump of warm lard topped with a Domestos vinaigrette sauce. It was absolutely foul. Quite the worst taste I'd ever experienced! My betel nut baptism had been enough for one day and, although the horribly sick feeling did subside surprisingly quickly, I decided that I'd be quite happy to never ever go anywhere near the stuff again.

NB 'Betel' nut is actually a slight misnomer. This package is, more correctly, an areca nut wrapped in a betel leaf -a type of vine leaf- and is 'usually' accompanied by lime and/or a concoction of spices.

During the first day in my Lahore hotel I'd received several warnings from fellow guests about things going mysteriously missing from rooms; and so I was more than a little concerned when I had to spend my first night in a room with a completely glassless window and a highly dubious looking lock on the door. I decided, as I'd often done in the past, that I'd sleep with my passport and money belt under my body, and the rest, I'd have to leave to chance. Most other hotel guests, being rather more experienced than myself it seemed, had had the forethought to bring along their own padlocks and chains. But, you know, I thought it rather a shame to have to resort to such a measure, thereby leaving the hotel staff in no doubt whatsoever as to your distrust of them. The trouble is, I suppose, that when you start out on an adventure like this, you can be either naïvely trustful (trusting everyone) or naïvely distrustful (trusting no-one). So on the one hand you're open to a multitude of possible friendships but also the odd crook; on the other...you're open to neither -because you've already assumed everyone to be a potential crook and guarded against it. Personally,

I'll take the former every time; -though admittedly the ideal path is probably somewhere in between.

Still, despite my slight concerns - yes, I did have them- by the end of a whole week at the hotel, I'd lost absolutely nothing. This seemed even more remarkable since, over that same period, just about every one of my fellow travellers had experienced at least one loss or more. Now, I'd liked to have claimed that this was perhaps due to my more trusting attitude toward the hotel and its staff but alas, I can't help thinking, if truth be known, that there may have been an altogether different reason. You see, at this time, all foreign nationals staying in Pakistan were able to obtain vouchers from the government in order to buy alcohol which of course, as their religion dictates, was banned to the local Muslim population. Not that this prohibition prevented a good many Muslims from wanting to get their hands on the stuff; and so, consequently, there was always a thriving black market for spirits, and at greatly inflated prices. This naturally created a business opportunity for some entrepreneurial middle men to cash in on. The game, as a tourist, was this:

Firstly you have to go and get your alcohol vouchers at the local office -at what department I don't recall- for this, all you required was a foreign passport, an address in Pakistan and the money to buy the drink. You then find an upmarket International hotel -one with real glass windows- where you could walk in and buy two bottles of whisky (preferably Johnny Walker, as that was the favoured brand). This, as a foreigner, was the monthly allowance that you could obtain with your vouchers. You'd then take the bottles back to your own cheap hotel and sell them on to the proprietor at double the price you paid for them. Simple! It was, of course, possible to obtain a much higher profit margin by hawking this unholy of vices on the streets; however, I was reliably informed by others 'in the know', that by doing the deal with your own hotel, you could pretty well guarantee the safety of the possessions in your room; a sort of honour among thieves and black market racketeers I suppose. Well, rightly or wrongly, that's exactly what I did and...it seemed to work for me! Either that or I just got very, very, very, very lucky!

Of all the sights in Lahore that emphasise the many differences in culture between East and West, perhaps one of the more obvious and extraordinary (to Westerners) is the sight of an adult man walking the streets hand in hand -or more usually little finger in little finger- with another. Of course, in the West we are quite used to seeing such a show of friendship amongst girls, but between Western macho males it is something that even today is taboo in public (unless perhaps, you happen to come from Brighton!)

You know, personally, I've always felt it a shame that the average Northern European male -in particular- is so conservative with his affections; and it was interesting here in Pakistan to note the difference. That said, at this time I certainly had a great deal of deliberation as to whether all this finger entwining was simply a show of friendship and affection or perhaps that the difficulty for young men here in trying to court Muslim girls had led to a slight hormone imbalance amongst a certain proportion of the male population. (Should Lahore be twinned with Brighton I ask!) After all, each and every one of us, throughout our short and fragile lives, is undoubtedly susceptible to outside influences, and I for one don't believe that 'being gay' is necessarily purely a genetic thing; nor do I believe that any one of us is 100% male or female but simply somewhere on that long, long line between the two; but, well....that's quite another story.

The thing is, at the end of the day, whatever the truth about these men I saw in Lahore, I prefer to think that the former is true; that the personal contact between them is nothing more than a sign of friendship, a bonding of two pals. This isn't through reasons of homophobia at all, but quite simply because I rather like the idea -at least- of males being able to display their emotions, not only towards females but towards other males   i.e. my philosophy in life has always been: I'm a human being first…and a male second!

One typically sunny morning in Lahore, the strength of my slightly conservative Western upbringing was put to the test.   I'd been passing the morning in the shade of a market stall casually chatting away -in English of course- to a local stallholder. Shortly, we were joined by a couple of his friends, and after the inevitable protracted introductions, this chap invited me to walk with them -I forget where exactly but that's beside the point. The point is: that we ended up walking along a busy street in the centre of the city…hand in hand! Now obviously, the initiative for this came from him, but he did it with such nonchalance, so very casually that it happened almost before I was aware of it. We were just walking down the street and, without ever pausing from his chattering, he simply took hold of my hand and continued on; and all without either him or his friends so much as batting an eyelid…so to speak.   It seemed to this man the most natural thing in the world. And whilst it's true to say that,

81

at that very moment, I didn't feel entirely comfortable about the situation, I'd also certainly no wish to offend him whatever the reason he was doing it. And so we continued, gaily on our way...oops! I mean...umm, merrily on our way...or was it? Oh I don't know, we continued anyway.

N.B. Regardless of what is or isn't true, it strikes me as quite appropriate anyway -amongst such a cricketing nation- to introduce a Freudian slip!

Over the next few days I had a great time chatting to all the English speaking locals. (I'm always a little reluctant to use the word 'natives' as, in the Western world, it still tends to have a slightly derogatory ring to it.) One such man was Abrahim, a man in his early thirties, who'd clearly had a fairly good education and who'd set up his own small business as a wool merchant. And when I say small, that's exactly what I do mean; for his shop was no more than eight feet wide and thirty feet deep. This in turn, was sandwiched between an equally small greengrocer's and a flour seller's.

Now, Abrahim employed just one young boy who, in the course of long days spent filling sacks with raw wool, looked very much like he'd actually produced the wool from his own body. In fact, what with his Velcro-esque shirt and trousers coupled with a slightly elongated dark face and mass of fuzzy hair, I can honestly say that never in all my life have I seen anyone -who wasn't a sheep-look quite so 'sheepish'.

I liked Abrahim and during the course of the following day, we discussed every subject imaginable from cricket to...well, cricket -with just a garnishing of culture and politics for variety! Then by late afternoon -ironically, just when the heat was tolerable enough to work in- Abrahim decided that it was time to shut up shop and he invited me to come back to his home and to meet his family. This I considered for a full millisecond and then accepted wholeheartedly. You see, I'd heard so much about Eastern hospitality in the past and now that I had the opportunity to sample it first hand, I really relished the thought. So, after a brief conversation with Abrahim, we agreed that the best thing to do was for him to pick me up from my hotel "just as soon as he'd got out of his 'wool' suit and cleaned up a bit". He also suggested that perhaps I "might like to bring the two English girls along with me?" (I'd perhaps rather foolishly mentioned the Ramsgate girls whilst chatting at his stall). So with that, I went off back to the hotel to tell the girls about the evening's plans and then retired to my room to lie on the bed and do a bit of swatting up on Pakistan and its history...just in case I should be put on the spot by one of Abrahim's family. Well, swatting up was the intention anyway. Unfortunately, these swatting sessions -of which there were many- would invariably turn into long and protracted bouts of semi-comatose ceiling starings, as I'd gaze into nothingness trying hard to digest at least a fraction of what I'd experienced that particular day. Still, either way, at least I was learning something, no matter how useful or useless it may have been. Mind you, and I don't want to go off at a tangent here but, I suppose learning only really counts as learning if you can recall the information later. They say that a young mind is "like a sponge"; well, in my experience, as soon as you remove a sponge from whatever it's just sucked up....it loses it equally as quickly!

Later, as promised, Abrahim and a friend arrived at the hotel on a couple of scooters. They were both far too polite to comment on my choice of hotel, though it was quite obviously not what they'd expected of a Westerner. It seemed fine to me, but for these two, why, they'd hardly set foot in the foyer before turning toward to each other, and in unison, were quickly engaged in a bit of none-too-subtle synchronised eyebrow raising. Then, Abrahim caught my eye and hastily beckoned the three of us out into the street. Next, we all mounted our motorbikes and were whisked through, what was now, a slightly less frantic city centre; me riding pillion behind Abrahim, and the two girls squashed up behind his very contented looking friend.

After perhaps fifteen minutes of deft weaving through a conglomeration of cars, trucks, buses and cricket outfielders -yes, it was less frantic but only relatively so- we shortly entered a maze of side roads and at once the cacophony subsided to a gentle hum. Then, soon the roads became smaller and smaller and in no time we were right in the heart of a bungalow filled suburb and pulling up outside the very neat and tidy middle class looking home that was Abrahim's.

As we all dismounted and began to approach the bungalow, we were politely ushered ahead by our host; the door then opened and a small but expectant welcoming party quickly formed itself into an orderly queue and we were formally introduced to everybody in the room. This in itself took a fair amount of time as, although there were just the three of us, there were at least eight of them. And now, all of 'them' were introduced individually to all of 'us'. This home team was made up of Abrahim's wife, his young son and daughter, the wife's friend and no fewer than four of Abrahim's male friends. Of course, whilst these introductions were all necessary protocol, they didn't really serve any practical function as nobody in the room was likely to be able to even pronounce anybody else's name, let alone remember it. Still, we went through the motions all the same and I smiled and shook my way along the line and hoped I'd get to the last one before it was home time.

Once inside, I noticed that the front door through which we'd entered, led not into a hallway but opened directly onto a large square-ish sitting room. Here, as is the case virtually the world over, all the furniture was focused towards a television in the corner. Abrahim was clearly proud to be able to introduce the three of us to his family and beamed as if he'd just shown up with a brand new sports car. But, you know, although it was nice to meet them all, it was quite a strange moment really. It appeared nobody in the party could speak a single word of our language, or indeed we of theirs. Therefore, the whole protracted performance, though animated, took place in near silence, and once again I felt an immense feeling of frustration at not being able to converse in somebody else's language. Certainly, both parties tried their damnedest to convey what they could through smiles, head waggles and other assorted gestures, but somehow it just wasn't the same.

Anyway, after what seemed an age, I'd almost finished grinning my way down the welcome party line when, to my left, Ramsgate Sue -the last in our line- was finally introduced to Abrahim's wife.

"Eeeeeeeeeeeeeek!" Immediately the wife set eyes on Sue, a great high-pitched shriek rang out as if she'd just had one of her stubby little brown toes squashed by an oversized brahmin bull. Well, like me, Sue stepped back, slightly stunned and perplexed, and it was only after an awful lot of pointing and gabbling that it became clear what all the excitement was about. After such a reaction, I thought at the very least Sue must have had something monstrously large and foreign growing out of the centre of her face but no, all it was, was that like Abrahim's wife, Sue also wore a stud in her nose! Soon, the girlfriend and daughter were also pointing and shrieking with delight, almost jumping up and down, crowding round Sue and examining her nose in close-up. In fact, all in all, it caused such an incredible stir amongst these people that, for a brief moment, I felt rather envious that I too didn't possess something similar to bridge the cultural gap; a henna tattoo perhaps or, like busty Sue, a small silver nugget stuck up my nostril.

After what seemed like the best part of a evening had past, the formalities were finally over and, still with much excited and incomprehensible chatter at Sue's stud, the girls were then ushered away into the next room by the hostess and her entourage. I, meanwhile, was given a seat amongst the men who very quickly regrouped into a tight little semi-circle around the TV. It was quite apparent, by the random twitching and uneasy shuffling in seats, that every one of the men around me shared my frustration at not being able to communicate, and so there followed a slightly awkward period of silence, as pairs of eyes and broad, slightly false smiles shifted between me and the raucous incomprehensible quiz show that was blaring from the television screen.

Several exceedingly long minutes later and I realised that the quiz show was definitely winning the battle for their attention. Hardly surprising I suppose given that, however mind-numbingly boring the quiz may have been, it must have seemed infinitely more exciting than some dumb Westerner who couldn't even speak their language. And so, as a consequence, all eyes bar mine now became vehemently glued to the screen. Sadly, Abrahim, the one person who could speak good English, was also soon hypnotised by the television screen and I was left wondering what the hell this meeting was all about. I suppose this feeling was further exasperated by the fact that I'd had such high hopes, such high expectations in the first place; I just felt so terribly disappointed.

Meanwhile, from the room at the back of the house, I could hear whoops of laughter from the girls, and as the time dragged on, though I knew that it would be so very wrong, I now longed to join them. I looked around at all the men realising full well that, even though I might as well not have existed, I was expected to stay exactly where I was. For the next half an hour I did just that. Not so much as one eye left the television screen for a single second until, finally, and regretfully...I could stand it no longer. I got up, left my chair and sloped off to see what all the excitement was about in the other room.

The door to the back room was slightly ajar and, as I looked in, there were dresses and materials scattered all over the place and about them a wonderfully happy atmosphere of boisterousness. Immediately, the women turned and saw me standing in the open doorway and I wondered how I would be received. To my surprise and great relief it didn't seem to matter a jot to them that I was there. They simply carried on laughing and chattering away and getting the girls to try on their traditional costumes (without exposing any flesh of course!) It was wonderful; everything so totally relaxed and natural. Unfortunately...the same couldn't be said of the men. For no sooner had I left them to look in on the girls, than the quiz show was completely abandoned and I became the subject of a somewhat heated discussion. Well, it didn't require any sort of language at all for me to realise that I'd obviously caused considerable offence to these people. And it's true to say that frustrated and bored though I may have been, I did feel more than a twinge of guilt at having perhaps abused my friend's hospitality. The strange thing is that though these men were certainly angry, it wasn't so much directed at me for being so rude, but at themselves for not having been more attentive hosts. (I learnt this later from Abrahim!)

Anyway, whatever the ins and outs, the rights and wrongs of the whole thing, the net result was that the three of us were shortly escorted back to our hotel. Nothing much was said between Abrahim and myself either during or after the journey, but, you know...it didn't have to be. We were both clearly very sorry about the whole incident but agreed anyway to meet up at his shop the following day.

The next morning I was up, washed and changed and went down to the reception area to do a bit of reading. A couple of other young travelling-types lolled around with a similar idea, enjoying a lazy few minutes draped randomly and haphazardly over the scattered chairs as if they'd fallen into that position from three floors up. It was hardly luxurious here but enjoyable nonetheless; a nice little quiet and shady communal spot shut away from the city as it was; whilst outside, the world buzzed, squealed and spluttered in the brilliant sunshine.

One of my fellow lounging hotel guests was Michel, a young French/Swiss chap of about twenty one. He was slightly built and had a generous mop of shoulder length, wavy black hair which, even without the platform footwear, gave him the appearance of a 70's Eurovision Song Contest singer. His voice was soft but as husky as a lifelong Gaulloise smoker, and when he spoke it was with such a broad French accent that it wasn't always clear whether he was speaking in English or French. Michel had apparently been 'on the road' for some time now, and keen to boost his dwindling finances, had been looking into the possibility of importing sapphires from Sri Lanka into Switzerland, naturally at a vast profit. Well, to me this all sounded a terrific idea and so, with ears cocked like a fennec fox, I started to listen intently to all that I was told, conjuring up all sorts of romantic images of myself becoming the next big sapphire importer. "Just how did so many people whom I'd met become so 'apparently' worldly wise with so few years behind them", I wondered. It was amazing. People like Michel here seemed to have the whole thing worked out. I'd thought before that I wasn't doing so badly, that I'd experienced a few things, but now it made me wonder what on earth I'd been doing all my life!

Meanwhile, back at the story, Michele assured me that if I was at all interested in becoming a gem importer, then there would be absolutely no problem in me following his lead. He then handed me a small scrap of paper, torn roughly from the corner of an old school exercise book, and on it were written the words 'Double Cutting'. This, from what I understood, was the name of a small village in Sri Lanka where I should buy the gems to take back to Europe. (Further on in the trip, it would transpire that I'd somehow completely misunderstood Michel and that a chance meeting with a very large and hairy Australian would lead me to something altogether different).

Later that same morning I met up once again with Abrahim at his wool shop. Nothing was said by either of us about the previous day's incident and, to his great credit, I was greeted as if it had never taken place. He then introduced me to yet another friend of his who, on learning of my nationality, greeted me with those all too familiar words,
"So, who you think is best: Imran Khan, Kapil Dev or Ian Botham?" Now, in these situations I would almost invariably stick up for 'Beefy' and, as always, there would then follow a lengthy but light hearted discussion as to the various attributes of 'the big three'.* Not that I was the best person in the world to ask about cricket you understand. After all, whilst playing for the school team, I once bowled a ten ball over because I couldn't quite figure out when to release the ball from my grasp. On the plus side, this did at least have the effect of making the batsman extremely nervous, though unfortunately...not the one I was bowling to! Anyway, however chequered my cricketing history, here in Lahore, it was always assumed by just about everyone I met, that my being English automatically made me a cricketer and a good one at that.

* When sticking up for 'Beefy' I'd invariably comment to people that I thought he was the "better batter" (yes, I do know it's batsman). Though, if Botham had known of Kapil Dev's incredible reputation here, I suppose he may well have been a slightly "bitter better batter"....Actually, come to think of it, I reckon he was also the best bowler and therefore perhaps...not only a "bitter better batter, but a better bowler". Just a thought!

CHAPTER 8

- MOSQUES, RIVERS AND CRICKET MATCHES -

In Lahore

Now as luck would have it, this new friend of Abrahim's just happened to play for a local cricket team and they were due to play a game the very next day. Well of course, it was quite hopeless trying to turn down the invitation to join in, and anyway, although slightly dubious about my prowess in that direction, I relished the chance to be a part of a proper game in a foreign country. Rather frighteningly though, it did occur to me that I'd hardly put bat to ball since my school days. But when I tentatively let this slip out, it just didn't appear to matter to them one jot. I was, after all, an Englishman and therefore a cricketer; an Ambassador for my country and for Beefy Botham and the boys back home.

Well, the match was set for the following morning and once again my new friends insisted that they would be there to pick me up from the hotel. So, with that, I thanked them, we said our goodbyes and I wandered off with an extra spring in my step ready to explore a little more of Lahore.

I have to say that, for me at least, the very best part of travelling is simply to be amongst different people doing different things, and far from being time wasted, I enjoy nothing more than to sit back and people watch; soaking up the sights, sounds and the smells of what for them is everyday life, but what for me is sublimely…different! Of course, that's not to say that I don't also enjoy a lot of the more usual highlights of a particular place. Take the Badshahi Mosque for example; one of the greatest and most memorable sights in Lahore or in all Pakistan perhaps; and this, a sight that I came across purely by accident. The Badshahi, whilst surprisingly little known in the West, is one huge, great, beautiful, red-tinged conglomeration of onion domes and minarets. Everything here on such an enormous scale -with supposedly the world's largest enclosed courtyard- and yet, despite the hordes of Islamic faithfuls who visit daily, it still remains spotlessly clean.   In fact, as a tourist sight I thought it rather special, and I was more than happy to while away a long morning there; to do what? Well okay, yes, mostly to simply people watch but, you know, how nice to be able to do it in such beautiful and awe inspiring surroundings.

I greatly enjoyed my time at the mosque, and after leaving it, started walking back to the hotel via the river which snoozes its way lazily through the city. The water was very low at this time of year and small farming families had erected make-shift shelters of wood, cardboard and plastic sheeting along the exposed river banks, taking full advantage of the new space available.   Everywhere, fresh new grass had sprung up all over the distended mudflats and handfuls of bony cattle and goats grazed happily away. Here and there young children were splashing and frolicking about in the silty Indus as carefree as newborn lambs, whilst their elder sisters shuttled back and forth between river and their ramshackle straw huts, heads laden with giant metal pots full of river water. It was a wonderfully timeless and rural scene. Everyone appeared so deliriously content with what little they had. But I couldn't help wondering what would happen when the river rose again and their homes would surely disappear under several feet of muddy water. Perhaps for them it's just become a way of life: commuting as they must between the permanent and the temporary river banks; taking full advantage of the fertile ground when it becomes available and then retiring to the more permanent edge -homes and all- when the water returns; scuttling up and down the banks each year like sanderlings on a tidal mudflat.

I wandered for a mile or two along the riverbank under the searing heat of the afternoon sun. There was no cooling breeze coming off the river, none at all. Everything and everybody moved about as if with a post stag-party hangover, save the children of course, who laughed and cavorted unceasingly in the water. Elsewhere, kites sat out the heat in lofty treetops, and buffaloes, with their dull expressions of resignation, took well-earned wallows before returning for the long hard afternoon session in front of a plough.

Away from the river I walked through a local marketplace. It was an everyday needs type of market with rows of fragile and rickety stalls full of soap and dustpans, and despite there being no shade whatsoever, it was still very much in full flow. I strolled on down the centre aisle then, unusually for somewhere so far from the city centre, I picked out the blonde head of a Northern European poking up above the busy thicket of black ones. Feeling curious, I went over to introduce myself and it transpired that the blonde head belonged to a German who, like the Frenchman I'd met back in Istanbul, was attempting to cycle his way around the world. Unlike the Frenchman however, whose bike had spent its last thousand odd miles on top of a bus, he'd already successfully managed to get this far under his own steam -or rather, his own pedal power- and so I looked forward to hearing about what must surely have been, an incredible adventure.

Well, as I discovered, apparently this German had just spent the past couple of weeks cycling up the Indus valley, all the way from Karachi, and had stayed with local families the whole of that time. And, all of these families, without exception, had taken him in and refused to accept anything whatsoever in the way of payment for their hospitality. So, in the course of a fortnight, this German had spent precisely...nothing!

Now, I'd heard of similar tales in the past, particularly - and paradoxically- in countries whose people could least afford such generosity. I also knew that the more basic the form of transport you choose to take, the more empathy you are likely to feel from the people you meet (in this respect, cycling perhaps coming a very respectable third to walking and horse-riding in the transport pecking order, but very much ahead of any motor driven vehicle.) But there was something about this chap that I didn't feel entirely comfortable about. You see, his reaction to all this unbelievable hospitality didn't appear to be one of astonishment and overwhelming gratitude. On the contrary, he appeared strangely nonchalant and cocky even, as if to say, "Hey look, I've managed to get by without paying a cent, but you know what, it was a pleasure for 'them' to meet me!" This gut feeling I had was further re-enforced by the German's very next action, for as we walked along the street at the edge of the market, he casually picked up an apple from a nearby stall and barely managed so much as a glance towards the stall owner as if to say, "Well, you don't mind do you?" before walking on his way. Consequently, I was left wondering just how hard this chap had tried to repay all the generosity that had been lavished on him over the past two weeks. Of course, it's quite possible that I may be doing him a great injustice but umm…I think not!

Still with this thought in mind we walked on. I'd already decided that I didn't really want to spend any more time in his company, but just then, the German's conspicuous form attracted the attention of a couple of teenage boys who ran over towards us. They were well dressed and good looking lads, these two, brothers in fact, and both of them spoke excellent English. Then, no sooner had we exchanged greetings with them than they enthusiastically encouraged us to accompany them back to their home. Well, in the light of my lingering negative thoughts about the German I felt a little pulled apart about whether to go or not, and secretly I wished that Hans would just 'get on his bike'. But, at the same time, I felt reluctant to miss out on this opportunity for some local contact and so I temporarily pushed my feelings aside and decided to join them.

Somewhat annoyingly, the two boys were clearly impressed by this giant blonde German and excitedly ushered him along the busy street, zigzagging between fruit and spice laden stalls whilst I, in the background, followed on. Then, we were taken off down a shady side road and led up to a very parched and patchy looking façade, beyond which lay their modest home. Just as we arrived, a small plump woman with a small plump face opened the door and smiled warmly. She led us into a tiny, square, windowless interior where we were invited to sit down on what little furniture they had, and were offered the obligatory cup of tea. Shortly, Mohammed -the two boys' father- entered from another room carrying a lit candle which he placed carefully on a shelf, before turning and welcoming us in near perfect English.

Like his wife, Mohammed was diminutive in size, standing little more than five feet tall and, even by local standards, so drably dressed that he could easily have passed for a Dickensian pauper. He also sported an equally drab and coarse woolly hat over a balding head and shuffled about in a homely pair of dust coloured sandals. But, much more noticeable than all this, Mohammed wore that wonderfully warm and deeply contented face of an old man who'd been through a great deal but had at least found some of the answers.

You know, I always find it hard to make any sort of a guess at people's ages when they live in tropical regions because, for those who've had to make their livings in the open air, the tropical sun can be so mercilessly ageing. (Though, if pushed...I'd say that Mohammed would've been about sixty!) Anyway, he was an immediately likeable man; sort of calm, kind and paternal, and I couldn't help but take a real shine to him. But not only that, for it turned out that we also had a little in common, as both of us had made our respective livings working with wood. The medium in which we worked though was about as tenuous a link as we could have had; for whilst, at

97

this time, I was simply a carpenter working on houses and occasionally knocking together the odd bit of rustic furniture, here in a dark little box of a house, tucked away in a quiet corner of Lahore, lived as skilled a wood sculptor as I've seen in my life. And not only that, but because Mohammed was old enough to have been around during the British occupation, he also spoke my language and so was able to talk to me about his work; a tremendous bonus for me...even if the information did take a little prizing out of him. Not that he didn't enjoy chatting to me at all, I believe he did, it's just that Mohammed was such a delightfully modest man. In fact it wasn't until much later -after yet another round of tea- that I managed to persuade Mohammed to actually show me some of his sculptures. This he agreed to do, and as he led me from the dingy room to an even dingier little room to the rear of the house, once my eyes had become accustomed to the gloom, I found myself being stared at by all manner of intricately carved forms lining the slatted shelves. These sculptures were quite unbelievable; just so wonderful, every one of them. Everything from lolloping buffalos straining against the plough to wizened old men with devout and drawn faces; beautiful, pert breasted, water-bearing girls in all sorts of positions, and a large effigy of Christ on a crucifix so detailed that, not only could you count every single emaciated rib, but also, every protruding vein which ran among them. Each and every man, woman, beast and object was a glimpse into local life -apart from Christ of course- a brief moment frozen in time, dwarfed and then painstakingly hewn from timber.

It was evident that, though remaining thoroughly modest throughout, Mohammed enjoyed showing me his work;

and before I left he said that he'd have liked to have given me one of his lady water bearers which I'd so admired, "if only they'd been finished"! I told him what a really kind thought it was and that I would've dearly loved to have had one "if only one had been finished". Secretly though I thought "God, never mind a finished lady water bearer, what I wouldn't give for one barely started"! (Most were pretty near to finished anyway and all...quite, quite beautiful.) Still it wasn't to be. It was time for me to leave. We walked back into the room where the others were still sitting around and chatting. Then shortly, Hans got to his feet and, without so much as a word of thanks, made for the door and stepped out again into the sunshine. I thanked Mohammed so much for showing me his work, thanked his wife for the tea and then left...in the opposite direction to the German. (I later learnt that Mohammed had been commissioned to do sculptures for a museum in Karachi.)

The following morning I awoke to the usual cacophony on the streets below my glassless window. Then, realising the time, I ran downstairs to reception and, as promised, was met by my new found cricketing friend. Shortly we then sped off down the road in his ancient but lovingly cared-for family saloon, and drove through the city to the cricket ground.

When we arrived, the entrance to the ground was distinctly plain and unremarkable, which seemed to me a shame for somewhere that would obviously provoke such passion on a regular basis. (Actually, I'm not quite sure why I remarked that it was unremarkable...or even if that's possible!) The ground itself was sandwiched between a variety of middle-class suburban houses, all of them painted in multiple shades of white, and every one of them, though undeniably neat and tidy, with a biscuit coloured 'plimsoll line' running all the way around their base; a sort of plinth, peppered with splatterings of mud which had dried on after the last rare deluge of rain and which nobody could be bothered to clean off.

Once inside however, though the cricket ground entrance may not have been terribly grand, the real surprise was what now lay before me; for instead of the parched and knobbly patch of baked earth that I'd anticipated, here was a brilliantly vibrant swathe of green as flat as a billiard table; a luxuriant and lovingly cared-for oasis nestling in the heart of frantic and dusty Lahore. It was quite astonishing, but as welcome as it was surprising. Shortly, we walked over and stood around in the awfully-frightfully, frightfully-terribly English looking cricket pavilion discussing the ground and all its facilities. It was a hot and humid day, and but for the oppressive heat, could just have easily been a summer's Sunday morning in a Home Counties village as in a busy city in central Asia. Meanwhile, everything outside the ground was obscured or shut away by the high surrounding wall: every site, out of sight and even the city sounds muffled to a faint murmur.

Fifteen minutes later and the other men started to appear. Shortly, I was being introduced to the rest of the team as they slowly entered the ground in their ones and twos and began filing into the changing room, each of them sporting a dazzlingly white set of shirt, trousers, shoes and teeth. Then, when they'd all assembled, a short team talk followed and it was decided that the normal 'sixth bat'

100

should drop out and that I should take his place in the team; and, not only that but, that the sixth bat should lend me his complete outfit of whites, minus the teeth. Well, though keen to play of course, I honestly, honestly tried my damnedest to turn down this wonderfully kind and unselfish gesture but, the team would hear nothing of it.

So, within a few minutes, all was set and the match got under way. My captain put the opponents in to bat, and after a few hours we'd managed to get them all out for…I don't quite recall, but not a lot. Well, the next thing that happened was the truly remarkable thing for, without going into greater detail, what transpired -or was it, what was 'conspired'- was that our batting line-up did rather well and when my time came, I duly went in to bat at number six with our team needing just six runs to win. So, there I stood at the crease; the field was set; all around waited with baited breath. The bowler prepared himself, ran in, let go of the ball. I stepped forward, made a sort of lunge; the ball zipped through past my bat and off flew one of my bails (to non-cricketers this may sound incredibly painful but it really isn't; please stay with me.)

A half-hearted cry of 'Owzat' went up from a couple of close fielders. But before I'd even had the time to feel hugely embarrassed, up shot the umpires arm with that face-saving pointy finger.

"No ball", he exclaimed, in a calm but authoritative voice. I looked around me; there didn't appear to be a strong objection from the bowler or from any of the fielders; just a bit of light incomprehensible chatter. Well, what could I do but go with the umpire's decision. I'd been judged 'not out' and I wasn't about to argue. So, with that, the bail was replaced on its stumps and we started again. Now this time it would be different, surely, wouldn't it…please!

The bowler set himself once again; he turned on his mark and started back down the pitch toward me; he then speeded to a slow canter, released the ball and 'thwack'; I cracked the ball down the leg side, cried,
"Yeeeesss!" and we managed to run two runs. What a relief! A generous applause rang out from the pavilion.
Then, with the field back in position, the ball was returned to the bowler, the bowler reloaded, once again turned the corner and came jogging in toward me. He then started to pick up speed, running faster and faster; increased to a gallop; brought his arm up; this time releasing the ball just that bit later. I quickly went onto the back foot and, 'tonk' the ball flew down the offside towards the boundary, whizzing through the grass and clonking against the wooden fence and…it was all over! Don't ask me how but I'd somehow managed six runs off two balls for our team to clinch the match. Amazing! Absolutely amazing! I strode back to the pavilion surrounded not only by my happy team mates but the whole of the away team all gleefully chatting and applauding. I smiled appreciatively, glad to share in our side's victory. But you know…yes, of course it was all quite wonderful but well, I couldn't help feeling slightly embarrassed and humbled by these peoples' sheer warmth and generosity. For to this day, I have never been able to quite fathom whether or not the whole game had been rigged in my favour. I really and honestly don't know but…I've a sneaking suspicion that it may have been!

Before leaving Lahore to head for India, I was to meet up with two Englishmen named Dave and Steve, whom - though I didn't know it at the time- I'd end up spending the whole of the following month with. The Ramsgate girls had already left Lahore by this time, once more rattling along in a Delhi bound bus, care of the British taxpayer. This was the last I ever saw of Sue and Julie, and I sometimes wonder just what they're doing and whether or not their bus trip to India made any difference to them as people. I do hope so…it's a bloody long way to go for a bit of sun and a biriany!

CHAPTER 9

- GOLDEN TEMPLES AND HOLY COWS -

Amritsar to Agra

When the train bound for India chugged in and slowly squeaked to a halt at the platform, Dave, Steve and I boarded our allotted carriage, slung our packs up into the racks above and had already completed our introductions before the train had pulled away from the station. Then, as we slowly gathered speed and the breeze from the window cleared the city dirt from our throats, town houses gradually gave way to slums, slums became urban, litter-strewn wasteland and then the urban wastelands blurred into the greens and browns of rural Pakistan.

Dave and Steve seemed a bright young pair of Englishmen; they were both in their early twenties and both had benefited from a University education, which sadly I had not (the closest I came to this experience was when sharing a house with three beer swilling, toast burning drop-outs named Lurch, Throbbing Gristle and Porno-Pete…don't ask!) But, apart from the more obvious common denominator -namely our lust for travel- we quickly realised that we shared a joint fondness for chess and Scrabble. This, though undoubtedly trivial, was to stand us all in good stead, for during the days that followed, many an hour was spent stooped over one board or another whilst the parched plains of the Indian subcontinent drifted slowly by. Periodically, we'd take it in turns to look up, snatching brief glimpses of life just outside the carriage window, all the while pondering another move: there, a naked runny-nosed boy chasing a squealing pig through a flurry of chickens; an old two tone buffalo -dust above, mud below- stands nonchalantly chewing the cud. Knight takes king's pawn...check!

The crossing into India must have been fairly easy and uneventful for, in all honestly, I have little recollection of it. Our first port of call in India though was to be the Punjabi city of Amritsar (The Punjab is India's Sikh state and, as such, is home to one of India's proudest peoples.) The three of us had long since established that we wanted to travel more or less the same path as one another through India, and so had decided to stick together...at least for the foreseeable future. Apart from the companionship that this gave us all, it also allowed me to pick the brains of my two travel mates. This was particularly timely since we were about to pull into such a famous and holy city.

Now, undoubtedly the number one 'must see' in Amritsar is, of course, the Golden Temple; the absolute holiest of holy shrines to the Sikhs and with a building and setting to rival any in the world. Naturally, when we arrived, the first thing to do was to find a place to stay about as central as we could sensibly afford and, as luck would have it, managed to book a room on the very top floor of a hostel...right next to the temple complex itself. This meant that, although unable to see the actual temple from my bedroom, if I were to go into the bathroom and stand with a slight crouch astride the wc, the beautiful and enigmatic Golden Temple was framed absolutely perfectly by the tiny glassless window. So whilst the hostel was hardly one of star laden quality, our toilet most certainly was, for it was surely the ultimate loo with a view.

I was up extra early the next morning and spent all day sleepily wandering the temple grounds. Despite my feelings of teenage-like lethargy it was an awe inspiring place: a gigantic swathe of spotless and blindingly white marble -polished by the feet of thousands- surrounding a huge, shallow pool of water; and at the centre of this pool, an absolutely sublime centre piece; the very intricate and very Golden Temple. The access to this was via a marble walkway which led out from one side of the pool to the temple in the middle -rather like a long, low drawbridge leading to a castle. Unfortunately, as a non-Sikh, I was forbidden entry to the temple itself and so I stood just outside and watched a young Sikh chap who sat cross-legged on a mat totally absorbed in some mega-thick, presumably religious, tome. I've no idea what it was he was reading of course, only that the book looked pretty important and that it appeared to be rather handsomely bound in leather. (In fact, the very first time in Asia I'd ever witnessed 'Hide and Sikh'!)

I'd have loved to have gone inside of course but, though I couldn't actually enter the temple, it would be hard to imagine how the inside could possibly be any more impressive than what can be seen from the outside. The combination of brilliant white marble and shimmering gold to some may seem a little garish, but the contrast is undeniably stunning and, to my mind, could only be improved by doing exactly what the Sikhs did: take one temple, put it in beautiful surroundings and then...just add water. For me at least, this place is quite simply magical!

I'm told that Sikhs come from all over the world to visit

the Golden Temple and indeed it was no problem finding someone to talk to in English about the Sikh struggle for independence from India, and how they tried to set up their own independent state. In fact, the very day I was there, I witnessed a party of school children parading around with their colourful silk banners, reminding people that though the Punjab is a part of India, "it may not always be so!" I also couldn't help noticing that amongst these banners there were reminders of perhaps Amritsar's darkest period in recent history when a whole congregation of men, women and children were massacred on the orders of a single officer during the British occupation. This event was later covered, of course, in Richard Attenborough's film Gandhi; an event about which I found it quite impossible to contain my feelings. In fact, on first witnessing this particular scene in the film, I stood up in tears amid a crowded cinema audience and shouted "You bastard!"...much to the surprise of both my mum and all of those around.

The journey down to Delhi was a long and stiflingly hot one. Even the movement of air afforded by the glassless windows was as hot as a freshly baked chapatti; the heat seemingly all the more oppressive knowing that the cool foothills of the mighty Himalaya lay only hours by train to the north-east. It felt excruciatingly frustrating being within a very long stones throw of these great mountains and yet not even lay eyes on them; but I thought to myself, not for the first time, this would have to be something for the future. Not that I was complaining...much. Indeed, I fully recognise that we all have to make choices at times, especially when travelling, and especially as virtually all of us have the restraints of time or money; or more usually both. But well, isn't it just so teasing, so tantalising when you know full well that there's a wealth of wonderful sights 'just up the road' and you've no hope of seeing or experiencing them. The problem is that, 'just' is very relative in terms of time and distance, and come to think of it -in this part of the world- so is 'road'! In any case, we didn't go; we decided to head south so, for the moment at least, that was that.

Throughout our journey down to Delhi our board games would invariably draw quite a crowd, and this of course, was a great way to engage the local people in conversation. These interactions were, without doubt, one of my favourite pastimes, but because a good many of the passengers were rural people, the conversations we had were conducted with varying degrees of success. This was mainly because they would often be carried out in half English and half Hindi; that is to say, us speaking all English and them, all Hindi. Still, if nothing else, it helped pass the time, and after numerous chess and Scrabble sessions and numerous cosy incomprehensible chats, we eventually pulled into Delhi Station. I then stepped down from the carriage tired but quietly triumphant, not because of managing at last to take a game of chess off Steve, but at reaching what, for me, was the greatest milestone of my journey so far...the wonderfully enigmatic city of Delhi.

I suppose I really should have demonstrated a much greater satisfaction at having reached this personal landmark but, for the moment at least, the long days of travel had sucked any life and enthusiasm from me. So, whilst I did genuinely feel quite pleased with myself, outwardly I probably looked about as happy as a three-toed sloth with piles. Not that my demeanour deterred the throng of waiting taxi drivers in the slightest. For no sooner had they clapped their beady little eyes on us than they surged forward as one, promptly surrounding us, eager to lighten us of our loads and at least some of the contents of our wallets.

Now, under normal circumstances, this wouldn't have been a problem; we'd have simply and politely declined the offers of a lift, waving away all the attention with a shake of the head and a cheery smile; but today, well, we just weren't in the mood. There were many times for friendly rebukes but this just wasn't one of them. We were hot and tired and, though I'd already lost weight on this trip, it now felt that my pack had actually gained it. All I yearned for at this precise moment was a bed...anywhere! Unfortunately, there was absolutely no other way out from the station but through the scrum of eager taxi drivers and so, using our packs as battering rams, we unashamedly and unceremoniously parted the noisy crowd and, as we forged on ahead, a straggle of them clung on to us like limpets to warships. Then, one by one, as each lost his grasp, they'd fall off and ride along in the wake of already displaced taxistas. Finally, there was one left; the very last taxi-driver. He put up a brave and spirited fight but just couldn't sustain it; though as dogged as a spider on a wing mirror our surge was just too much for him; we quickened our pace a little; his knuckles whitened; he grimaced, gritted his teeth, and then at long last lost his determined grip on my rucksack before spinning off into the crowd. We were free. Without looking back, we hurried from the pack, into the main street and off across the other side of the road.

The sun was oven-hot now; the city though, still teeming with life. We longed for the first little hostel that could offer us shade and a bed. We sweated our way for a few hundred yards along a busy street and then snuck down the first quiet little alley we could find. Then, lo and behold, and to our great relief, that little hostel appeared right on cue.

On offer within this particular establishment were three single rooms, all with running water: sometimes, electricity: maybe, but beds...yes, beds! There was no need for discussion whatsoever; we took them without batting so much as a parched eyelid; and, once we'd signed in and had been handed our keys, I followed the boy up to my room. Then, I slung down my rucksack and the boy closed the door behind him and disappeared back downstairs.

I looked around. The room was sparse to say the least, and could only be described as a bedroom because...it had a bed in it! In fact, the only other 'non-living' thing in the room were the huge drifts of dirt and dust piled up against the walls, like someone had installed miniature mohair skirting boards all around. Still, I thought, what do you want for the price of a handful of Black Jacks, right now I just couldn't care less. I pulled back the single off-white cotton sheet, ousted a rather surprised looking cockroach from the bottom of the bed, and slumped heavily into a horizontal position. Then, before I could even begin to wonder what miracle of nature it was that stopped the gecko above from falling directly onto my face, I was in dreamland.

Now in the big city, both Dave and Steve had their own separate things to do, and so I spent the next few days mostly alone, wandering the streets of Delhi, seeing a few of its sights and overdosing on what, for me, was a pleasantly but exceedingly different culture.

It'd already become fashionable by this time for travellers to say things like "Well yeah, Delhi's okay but after all it's just another city!" And I daresay that I too have probably been guilty of similar thoughts in the past. After all, cities are often thought of simply as places to fly into, meet fellow travellers and collect mail, before moving on to experience the 'real' country, rather than being destinations in their own right. However, it's easy to forget that a huge proportion of a country's population live in its cities -through choice or otherwise- and, as surely a major reason to travel is to meet and observe a country's people as they go about their daily lives, then in my book, this undoubtedly makes cities important places to experience.

That said, what was my first port of call in Delhi? Yep...the post office! Well, it had been a long time since hearing from anyone back home and being that I was in a major city, I was eager to hurry along to the main GPO. Now, this was to be my very first experience of how things in India are not always as straight forward as you might expect. For one, I had as yet no experience of the golden rule of Indian urban orienteering; namely, that if ever you want to find somewhere, then it's necessary to ask at least three people the way. If by some chance all three opinions agree, then there's an even money chance that it just could be right. If, on the other hand, just one of the three disagrees...keep asking! Not that the people here are necessarily ignorant, disgruntled by the colonial period or generally out to get you; on the contrary, usually all they want to do is to please you. The fact of the matter is, the average person in the street would far sooner give you a positive answer -even if it's a wrong one- and have you go away happy,   than give you a negative answer...and have you go away unhappy. Confused?...This is how it works.:

First approach: You go up to a local and say,
"Is this the right way to Ravi's Rock Shop?" He will almost certainly smile, waggle his head from side to side in that inimitable Indian fashion, and confirm that,
"Yes, this most definitely is correct!" Well, you may, if you're extremely lucky, arrive at where you want to go but, it will almost certainly be...luck. However, having tried this approach on several occasions without ever coming even close to your chosen destination, you may begin to get a little wiser and wish to try the second and slightly more rewarding approach,
"Excuse me, but 'which' way is it to Ravi's Rock Shop?" Now, this may well provoke the same positive and unfaltering response but on occasion, may just cause the person concerned to ponder a second or two for a more considered answer. However, and this is important; now comes the psychological waiting game for, if at any time during that brief pondering session you lose patience and suggest,
"Umm, is this the way?" then I'm afraid all is lost and you're back to square one because, as sure as eggs is eggs...he'll agree that,
"Yes, that is indeed the correct way!" No, the idea is to hang on long enough for him to make up his 'own' mind about which way it might be, thank him for his answer - which indeed may still be the wrong one- and then go on your way. You then repeat this process over and over until

you can get at least three people to agree with each other. Then, and only then, if you're lucky enough to find three people who are all of exactly the same mind, I'd say that your chances of arriving at Ravi's Rock Shop without having covered every single back street of Delhi are, well…reasonable!

Anyway, as things panned out, I eventually, through trial, error, error and error, found my way to the GPO only to discover that all International mail is kept at the GPO in…'New Delhi'. This, naturally, is a good distance away from where I was in the old city, but is, in fact, the real capital of India. But, unlike so many modern cities which have grown up around a small and ancient centre, New Delhi isn't so much a city with the old heart contained within it, but rather a big new city with…a bit on the side! And, of course, as is often the case from an economic point of view, the old original city has become very much the poor relation between the two and, rather like an old aunt confined to a small annex at the back of a large modern house, old Delhi goes about its business as it has done for hundreds of years with its wealthy carer only really caring when absolutely necessary!

The result of this is that whilst the old city contains all the bustle, the history, the culture, the pleasures and pains and the blood, sweat and tears of millions; just outside of all this mayhem, the money people of New Delhi look on from a safe distance: managing, administering and pushing paper about in a fume free, beggar free, air-conditioned, but frankly, rather sterile zone. For me though, there is simply no contest; I'll take the old every time. For though I truly believe that there is good to be found in almost everything, everywhere, if I'd wanted to stay in the 20th century...then I might as well have stayed at home!

Anyway, where was I? Oh yes....Still feeling excited about the prospect of getting some mail -though a little less so after all the morning's trials- I decided to fork out on a taxi and get over to the New Delhi General Post Office before closing time. This I did and, on arrival, I tracked down and joined the queue at the 'Poste Restante' section. (This was formally a section contained in all major post offices worldwide, where you could both send and receive mail!) When my time came, I gave my name and anxiously looked on as the postal worker behind the desk grabbed a large handful of letters from behind him, and began flicking through what I could plainly see was the 'M' pile. By craning my neck over the counter I could just catch a glimpse of the upside-down names on the envelopes, and every time I recognised one as my own I let out an enthusiastic "Yes!" Then, to each of these excited cries, the post office worker, barely faltering from his fast fingered pace, would place my envelope to one side and then carry on thumbing through to the end of the batch before straightening the pile and returning them to their correct little cubby-hole.

Now, I'd been forewarned by other travellers that, if expecting mail, it was always prudent to explore a variety of other possibilities when at the post office, and so whilst there, I also asked for the contents of cubby hole 'G'. (I had, of course, already covered 'M' for Mobsby...which coincidently also happened to cover, 'M' for mister, master, missus or Mahatma Gary.) But though this request didn't seem an awful lot to ask, it became quite clear that to thumb through two cubby-hole's worth of letters was way beyond the call of normal duty. The postal

114

worker looked up disapprovingly and let out a long and audible drawn out sigh before grabbing another pile and briskly cantering through 'G'. Of course there was a time when, at most GPO's at least, you could ask for any old pile of letters and thumb through them yourself. Unfortunately that seldom seems to be the case these days; something called progress I think. Though whether this is an improvement or not is most definitely...questionable. All I know is, it deprives people like me the unquestionable excitement of the hunt!

NB Since writing this, of course, the whole idea of leaving letters all over the globe at Poste Restante offices has largely been superseded by the advent of computers and e-mail.

Meanwhile, back at the post office...satisfied that I'd explored all 'logical' alternatives, I then handed my passport over to the post office worker who, in turn, scrutinised the name in it and methodically compared it with the names written on all the envelopes. Thankfully, these appeared to be a good enough match and so he tapped my letters into a neat little pile, handed them over and I skipped out of the post office joyfully clutching my five letters...no less than three of them from the 'G' pile!

It was so nice to hear from my family again and to hear a little about what had been happening back home. Though invariably this wasn't a great deal; normally stuff like, "had my hair done last week"; "went to Tesco's" and, "your grandad's knocked another cyclist off his bike!" The worst and most important news for me though was that there was no sign of the money from my mum that I'd been so hoping for. I had so far managed to come all this way on the two week's wages which I'd saved up over a period of…two weeks; but by now, my wallet was looking decidedly anorexic. Even more disappointing was that I'd actually taken the trouble to think several weeks ahead and asked for the money to be sent to me here in Delhi -albeit via a bogus ransom note containing one of my fingernails from a 'Sheik Zee-dripsov', when I was in central Iran. (She'd been a little worried about my travelling through Iran so, it seemed appropriate!) Still, there was nothing for it; there was no money and so I'd just have to hope for some a little further down the line and, in the meantime, tighten my belt a bit. This is only metaphorically mind, as otherwise I would've had to go out and buy a belt in order to tighten it.

I enjoyed my few days in Delhi and each night happily returned to my new bug-less bed totally drained of energy. Physically, this was simply from the long and continually aimless wanderings under a searing sun; but, you know, it was mentally that I found Delhi to be even more energy sapping. This wasn't necessarily because of all the hassles involved in doing just about anything, but because of the sheer and constant bombardment of so much information from so many different sources. Everything around is so incredibly mind-boggling, so eye catching; from the gaudy shop fronts, posters and magazine stalls, to street jugglers and bellowing vendors pushing homemade carts; bumper to bumper cars, buses and bikes interspersed with take-your-life-in-your-hands road-crossers; beggars, nonchalant 'holy' cows and the odd garishly painted elephant. Everything around was so new, so much to take in. It's all just part of the ordinary, yet somehow extraordinary, everyday lives of the people of Delhi. I found the whole experience totally and utterly absorbing.

As previously mentioned, I find it's always a great experience to be invited into other people's homes, and particularly when they come from such a vastly different culture. This sadly, I never actually managed in Delhi, but just by being here I felt that I'd been invited into the homes of millions. For many of these people's lives are lived out on the streets, day after day, for all the world to see; rather as if some Hindu God had suddenly removed the front from his gargantuan doll's house. Of course it's not only the private lives of Indians that are so public though, but also every conceivable business you care to mention.

Here you can experience everything and anything that could possibly be charged money for; anything from: shoe-shining, foot massaging, palm reading, hair de-nitting, tooth pulling, ear cleaning and nose-hair clipping. Or if none of these appeals, you could always just pay a few rupees, stand on the street and watch a skinny little Indian holy man sit in an excruciatingly uncomfortable position all day long, looking for all the world like an old second-hand deckchair which somebody had tried to erect but had failed miserably.

Though in Delhi for only a short period, I was to experience a number of different things for the very first time; notable amongst them, an Indian-style shave and haircut. "But, just how different can a shave and haircut be", I hear you ask; well quite, actually. And although my particular experience all started fairly normally, I certainly hadn't been prepared for it to happen out in the street;

117

neither was I ready for the Spaghetti Western type cut throat razor which was used. Granted, this tool may be nothing out of the ordinary for some people, and is even preferred by some barbers in the West but, for me at least, the encounter was a totally new one. So, for the uninitiated 'electro-type' shavers like myself, this is how it's done...in India:

Firstly, you take the chair -invariably sited on a busy street- and, once the finances have been agreed, the barber produces a tablecloth-sized towel and drapes it around your neck and shoulders. Secondly, he vigorously knocks up a fresh batch of shaving cream into a frothy lather and briskly slaps it about the bottom half of your face with his brush before unceremoniously scooping excess fingerfuls of foam from your nostrils and wiping it on the towel. He then leaves the chair, disappears somewhere behind you and goes about sharpening his razor on a kinkily-thick leather strap. This rhythmical sound of metal on leather seems to be the cue for all passers-by to stop passing by and to gather together in a huddle and form a neat little semi-circle around the front of the barber's chair. (Though I doubt the barber ever plays to a full house if his chair isn't occupied by a Westerner!) Then, with razor sharpened and crowd in place, the barber eases back your head and, with a firm hand holding it at precisely the desired angle, checks that his audience is paying full attention and goes about rasping away the foam and stubble with deft flicks of his razor.

Now, as I've said before, this may all sound quite normal to some and I've had no other similar experiences to judge against this one. However, I feel quite sure that the speed and absolute theatrical flamboyancy with which my barber did all this, just can't have been normal. I also

118

have an inkling that the capacity crowd may have had some influence here. Whatever the case, the gathered crowd seemed suitably pleased by the performance and, as for me well, I was hardly in a position to complain even if I'd wanted to; particularly as the barbers cut-throat was being wielded up and down just a Rizla's thickness from my jugular. (Paradoxically, this wielding of the razor-sharp razor made me want to swallow hard out of sheer terror, but I daren't for fear of suffering a serrated Adams apple!) For the barber though, it may well have been all in a day's work; but this man was nothing if not a showman and, in this show at least, there was very much only one star! In fact, had he chosen to renegotiate the price at that very moment, I'd most certainly have paid ten times the few rupees he'd asked.

Anyway, the next stages of my shave allowed the barber to call on a few more props for his act; namely, a second smaller towel for even more excess foam, a large block of ice and lastly a small bottle of lavender water -or at least I think that's what it was. And by the time these were in place there was no doubt about it, he had the audience in the palm of his hand. He shook out the second towel like a seasoned bull-fighter, threw it over my whole head and proceeded to vigorously de-foam my chin, my cheeks and every single orifice from the neck up. The trouble is that because the towel felt more like an oversized Brillo pad, this over-enthusiastic rubbing left me feeling exceedingly raw around the chops. But oh, what relief; what blessed relief when next the ice was applied! This huge block -the size of a Tupperware lunchbox- was gently rubbed all over my smarting chin and felt like pure heaven. But just then, just when I thought we were nearly there; that there was to be a happy ending to all this...the 'lavender water' appeared! I suppose I should have suspected that it wasn't all over by the look of expectancy on the crowd's faces! As the barber half emptied the bottle of his 'special' potion into a cupped hand and rubbed his hands together, the whole crowd seemed to lean forward as one. The reason for this soon became obvious, for then...he clapped his two hands to my two virginal cheeks and briskly rubbed in the contents. Jeeeeeesus; the pain...it was indescribable! I let out an audible gasp and gripped hold of both edges of the chair as if on a roller coaster...God, it was excruciating! (Strange how one becomes religious at times like these.) Then, as a small lake quickly welled up in my right eye, I tried unconvincingly to turn a wince into a smile, but it was futile; much to the amusement of all around, a tear the size of a gobstopper burst its banks, ran down my cheek and blobbed into the dust below.

Now I feel sure that not every shave on the street can be like this one, and I daresay that there are barbers around who are capable of making the whole experience pleasurable even; but well...let's just say that I wouldn't be rushing back to this one!

Anyway, after my shave, the haircut was really nothing much out of the ordinary, an anti-climax even. And so, because of this, a good many of the happy and sadistic crowd dispersed and went about their businesses. What did make it different however, is not the haircut itself but what followed; for there was no, "Have a nice day Sir," or "something for the weekend Sir?" no, just simply, a full blown head and neck massage. Why, no sooner had the scissors been tucked away than the barber suddenly came at me from behind, clamped both hands down on my shoulders and began pushing both thumbs inward towards the centre of my neck and drawing them strongly and slowly out again towards my shoulders, before repeating the process over and over (not bad so far). He then placed one hand on top of my head and the other under my chin and eased my head round to one side to the absolute furthest point it would comfortably go; then, with a nauseating 'clonk', he suddenly jerked it sideways just that bit further. God! Ugh! What a horrific sound! I couldn't believe what was happening!

Next though, before I could even start to have any thoughts of scarpering off down the road, it was repeated to the other side with that same horribly, horribly sickening 'clonk' Aaaargh! But this still wasn't the end of it; for then, with the whole of my head in both hands, he began to vigorously throw it back and forth, back and forth in rapid succession, like a frustrated monkey trying to get milk from a coconut. Christ Almighty, I felt as if I was in one of those films where some religious fanatic is trying to rid a child of the devil. "Bloody hell" I thought, I only came here for a cut and shave.

"Enough, enough...STOP!!!!!!!" I leapt out of the chair, paid my money -somewhat reluctantly- thanked the psychotic barber and went on my way. True, I'd never felt so fresh faced, light headed and loose around the shoulders but, you know what, for days afterwards, I could still hear that sickly dull clonk in my ears from having my neck graunched about from side to side; the sort of sound a train door makes when being slammed inside a distant tunnel, except that this time, the noise was happening somewhere in my head!

As I walked down the street, my new super-soft, hairless chin felt sort of new-born and vulnerable amongst all the dust and fumes of the city; I felt, as you would with a young animal, that I needed to guard and protect it. It'd been a ghastly ordeal and one which I'd be positively ecstatic not ever to have to repeat, ever again. But you know what? In a bizarre sort of masochistic way...I was glad to have had the experience.

Of all the visual indications that the British were once here in India, some of the more obvious are to be found on the roads. For although there may seem to be every type of transport imaginable vying for every inch of tarmac, it is the distinctly Morris-looking cars still ferrying the more affluent around, that hit you most -both metaphorically and alas, all too often, literally. It was quite strange seeing all these old jalopies in the flesh though, as the only other times I'd seen them in such numbers, they always appeared in various shades of grey -courtesy of Elstree studios. (In truth these Indian cars aren't actually Morris's at all but a rather grand look-a-like called the Ambassador -made by Hindustan Motors- which was based on the Morris Oxford...but enough of all that.)

Yet, this wasn't the only vehicle which had forgotten that it was out of fashion here; for listen hard through the cacophonous discord of sound on the streets, and if you can pick out the distant base tones of an old motorbike approaching, in all probability, it will be those of a Royal Enfield, that ancient - still produced- and still refreshingly un-modern motorbike which roars around the country just as it has since the days of Gandhi.

Of course, most of the local populous have to make do with rather more humble forms of transport. For many this still means Shank's pony; but, for those lucky enough to be engaged in any form of employment, a myriad freight laden bicycles pick their way through the melange of pedestrians, every one of them in various states of disrepair. Meanwhile, a plethora of antique, fume-belching buses, criss-cross the city full to over-flowing, and everywhere people, people, people.

If there is any sort of order to all this then it's hard to see. The general rule when using the road appears to be, 'Give way to the right'; the right, invariably meaning, those who have somehow acquired the right to drive a bigger vehicle than you have! Indeed, the only single exception to this seems to be when confronted by one of two things; a man in uniform or...a cow. Now, the uniform thing is pretty easy to understand; the cow perhaps, a little less so (if only I'd brought along my pantomime cow outfit, I'd be quid's in!)

I had of course learnt about the cow being sacred in India, but I wasn't quite prepared for the extent to which this 'recognition of greatest' applies on the road. On more than one occasion, away from the city centre, I was witness to an oversized, carefree and contented looking bovine taking up a position smack in the middle of the road, casually chewing the cud, whilst the rest of India simply treated it as a small but much revered roundabout. You know, I never once saw a single person attempt to shift a cow or even so much as blast a horn -no, not that one- in frustration. In fact, on one occasion, I was stood at the roadside and watched as this humungous, white, straggly-horned beast, sauntered out of somebody's doorway, walked straight across the road -causing two vehicles to screech to a halt and change direction- and continue right across into somebody else's doorway on the opposite side of the road. Quite amazing! I'm not quite sure what cows have done in life to have achieved such an elevated status, but they certainly seem to have things worked out.

One job that I really had to get done whilst in Delhi was to send home my growing collection of souvenirs. I had, by this time, managed to acquire rather more bits and pieces than I cared to carry around in an already over-laden rucksack and, being as I was in a major city, this seemed a good opportunity to lighten my load. I was especially keen to lighten myself of the two Pakistani prayer mats that I'd bought back in Lahore and which were undoubtedly going to come in, 'oh, so useful' back in England!

Rather surprisingly…or not, this one little task was to take me well over half a day to complete. Okay, so admittedly it's only a case of…finding a box to suit your contents; getting the package weighed; writing exactly what your box contains on the outside; having a post office worker copy all this information meticulously in a book; leaving the building again to find someone to specially sew the package up in cotton cloth; resealing it and finally retying it but…when each and every one of these stages is preceded by an extraordinarily lengthy queue and it appears to be a closely guarded secret as to what the next stage is, or what queue leads where, then…time can drag somewhat.

All this though, is part of the experience of India; and had I not known before that Indian bureaucracy is legendary throughout the entire world then I certainly did now. (I realise, of course, that this is also something inherited from the British, though they do seem to have taken things to a slightly different level.)

It's not only the postal services that can be a little testing though. In essence, India, although a vast and fascinating land, is the ultimate lesson in patience; where Western and Indian concepts of logic can seem about as far apart as cornflakes and onion bhajis. No greater example of this can be found than at the railway stations, where you can usually find a good assortment of long but surprisingly orderly queues awaiting tickets to a variety of indecipherable destinations.

Now naturally, before joining a queue, it's not only prudent but essential to go through the tried and tested method of orienteering that I've already spoken about: namely, that of asking at least three different people which is the correct queue for your chosen destination before actually committing yourself to one. And, of course, I did try this on several different occasions and well, I defy a saint even not to become just a little frustrated when, on finally reaching the ticket counter after an hour's wait, you are told that the queue you want is actually the equally lengthy one right alongside. Not that I want to give the impression that this sort of incident is an everyday occurrence but well, it did appear to happen rather too often for me to consider myself plain unlucky. Obviously, some such misunderstandings can be attributed quite simply to the lack of a common language or even to misinterpretation but, as a tourist here, you just can't help feeling that there must be a candid camera hidden away somewhere or that you've just secretly auditioned for the starring role in some epic Brian Rix farce.

After a few days in Delhi we were ready to move on, and so Dave, Steve and I tried out a variety of queues and counters and eventually, after being rewarded with three second-class tickets, we boarded the train for the four hour run down to Agra; famous the world over as home to the Taj Mahal! By now we were well accustomed to being centre of attention on our journeys, and even if the sight of three white, slightly hippy looking strangers didn't do the trick, the chess board would always pull in a good crowd. Usually, once a game got going, it wasn't long before a small group would quickly congregate around the board and then, for the next couple of hours, we'd find ourselves surrounded by intent but bewildered faces, like so many medical students witnessing their first ever operation. Periodically, one of us would look up after a long considered move and smile, momentarily breaking the spell under which our audience was held. Sometimes there would be the odd quiet murmur from the few who understood the game; but, more often, the crowd just looked on, strangely silenced by curiosity and wonderment. Then, the only sound would be the clankity-clanking of the rhythmically swaying carriage...or the faint rustle of a hastily unwrapped bag of samosas.

Steve had been a history lecturer back in England and when he first told me this I'd thought little of it. History had always seemed to me quite an interesting thing to study but not the most useful of subjects in everyday life. It had always seemed good for say...teaching history, but little else. It wasn't until we'd spent some time together that I realized the real worth of his knowledge. After all, taken literally, the study of history is the study of absolutely anything which has taken place in the past, and being that we can only ever learn from the past, I had to concede that my initial thoughts were a little ignorant to say the least. And the more time that we spent together, the more I found myself learning little snippets of knowledge with every day that passed. A shame then really that I actually remember Steve more for a smile full of pureed biscuit than I do for all the history lessons. This is in no way his fault of course but rather the result of my completely unselective and infantile memory. And though I definitely prefer to remember Steve biscuit-less, I'm afraid I just can't help myself. Nevertheless, it takes absolutely nothing away from the fact that he was an extremely good and knowledgeable companion.

On arrival at Agra, we sought a bicycle rickshaw driver - or rather he and his mates sought us- and then we set off to find a hotel as near as we could to the famous Taj'. Incidentally, for those not in the know, a bicycle rickshaw is one of the most ubiquitous and simple forms of public transport to be found in India and consists largely of a bicycle with a small sofa attached to the back: this attachment, being just about big enough for three tight-cheeked Asians or around…one and a half Westerners.

The need for public transport in India does, of course, create an incredibly competitive market, with every rickshaw driver desperately vying for your trade; and so, when we were ushered towards a waiting posse of drivers and their rickshaws, we were fully prepared to have to hire one each. However, one ultra-keen rickshaw wallah absolutely insisted that he was more than capable of carrying two whole people, luggage and all. Well, a cursory glance at our bulging packs, hefty white bodies and then at his diminutive frame, gave me serious doubts but anyway, we agreed to trust his judgement and to go along with him; our only proviso being that Steve should follow in another rickshaw with all of our packs. This, he agreed to, and so off we went, Dave and I wedged into one vinyl sofa, and Steve close behind with the rucksacks in another.

Well, as brilliant an invention as the wheel might be, given the dusty, pot-holed and unsurfaced road which our driver opted for, he soon showed signs of flagging. The sun was beating down relentlessly by now and as we started up a small incline, our poor driver pushed and puffed, sweated and gasped, contorting every sinewy muscle in his body; straining away to the left and to the right and applying his full six stone at the zenith of every revolution of the pedals. It was a truly valiant effort but eventually, part way up the slope, the pedals could be coaxed no further; our little chauffeur grimaced one last gargoylian grimace and completely ground to a halt. He then jumped down and, without so much as a backward glance or a pause for breath, proceeded to 'push' the whole thing up the hill. Well, clearly I just couldn't let him do this, and anyway I was keen to see just how difficult a rickshaw wallah's lot is. Immediately, I jumped into the saddle and took over -much to the amusement of our driver- and against all odds, between him shoving and me pedalling, we just about managed to pick up a bit of steam. Soon, the gradient eased a little and I quickly beckoned him on board, and though a little reluctant at first, he leapt in the back alongside Dave and there he sat; knees tight together like a Catholic choirboy, bumping along with a coy but happy grin. (Please note that I refrained here from any jokes about coy choirboys on vinyl-clad rickshaws being, 'virgin on the ridiculous'!)

Though smiling, it was plain to see that our rickshaw wallah was more than a little embarrassed by this unexpected reversal of roles, and though I certainly didn't share his embarrassment, I sort of understood when he became only too eager to get back to the pedalling once we'd hit the flat again. In truth, I thought it such a shame that he felt that way about the situation and I desperately wanted to convey to him that he'd be exactly the same person to me whether in the front or back. Nevertheless, I respected his feelings and sat back down on my sofa again to enjoy the ride -the decision to regain my place in the back doubtless made easier by the fact that I was about to collapse in a sweaty heap.

So anyway, normal service had been resumed. Our little driver hit the pedals and off we went again: two young, hulking great tourists bumping along in a box, pulled by a tiny middle-aged Indian -with the colour and physique of a charred coat hanger but the strength of a youthful ox.

I'm told that the average life expectancy of a rickshaw wallah is around forty-five years old, and having been one for a full two minutes I can quite understand why. Now, I've met a number of travellers who abstain from using bicycle rickshaws on the grounds that, for the drivers, it's such a hard and demeaning life. Well, 'hard'...undeniably; 'demeaning'...I'm not so sure! All I can say is, in my view, until such time that some other solution can be found to employ and feed such a massively populous nation, rickshaw driving has to be a far less demeaning life than begging, which may, for many, be the only other viable option. The irony is, that those same conscientious objectors, the ones who knowingly refuse to support this way of life by not using rickshaws, are in all probability, the very same people who walk by without ever giving to the people who are forced to beg in order to stay alive.

Once we'd arrived in downtown Agra, we made a brief reconnaissance of the area and managed to find ourselves a suitable hotel close-ish to the Taj. Then I did a quick check of the rooms and, feeling reasonably happy about what was on offer, we moved in.

The word 'hotel', of course, is used very loosely when travelling in so called developing nations. For many years now I've been a life member of the Youth Hostel Association in Britain, and quite thought that this would come in jolly handy on my travels in Asia. However, it doesn't take long to realise that, in terms of both cleanliness and price, there is little to choose between the Youth Hostels and the myriad small hotels that can be found in nearly every town or city in these parts.

The usual routine when doing a 'reccy' of one of these hotels or hostels, was to do a quick check for running water and electricity -namely that both existed- that the bed had fresh and bug-free sheets and that the bedroom door -assuming that there was one- was lockable.* But, though first impressions would often convince us that all of the above were passable, by some cruel trick of nature we would frequently find that both the water and electricity were only actually guaranteed to work until you'd checked in and paid for that first night. What's more, the room might well seem totally bug-free, but I'm convinced that, all too often, it was simply that the resident bedbugs had been especially trained to retire to the underside of the mattress until nightfall, when they'd magically appear again –rather like Mr. Benn's shopkeeper- and indulge in a midnight feast of medium-to-rare tourist. Now, naturally, I am talking here about rather basic accommodation of the 'penniless student' variety, and it's usually fairly easy to find something a little better if you want to extend the budget a smidgen; it's just that, on this occasion, though neither penniless nor indeed students...we were gripped by the mentality of both.

* Whilst checking that the door is lockable it may also be wise to check that there is actually glass in the window; if not, a room on the ground floor probably isn't advisable. It also goes without saying -oops, too late- that if forced to accept a glassless window-ed, ground floor room...best not worry too much about the lockable door!

The Taj Mahal is undoubtedly one of the most photographed and famous buildings in the world. Therefore, having seen and heard so much about it, I fully expected to be a little disappointed. (Just as is usually the case, on seeing a film after all your friends have raved about it). I can honestly, honestly say though, that on my very first sighting of the Taj, I felt no shred of disappointment whatsoever -though that's certainly blown the Taj's chances for anyone reading this! In my opinion it is quite simply magnificent. But not only is the building itself stupendous, it also comes in a wonderful setting, with beautifully tended, tranquil gardens and a dreamy river that winds its way round behind. Unfortunately, the river wasn't quite so dreamy on this particular visit as it was nearly bone dry, but that's beside the point; I'm quite sure that in full fettle, it would have enhanced even this, surely one of mankind's most beautiful creations.

Of course, as with all the big crowd-pullers in the world, the vast majority of visiting punters probably spend less than two hours visiting the Taj which is rather a shame really; or a shame for them that is, as I personally am only too glad to see these people shuffle back to their coaches, leaving the rest of us to spend the day there in peace.

It struck me as rather odd though to witness the hoards of smiley, camera toting Japanese filing through the gates to the Taj. They'd be totally aghast at seeing this wondrous building in the flesh for a full thirty seconds, before ducking down and hiding behind their hi-tech lenses, eager to record it for posterity. In fact, it seemed to be far more important to them to get it on film than it was to actually see it in real life. Even more bizarrely, it wasn't the Taj Mahal that was the focus of attention at all; this stunningly beautiful building was merely an exotic backdrop to an endless procession of friends, as each took up his position in the group between Taj and camera. Every one of them with their matching outfits and matching haircuts, and all wearing that same surprised expression; you know the one: like that of a bunch of monks who've just taken a vow of silence and then been jabbed up the bum with a sharp stick. Then, after every photo, a few indecipherable words would be exchanged and each and every one of them would step out of the group to take his place behind the camera, until every possible configuration had been satisfied.

If, as a European, you happen to be in the same vicinity at this time, you will undoubtedly be asked to join in with this charade. God knows why but apparently, a carefully positioned Westerner in the group adds a little something to the picture. In fact, even as we speak, my grinning face can be seen peering out from mantel pieces all over Tokyo, or slapped between the pages of a thousand photo albums, sandwiched between a string of identical Japanese faces; the same people with the same smiles. Today: the Taj, tomorrow: the Red Fort. Just change your token

Westerner and your backdrop. As if an exceedingly low-budget film director had gathered a group of oriental extras together in a studio and added in the exotic location later.

I lay back on the grass soaking up the sun and listening to the birds which had been attracted by the pools of water and the luxuriant garden. It felt so calming, so relaxing and sleep inducing lying here. Picnic parties of Indians chatted quietly around me only adding to the atmosphere; the coach loads of tourists just a distant gabble. Although I knew that I was also one of them, for the moment that's how I wished to remain…just one.

CHAPTER 10

- PEDDLERS, SADDHUS AND CHRISTMAS AT THE OASIS -

Bharatpur to Pushkar

When I left England I had very little knowledge of India or indeed anywhere else on my route outside of Europe; neither did I know anything of all the travel guides that existed. And so it was with great interest that I read through a borrowed copy of the Lonely Planet guide to India. This was the very first guide that I'd looked at on this trip and, after having browsed through it for an hour or two, I may not have necessarily learnt a great deal about the country, but at least I was a teeny bit more qualified to judge, what for me, are the pros and cons of travel guides. Of course, some might say, "How can there possibly be a down side to gathering information?" Well, whilst that maybe true, having no prior knowledge of a particular place does at least mean that everything you encounter is surprising and refreshingly new -be it good or bad- and therefore, every journey a great adventure. However, by not reading up on a place, it can also result in a great deal of frustration. This manifests itself only after you've returned home, of course; when you see some unbelievably fantastic sight featured on television which, only a week earlier, you'd been within a hair's breadth of...and missed. Now, how bloody annoying is that!

For me, what was to follow could easily have been one such time had I not been fortuitous enough to be able to thumb through a guide book. It would have been all too easy to leave Agra and board yet another train going to who knows where; but simply by chance, I discovered that just to the west of here lay a national and natural treasure. That treasure was the Bharatpur Bird Sanctuary -a.k.a. Keoladeo Ghana Bird Sanctuary- a huge area of wetland that is unequivocally one of the best areas of its kind for bird life in the world, and therefore an absolute must for every single anorak-clad, binocular-toting 'twitcher' on the planet. Neither Steve nor Dave were particularly interested in birds -of the feathered variety at least- and so, at this point, we all agreed to split up and then regroup a couple of days further down the line.

So, the very next morning, with romantic images of a hazy Taj still floating around in my head, I boarded my first ever local bus in India. Now, experienced travellers will know that most buses operating in the tropics were built specifically for school children. This is not just metaphorically but quite literally, as they are often hand-me-down school buses bought from richer Western nations, whose companies have discarded them once they've become too uneconomical to keep on the road. Fortunately for them, the majority of indigenous tropical folk tend to be rather on the small side, and so, size-wise these buses are actually just the job. Unfortunately for any Westerner with more than six inches between knee and crutch, it is quite impossible to sit down and put both of your legs in the direction of travel and so, these seats will leave you with one of two options: either you sit with knees tight together and at a forty-five degree angle to your body thereby risking the disapproving look of your encroached upon neighbour, or you sit with both knees totally akimbo, thereby...risking the disapproving look of your 'still' encroached upon neighbour. Luckily though - for Western travellers- there seldom seems to be the same possessiveness of space in Asia as there is in the West. Not necessarily that they regard themselves as having no right to that space, but because they are conditioned through necessity to having to share it with people every single day of their lives.

It was a hot but mercifully short bus ride to Bharatpur, rattling through a dry and dusty landscape; a landscape that hinted tantalisingly at the great desert of Rajasthan which lay further to the west. Consequently, when we arrived, it was a blessed relief to get down from the bus and into the shade of a large group of acacias which surrounded the entrance to the reserve. For a place so incredibly rich in bird life, the small wrought iron entrance gates seemed somehow understated; the only real evidence that anyone might just want to see what lay beyond them was a gaggle of dark, slick-haired Indians across the road, excitedly beckoning to hire one of their bicycles. I hadn't really intended to hire a bike but this struck me as rather a good idea in view of the vast area there was to be covered; and so I crossed over to them and, as usual, began running the gauntlet of slightly desperate and identical sales pitches. This, of course, made what should have been a very simple transaction, into a lengthy discussion. Not that it was a tough decision; only that ideally I would have liked to have shared my meagre business about a bit. The thing is though, there was nothing to choose between any one of bikes on offer, and provided the wheels went round and the saddle didn't, I was quite happy.

Anyway, after several minutes of forceful but good humoured banter, I was still none the wiser and so I just selected a bike at random. Then, I handed over a few rupees to the excitable bicycle wallah, and the others -still in good humour- stepped back and busied themselves: squatting and chatting and awaiting the next fly to enter their web.

Which reminds me...how on earth do Indians do that flat-footed squatting thing without tumbling over backwards? I'm told that it's all down to having a far suppler Achilles tendon than we do -a theory borne out by the fact that the majority of Westerners who are able to it seem to be either Yoga teachers or children under the age of ten. In fact, the only other 'minority group' I've ever seen master it successfully are adult females who happen to be extremely well off in the chest department; more a matter of weight distribution though rather than elasticity. Mind you, having said that, I did, on one slightly drunken occasion, actually manage this position myself; but only with the aid of a pair of 70's heels, and by holding out in front of me, a large frozen turkey. For the Indians though, they seem to be more than happy to stay in this exact same position for days on end.

The bicycle I hired was, of course, quite ancient; the sort of 'sit-up-and-beg' type as used by the Wicked Witch in The Wizard of Oz. Its only real redeeming feature being that it did at least last the day in one piece...just. This was remarkable in itself as the bike didn't look so much a vehicle as what you might imagine the result would be, of a Meccano kit in the hands of a young Salvador Dali. It had clearly been fashioned from various bits and pieces of once quite presentable bicycles, but now, though still functioning, had metamorphosed into a sort of man-made metallic mongrel. However, these bicycle 'peddlers' didn't only demonstrate some interesting practical ingenuity when it came to cycle construction, but also an unusual flare for business acumen. It would seem that these men had learnt from the capitalistic West an invaluable lesson; namely, that free enterprise encourages competition and hence either pushes prices down or standards up. Well, the bicycle wallahs had taken on board this valuable lesson in economics and had come to a unanimous conclusion…to totally ignore it! Therefore, they'd reached a mutual agreement within their own little business group, that the bikes would be kept at the very same price and in an absolutely minimal state of repair.

Anyway, after buying my entry ticket, I cycled off down the dusty track on my Meccano bike and spent the rest of the day in absolute twitcher heaven. Huge marshy lakes spread out from the raised dirt tracks on every side of me, and everywhere you looked the trees were bowed under the weight of nesting storks and ibises. Waders waded through reedy shallows in their hundreds, brilliantly coloured kingfishers flitted from bush to bush in the foreground or were mirrored in the marshes as they perched on a favourite branch as if mesmerised by the still water below. After a while I was lucky enough to stumble upon two large pythons lethargically bathing in the morning sun; one of which lay sprawled across the middle of the path and which I failed to notice until the very last moment. Quickly I skidded to a halt, inches from creating two rather smaller pythons. The snake though, didn't appear in the least bit perturbed by its kiss with death, and even after being gawped at, stroked and photographed from every conceivable angle, appeared totally unmoved; perhaps quietly confident in its ability to dissuade a would-be aggressor should the need arise. Shortly, I decided to give it the respect it deserved and moved away, happy to leave it in peace and not in pieces. The python then quickly -or not, as the case may be- got back to the serious business of sunbathing.

It was a real and unexpected bonus to see animals other than birds in the sanctuary, and an even greater surprise when later that day I came across a nilgai, or blue bull, as they're more commonly known, blocking my way. A large and rather odd-shaped antelope, it too had decided to adapt to the heat by adopting a sort of serpentine lethargy. This strategy though, only became obvious after I'd dismounted from my bicycle at a distance and slowly advanced towards it on foot. Naturally, at some point, I'd expected it to turn tail and run, but in the end I got so close, I was very nearly in lashing distance of its extraordinary and lusciously long eye lashes. But of course, whatever its reasons for staying, this was a wild animal and as such, there was bound to be a limit to the nilgai's trust. He allowed me to close in just so far before letting out a sharp and indignant snort and dashing off through a thicket, only re-appearing again some way off across the water. He then looked back at me across the ripples from the safety of an island of trees and disappeared.

Before I knew it, my time was nearly up. The sun was beginning to sink into the shallows, tinting the sky and marshes first pink and then orange and crimson, before darkening to an almost beetroot purple. Hunched anthropoid silhouettes of maribou storks now stood motionless, high in the trees, and the last of the waders tip-toed stealthily through the still water and then vanished between tall reeds.

After a long day on the dirt road I'd become quite accustomed to steering with my handlebars at forty-five degrees in order to drive straight; after all, it was only a matter of practise. My trusty steed, meanwhile, had now acquired a new coat of fine dust; its chain hung as limp as a microwaved lettuce and my hands bore the grease marks of several changes. Still, it'd been a great day and together, we'd finally made it. We'd clonked and clattered and bumped our way through the gathering gloom, and were back once more at the entrance gate.

My little bicycle wallah was waiting patiently to greet me when I arrived, looking only slightly less dishevelled than his bike. I handed it back to him with thanks and wandered off down the road trying, as discreetly as possible, to adjust the severely jarred contents down the front of my trousers. What a wonderfully rewarding and satisfying day it had been -even if a little uncomfortable! I then managed to catch a late bus going roughly in my desired direction, hopped aboard and went to find Dave and Steve.

The following day the three of us headed out west and found ourselves in the famed 'Pink City' of Jaipur. Now Jaipur has a couple of outstanding and beautiful buildings but, in my view, is no more remarkable than any other town or city in the area but for the fact that its centre is well...pink. (It has stiff competition around here as just about all the towns are remarkable in some way!) This alone though certainly makes Jaipur very different, and though pink may not be the most popular of colours in architectural history, it's certainly a refreshing change from white or mud or muddy-white, and makes an excellent backdrop to the inevitable and ever colourful market stalls.

Colour aside though, I suppose the centre piece and most famous building of the whole city, has to be the so called, 'Palace of The Winds'; a quite strange but wonderfully dramatic looking stucco pyramid of windows and arches, and all of it naturally, quite pink. This palace is certainly a rare and unusual building, but it's only after actually paying your entrance fee that you fully realise what it is you've entered; for whilst the Palace is undoubtedly impressive from the front, the whole thing is largely a facade, a building so slim from front to back as to be almost two dimensional, like a vastly elaborate cardboard cut-out or a rather expensive backdrop to some great chapatti western.

Nevertheless, the Palace of the Winds, or Hawa Mahal - to give it its correct name- is undoubtedly unique and marvellous and well, I rather liked it. In fact, I found wandering its narrow arched corridors whilst natural sunlight flooded in from both sides, a charming experience. Certainly an infinitely preferable one to roaming around one of Jaipur's other famous buildings, the so called, 'Jantar Mantar'. Now this is quite another thing entirely. It lies just behind the Palace of the Winds and is erm...a sort of star-gazing contraption which I couldn't really fathom except, for some reason, it seems incredibly popular with the local monkeys (or macaques, I think they were). In truth though, this strange array of weird shaped lumps of concrete is actually an old observatory and was apparently used in order to predict all manner of things by observing the heavenly bodies. But whilst its function may be moderately interesting, it's the actual appearance which baffled me: more like an early skateboard park than an observatory. No, excuse my ignorance but, as far as I'm concerned, the monkeys can keep it. Mind you, it's just as well I think that because they seem pretty intent on keeping it anyway, and having seen them display their dental armoury at close quarters, I, for one, wasn't going to argue!

I liked Jaipur, with its hustle and bustle and all its pinkness, but isn't it always the bizarre little things that stick in the memory. For me, this wasn't the city itself but the arriving there. I'm not talking on this occasion about the actual train itself -for trains in India are always remarkable by any standards- but what came over the Tannoy system as the train pulled into the station. Sadly, very few of the trains seem to have the benefit of this in-train announcement system anymore, which is a crying shame; but for those that do, they give a marvellous insight into just what travel must have been like during the times when the British were still here with their exceedingly stiff upper lips. Why, it's almost as if they'd never left, for the voice you hear is far more forties BBC radio broadcaster than it is a modern day Indian railway announcer. It began just as we were slowing into Jaipur station; a frightfully, frightfully, terribly, terribly Indo-British voice announcing our arrival,
"We are now approaching Jaipur, the famed pink city. A city with beautiful sights and smells to delight and tickle your senses"!
And just to jazz things up a bit, this announcement was both preceded and followed by a synthesized fanfare played by some invisible chap on keyboards. This, in order to let the passengers know exactly when the

announcement was about to start or that it had finished. Well, of course it wasn't intended as such but, I have to say, I've never experienced on-board entertainment quite like it. Outstanding and priceless and...long may it continue!

You know, it's at times like these that I deeply regret not carrying some sort of recording device such as a Dictaphone but, then again, when you consider that I seriously contemplated snapping my toothbrush in half in order to 'travel lightly', I think maybe a Dictaphone would've been a tad extravagant in the luggage department!

Our next port of call was to be Pushkar, a place about which, like most other places, I knew nothing. However, somewhere entangled amongst the far reaching branches of the travellers' grapevine, this little place in the desert always seemed to crop up in conversation. And as it turns out, Pushkar actually has two fairly significant claims to fame, for not only is it famous in India for being one of the holiest of holy places; but it also plays host, every November, to possibly the largest camel fair on earth. Not that the earth is over-run with camel fairs or that this has any particular relevance...I just thought I'd mention it.

In order to get to Pushkar though, we had to pass through the town of Ajmer. Here, we had a brief pit stop born out of necessity -i.e. the bus terminated there- and so were hardly in town long enough to form an opinion of it before jumping on yet another bus. (Some would say we were hardly long enough anywhere). However, it 'was' long enough to bump into a nice little English family who'd just driven down from some place in the north –a location I don't recall- where the father/ husband was working. Well, when I met them they were sat round a table in a café, the mother and two children, chatting away together and the middle-aged father relaxing with a rather large whisky. When I introduced myself he seemed quite keen for some male company and, as luck would have it, turned out to be one of that rare breed of human beings; one who was genuinely excited to hear my travel stories. So, as it was, we ended up talking right the way through the afternoon -or more, me talking, him listening- and it wasn't until well after the children were nearly unconscious with boredom that I suggested that maybe I really should be on my way. Before I could leave the room though, he beckoned me back, poured himself another flagon sized tumbler of whisky, screwed the lid back on and handed me the remaining half bottle. Well, it would've been extremely rude to turn down such a generous offer wouldn't it; and so I gratefully accepted. Not that I was really a whisky drinker, but I felt sure that sometime in the near future something just might convince me to become one.

Later in the day, Dave, Steve and I hopped onto yet another hand-me-down school bus and by early evening we'd arrived in Pushkar. There seemed to be no shortage of accommodation here and so we decided to head straight for pole position by the lake, where we managed to acquire a room in a grand old place right on the water's edge. Then, by the time I'd sorted myself out and stepped back outside, scores of little houses around the shoreline were already lit up for the evening. From across the lake you could hear party sounds, the music and the laughter so amplified by the expanse of water and the still of the desert night, it could have all been going on right next-door to the hotel. Walking round the town, everyone here seemed so exceedingly happy. And apart from those who actually lived here, just about everyone appeared to be either Indians on a pilgrimage or second generation hippies who'd come here to 'find themselves'; though the difference between the two groups was both obvious and bizarre. For the hippies, of all places on earth, this surely had to be one of the easiest to find themselves because, from what I could see, most of them hardly moved a muscle the whole time they were there. It seemed the majority just sat around the lake all day in a trance-like state, all glassy eyed and totally motionless, like so many gormless garden gnomes round a giant fish pond.

As for the Indian pilgrims, paradoxically it was they who were the revellers here; partying away every night well into the small hours. However, for all their differences, it seemed the two did share common interests; for both groups were here in Pushkar for spiritual reasons, and both of them acted like they were drugged up to the eye-balls though in entirely different ways. The singing and dancing Indians high on religious fervour -enhanced by copious amounts of alcohol- the mystical young hippies high on well...anything they could lay their hands on. How very strange life can be!

NB In defence of hippies -second generation or otherwise- I have to say though, that during and indeed since this trip, I have witnessed hundreds and hundreds of people of all ages under the influence of grass, ganja, pot, hash, dope, marijuana or whatever you want to call it; but I have yet to see one single person become violent because of it. In this respect, smoking the stuff surely gives it a clear advantage over alcohol, from which I've seen some pretty grizzly results from some very respectable and ordinary people. Now, this may or may not be a good argument in favour of legalising cannabis but, for the vast majority of people, there's probably nothing to be lost by doing so. Unfortunately, as the 'against' lobby will argue, there is and always will be a certain number of people who want to take things just that step further and experiment with something rather stronger. Well, whilst that's certainly true, these people undoubtedly form a minority. I suppose the real problem is that, especially amongst the younger set, it takes a very strong minded individual to resist the almost inevitable peer pressure which will be put upon them to try other things: peer pressure, indeed, that can eventually become so strong and far reaching, as to elevate whatever it is they're taking into a trend or fashion. Something that's all too easy to see with the 'pill popping' that goes on around the clubs and discos of today. (God, I sound old!)

Another N.B….Actually, I lie about not having seen people getting violent on dope; subsequently I've seen a number of people in the Caribbean -in particular- who really should be locked away for good. But then, these weren't recreational users, they were people who lived on the stuff. Besides, I'm certainly not suggesting that these types of drugs should be available on the National Health - for who'd want to wait three years for them anyway- but it does make you think, doesn't it!

Meanwhile, back at the hotel the following morning, I awoke to the rhythmic shh, shh, shh sound of someone sweeping. I looked out of my window and below, an old woman was busy redistributing dust and sand around a small yard. As she went about her business, the whole time she was bent completely double at the waist; this being the only way to reach the ground with her small brush of twigs. Now, this type of brush can be seen all over the tropics and, though remarkably effective at getting the job done, makes you wonder why on earth somebody hasn't come up with a deluxe version i.e. one with a longer handle, so at least the user can stand upright. As they say, 'it's hardly rocket science'. It strikes me that the inventor must have been about as daft as the brush he invented!

Over in a small field next to the lake, a tall thin man with an oily rag of a shirt, tended a handful of goats. A little fat pig down by the bridge, oinked away and nuzzled a discarded plastic bag, blinkered as it was by its own ears. A moth eaten three-legged dog lay sprawled out in the sun on top of a bank of earth, waiting to be kicked by a passing child.

By seven o-clock the sun was already starting to climb the hill on the far side of the water but morning mist still hung above the sand of the surrounding desert, suspended like an enormous fine net curtain draped over the land. People were now gathering on the ghats -or steps- leading down to the lake, in order to welcome the new day and to perform their morning rituals and ablutions. It was a truly magical scene and one of those moments impossible to describe without a whole plethora of clichés. (Though, this of course is exactly what I have done, but where's the point of purposely avoiding a description which perfectly suits your feelings.)

Before most of the guests in the hotel had surfaced, I decided to climb the hill behind the lake to the small temple at its peak. I walked down to the waterside, crossed the bridge and up past the three-legged dog which, by now, was being mauled and taunted by a posse of only slightly healthier looking mongrels. It was such a sad and pathetic scene; the poor little wretched creature whined and whimpered away, and it was only when I shouted and drew his assailants' attention that he got any respite. Unfortunately though, this was at my own expense; for now, as I neared the bottom of the hill, the entire mongrel posse turned and started haring full pelt towards me, gnashing and snarling as they went. Well, this wasn't what I had in mind at all; it was terrifying! And it wasn't until I could see the reds of their eyes that I suddenly remembered...and reached to the ground for an imaginary stone. In an instant, the whole pack turned tail and fled, galloping away into the distance. Now, given these dogs' apparent bloodlust this may seem pretty remarkable -and it is really- but luckily I'd learnt this trick from way back, and the fact that it most definitely works is perhaps a sad indication that, in these parts at least, there are probably more stoned dogs than stoned hippies. Though in truth, this canine deception isn't solely confined to the dogs of India; I have subsequently, in fact, used this ploy quite often and, as yet, dogs the world over don't seem to have cottoned on to the old 'imaginary stone' trick. Let's hope they never do; for one: I hardly relish being mauled by a pack of mangy, rabid hounds; and two: if they were to ever get wise to it, we may all feel compelled to travel the globe armed with pocketfuls of rocks. And how embarrassing would that be, to risk arrest at a border post for ballast smuggling!

Once at the hilltop temple I kicked off my shoes, as is customary in most religious shrines, and put them alongside a well worn pair of yellow rubber flip-flops. This type of footwear, of course, is more associated with British beach resorts than with an Indian desert; nevertheless, the humble flip-flop has become so popular here that it's all but become part of the national costume. As such, I wasn't terribly surprised to find that this particular pair belonged to the temple guardian himself (that coupled with the fact that they were the only other shoes around!)

The temple courtyard, when I arrived, was small but quite spotlessly clean. And there within its centre, stood the temple itself; a tiny shrine of stone, its interior lit by nothing but a couple of candles. These revealed, as in all over the subcontinent, a gallery of rather gaudy pictures decorating the walls and featuring various Hindu Gods. Off to one side, the guardian and his wife sat cross-legged on a rectangular piece of matting quietly eating fingerfuls of rice. It struck me that theirs probably would've been a very meagre existence up here, were it not for the fact that Pushkar was now well and truly on the travellers' trail. This meant that, not only did they get a lot more visitors to the shrine, but that their son could also earn a reasonable living by going down into the village every day to sell his handmade jewellery to the hippies; thereby, being able to afford a little something perhaps, other than rice.

It was only from looking back from this temple that you could fully appreciate that really, the little town of Pushkar is nothing but an overgrown oasis. All around the lake below, tiny white box houses jockey for position like sugar cubes round a saucer, and behind them, a vast desert of sand and rock stretches away for mile upon mile in every direction.

Behind me in the trees, small families of monkeys groomed, sunbathed, chattered and played in characteristic fashion; the occasional bird flitted nervously from bush to bush just far enough away to frustrate any attempts at identification. It was a wonderful place to be, and all the more so for having it all to myself.

Later on, whilst still in Pushkar, I spent another lazy and carefree day walking around town. Everybody went about their business in the same relaxed manner, and it wasn't until halfway through the morning, I suddenly realised that today was Christmas Day. I went and sat down by the lake in the sunshine, then smiled to myself as I began thinking of my family back home. It seemed a little strange not to be sharing Christmas with them all, but as that was clearly impossible at that precise moment, I could hardly think of a better and more tranquil place to be.

Though a holy site, the growth of Pushkar can probably be attributed as much to tourism as to the growing numbers of visiting worshippers. Not that the two things are necessarily conflicting, on the contrary -as discussed earlier- whilst tourists and worshippers may be two quite distinct groups, it's not always easy to separate the two. Why, I lost count of the times I saw young Westerners still eager to find themselves, being led down to the water's edge by a colourfully painted Saddhu. These 'holy men' would give their charges a few flower heads to throw onto the lake and then treat them to a "special Hindi prayer" before leading them back up the steps and relieving them of their money; only a donation you understand!

Apparently, or so I was told, "the more you pay, the better the Gods will think of you" -a Saddhu's words, not mine. Now, call me a cynic but well, taking advantage of young mystic seeking Westerners in such a way doesn't seem to me terribly righteous or holy. Though I suppose, principles aside, such petty extortion has to be preferable to begging for a living, and having witnessed on no few occasions how the majority of budget travellers are so unwilling to pass on any more of their 'hard earned' cash than is absolutely necessary, perhaps these few locals can hardly be blamed for their little scam. Also, I'd like to point out: I say these few locals because, after all, that is what we're talking about here. There's no denying that a lot of genuine holy men do really exist; men who spend their whole lives daubed in gaudy colour but who are, nevertheless, totally devoted to their belief. I suppose the problem is that sometimes, as an outsider, it's just that it's near impossible to judge the morals through the make-up!

Another way in which an increasingly large amount of Indians seem to be making a living -particularly in Pushkar- is by dressing up as so-called Saddhus and asking for money simply to be photographed. This also is usually nothing more than a gimmick of which I too have been a victim, or more accurately should I say, a perpetrator! The reason I say this is because, although I knew full well that these men were no more holy than I was, I did actually give them money -albeit a little begrudgingly. But, though I say so myself, I did also get some extremely colourful and 'authentic looking' shots. And yes, okay, so maybe I'm guilty of encouraging what is nothing more than a cheap con trick, but well, sometimes we all need to take a step down from the moral

151

high ground; after all, how can you seriously object to donating a little money to a handful of rather entrepreneurial men when they live in a land with so few opportunities.

That evening, I went down to the ghats to watch the sunset. A young Indian couple over on the bridge were facing into the sun, held in each other's embrace. It was unusual to see two Asians displaying mutual affection so openly, and I thought to myself that they'd probably come from one of the big cities where the inevitable onslaught of modernity had softened the edges of their religious upbringings. Maybe even, I was witnessing their very first private moment together; perhaps being here alone away from their families, they were experiencing a deliciously new sense of freedom; for that's what it seemed...tender, loving and new! It was a wonderful thing to see though, and I felt just a twinge of envy; a yearning for something in my past. I sat down by the water's edge deep in thought.

It was getting late now and people had already gathered on the steps facing west, their faces aglow with the goldening light. A Saddhu -probably genuine- sat cross-legged on a stone block, motionless. He stared out across the lake alone with his thoughts; the streaks of red, yellow and white paint on his face and body changing hue with every passing second. An Indian in Western dress completed the atmospheric mood by playing out a haunting, chanting, rhythmical beat on a pair of bongo-like drums. Nobody spoke, nobody moved; until finally the sun had sunk into the rocks beyond the desert. Then, the drums stopped dead leaving a moment of magical and potent stillness; a moment of serene nothingness as I sat there in the dusky light.

It was a good few minutes before everyone slowly rose to their feet, and then each began to drift off into the night: the locals, back to their homes; the pilgrims to their all night parties around the lake; and us Westerners to congregate, yet again, in one of the many bars and restaurants.

Of course, with Pushkar being well 'on' the beaten track, it was more than capable of providing rice-weary travellers like myself with all sorts of Western standard food such as pizzas and pancakes but, as it was Christmas, I decided that if ever there was an occasion to celebrate, then this was surely it.

A small mixed group of Asians and Europeans had made a campfire away from the lake and so I went over and joined them in order to have a bit of company whilst eating my Christmas dinner. Obviously, as I'd only just this minute discovered that it was Christmas day, I hadn't really put a great deal of thought or planning into this festive meal. However, I did happen to have with me, a rather special and long awaited Christmas treat....no, not for me a succulent breast of turkey, not even a hint of ham or the whiff of a Brussels sprout but......two pot noodles and a half bottle of whisky! The whisky, of course, courtesy of the kind Englishman in Ajmer; and the pot noodles? I'd carried them in the bottom of my rucksack across two continents, all the way from Horsham to Pushkar. What a feast; Christmas would never be the same again!

Although I'd already had a brush with the hash smoking fraternity back in Pakistan, the stuff I'd tried there seemed to have had little effect on me at the time and so, sitting in a circle of fellow travellers on the floor of a very laid-back looking restaurant one night, I thought I'd give it another go. For one thing, I just loved that unmistakably sweet aroma of smouldering ganja and Pushkar, of all places, seemed the ideal place in which to experience…whatever it was that everybody else appeared to be experiencing.

There were perhaps eight or nine of us in the restaurant that night, and no sooner had we sat down on the loosely arranged coconut matting, than a couple of spliffs the size of descant recorders were being passed round the circle. Now, being something of a novice myself, when my turn came to smoke these joints I found that I was caught a little in two minds between wanting to go the whole hog - by taking back as much as possible- but at the same time, trying to save face by not totally passing out by the third round. Consequently, although inhaling my full quota of two drags per spliff on most rounds, there was the odd occasion when I would give it a miss completely and pass the little parcel on (perhaps subconsciously still waiting for the music to stop!) In any case, within no time at all, there was such a thick cloud of sweet smelling smog billowing about us that, had I abstained totally, I might well have reached a passive high anyway. The thing is, and I can quite honestly say this with hand on heart, the whole thing didn't really do a lot for me. Okay, I suppose I felt pretty mellow, but then I didn't think I had a problem in that direction anyway.

Peering through the dense fug, I looked around the circle of faces and wondered if I too was wearing that same happy but slightly glazed expression. You know, the expression that says, "The lights are on but…there's somebody else at home!" What was it that these people were experiencing that I wasn't? And in all honesty, how could it possibly be any more calming or more wonderful than some of the things I'd already seen and experienced in reality. I left slightly earlier that night. Besides, I'd already decided that I wasn't really cut out to be a fully paid up hippy, and especially if it meant spending every waking hour sitting in that obligatory cross-legged position.

NB On a subsequent visit to Pushkar, I spent an evening with friends at that very same restaurant. One chap had brought with him a litre bottle of 'bang lassie,' a potent mix of yoghurty milk and hashish, with both the colour and taste of muddy water. There was plenty to go round that evening, but only two of us actually drinking it. We chatted, ate and drank...ate, drank and chatted; sipping our lassies through plastic straws. After one large glass I'd definitely acquired that mellow feeling; after half a litre of the stuff -unlike previous experiences here with smoking- the effect became quite extraordinary. There was clearly some magical ingredient in this muddy water that gives the drinker the humour of a seven year old. This became obvious as the evening went on. You see, we'd been discussing the Pushkar camel fair, and I remember thinking how wonderful it would be if the fair were on right now, and if those camels were to pass by the restaurant so that I might toss my plastic straw under the last one's foot...yep, just so as I could say "it's the last camel that broke the straw's back!" Umm, pathetic maybe; infantile certainly; but the thought alone was enough to transform me into a gibbering, hysterical heap. The fact that nobody seemed to share my hysteria, of course, only made things funnier. I was quite simply uncontrollable. Now, to be perfectly honest, I don't normally like that feeling of lack of control but well, if this were always to be the result, then bugger legislation, muddy water should most definitely be available on prescription!

I felt a terrible reluctance to leave Pushkar with its odd but happy blend of travellers and devotees, and wondered if it would always contain that same irony: the Westerners serenely calm and mystical; the Indian pilgrims with their riotous all night parties. What a strange but happy contrast they are; each finding fulfilment but in bizarrely different ways; hand in hand every night, "All we are saying, is give peace a chance, but for God's sake...turn the music up!" I fear it will all eventually change but, I rather hope it doesn't.

Udaipur was just another big town but one which has been made famous by the presence of one very special building; that being, the Lake Palace Hotel; a quite beautiful ex-Maharaja's palace floating, funnily enough...in the middle of a lake. The Lake Palace is one of several extremely beautiful and grand old palaces in Rajasthan which were once occupied by their obscenely wealthy owners and dutifully cared for by armies of minions. Now however, times have changed quite dramatically; to the extent in fact, that many of the current inheritors have had to look to tourism in order to make ends meet. Well, this may be sad for hopeless romantics hankering after a by-gone era and, even more so perhaps, for the current owners; but undoubtedly, it's fantastic news for the non-budget traveller or, even more, for the budget traveller craving a rare bit of opulence. Sadly, at this time, I was most definitely one of the latter but worse still, didn't even for one night, have the means to quench that craving. (These places are great on the eye but not on the wallet.) My only hope is that they don't change beyond recognition and that they continue with their Maharajas in residence until I eventually have the means to stay there. I'd just hate to see the Umaid Bawan in Jodhpur become a Travel Lodge; its pristine lawns turned to tarmac with a bottle bank stuck in the corner. If only more money was put aside to construct buildings such as this one. Surely to God, it has to be better than say…splashing out on an oversized jamboree tent in the middle of London. (This 'masterpiece' of modern architecture was undertaken rather later than this journey of course!)

By this time, I'd realised that we were following a pretty well worn path through India; a path that was becoming more and more worn, due largely to the Lonely Planet guide book to this area. Now I know I've mentioned guides before but, I'm going to again. The thing is, they can be both friend and foe for, as I've said, whilst travelling without one can result in every wonder around every corner being refreshingly unexpected; well, to return home and discover that you've missed something quite unbelievable by only a gnat's whisker, can be more than a little frustrating. However, it can also be said that a good guide book will eventually 'kick itself in the teeth' by extolling the virtues of unspoilt places until…they're spoilt. I think that on the whole though, I would have to be pro guide, as these books undoubtedly provide valuable information but, and this is important, information which doesn't necessarily have to be followed. So, if then as a traveller, you wish to be alone with nobody but local people in unspoilt places, then I suggest that the best way in which to do so is to thoroughly read through every single guide book available, and to go everywhere 'not' mentioned.

One place given scant publicity on our route was Chittaurgarh; a raised plateau amid the flat plains to the south of Rajasthan. It'd been the scene of many old battles in India's colourful history but is now a haven of tranquillity, with nothing but the occasional vervet monkey scrambling about in a stumpy tree, or a couple of orange-turbaned, wizened old men chatting on a rock to bring the place to life. Meanwhile, the plains below drift off into the midday haze as far as the eye can see. But all about the eerily silent plateau, crumbling ruins still litter this old fortress in the sky, reminding us of a more bloody and turbulent past. How many thousands of men must have died out on these plains trying to take possession of this natural stronghold? How many wives must have suffered the horrific death of being thrown onto their husbands funeral pyres alive? For it may seem inconceivable now, but in days gone by this was the way of things here. A time when a wife was little more than a possession, a mother to the all important son and heir; a live-in servant and pleasant distraction from the rigours of life. God, how times have changed! Okay, so there are certainly parts of this world where 'sexual' and 'equality' are still dirty words, but thankfully the days of using widows for firewood have long gone. (In fact, in my experience, it is far more likely us men who'll get a roasting for well, just about anything, from forgotten birthdays to unnoticed hair-dos!)
But strangely, though an abandoned practice, I'm told that

here in this part of India, it's still customary for the new widows to abstain from attending their husbands' funerals so as to avoid having to be barbecued in this somewhat barbaric tradition. Interesting to note then, that because the religion and traditions are so very strong and deep rooted, it's thought preferable to avoid the consequences of your husband's death by staying away, rather than to alter the tradition, itself a way of life that has existed for generations.

Here in the West meanwhile, it seems that there is less and less need to believe in someone or something which isn't tangible; and it would appear that the more 'financially' wealthy a society becomes, the less it relies on some form of religion. In fact, in recent times, even in the Muslim world I've witnessed young men rushing to their mosques on mopeds at the call to prayer; this being very blatantly out of duty rather than from a heart felt belief. But then, I suppose, many Muslims do at least have a sense of duty, whereas in large sectors of the West, religion has all but died out. This disintegration of belief or reliance on something 'intangible' seems to reach its lowest ebb when a given society has attained a certain standard of living, i.e. has no apparent need of a 'crutch'. But beyond that, bizarrely, it would appear that people who have nothing more to worry about or to strive for, then create their own stresses in life and revert to the need for something to believe in. This is best seen perhaps, in the United States where, not only have a lot of individuals and communities turned back to religion, but if they don't find one which suits…they simply create a new one which does!

Religions of course provide a whole armoury of double-edged swords in that, throughout history, they have in one way or another, been responsible for both uniting and/or killing most of the people who have ever lived on our planet. As far as I am concerned it's all quite simple: if any belief whatsoever causes people to live in harmony with one another...then it's a good thing; if it doesn't...then it isn't! From what I can make out, the message that comes across from all major religions and their teachings is quite simple and clear, "Hey, lead a good and honest life aye. And if, along the way, you can help others to do the same then...that's just great!"

CHAPTER 11

- CAVES, THIEVES AND TICKET INSPECTORS -

Ajanta to Bombay

Some way south of Chittaurgarh lie the Buddhist and Jain caves of Ellora and Ajanta. Not the natural stone-age home variety, but ones that have been hewn out of the rock by generations, once again, all in the name of faith. Now, I use the word 'faith' here because Buddhists generally prefer to think of their beliefs more as a philosophy, a way of life rather than as a religion. Though traditionally, as Buddhists believe in a God, how you can separate one from the other I'm not quite sure. Also, by its very definition, any religion involving a non-tangible god is, of course, a faith but...I don't really want to get too heavy here.

Anyway, there are several fairly basic looking caves in these two places, some containing nothing more than a single effigy, but others, virtual galleries of marvellously intricate stone carvings. All of which would normally be near invisible to anyone entering -for there is neither man-made lighting nor the cave-mouths wide enough to allow enough natural light in. However, true to form, there was somebody present here to take full advantage of this very fact; and so, wherever we went, we would inevitably be closely pursued by a young Indian boy toting a large foil covered board. And each and every time we entered a cave, within seconds, its interior would magically be lit up as sunlight was bounced in off a home-made mirror, revealing beautiful and ancient rock sculptures. Whether these boys were being employed as official guides or whether they were simply being entrepreneurial and showing ingenuity I'm not sure, but they went about their business in such an unhussler-like and laidback fashion that, once we'd done the rounds, we were only too pleased to give them a few rupees by way of a tip. It was just so nice not to feel under any pressure and to be treated well, more as friends than tourists. Their attitude, I suspect though, was born out of the fact that these boys were very much from a rural community and as such, had yet to have their lives and ideals tainted by the faster pace; the aggressiveness of modern city life. It was also refreshing to see that these caves, which have remained so wonderfully natural looking for so many generations, have yet to be spoilt by the introduction of electricity. How long this will remain the case is anybody's guess; and I daresay that, even as I write, a thousand fluorescent light bulbs may be illuminating every shadow; coca-cola sellers leaping out from behind every finely sculpted pillar, and boys with real mirrors asking for real money; I dearly hope not.

The Jain caves meanwhile, are either enclosed and cave-shaped like the Buddhist ones, or are beautifully handcrafted open-air temples; the rock sculptures even more intricately carved or some may say 'over the top' than the Buddhist ones. Whether this greater attention to detail is for any particular reason I'm not really sure, but it's interesting to note that this is also a reflection of how both groups seem to live their lives. That is to say, the Jains may have similar beliefs to Buddhists but have taken things just that bit further, and particularly when it comes to the 'respecting forms of life other than their own' part of the philosophy. Now, I'm very much for preserving life of all kinds -apart from, that is, every single bastard mosquito on the planet- but I think maybe the Jains have gone a little too extreme on this one! I can respect various reasons for becoming vegetarian, but to wear gauze over your mouth in order not to breathe in the microscopic animals in the air? This, for me, is well…just too much. Like so many things in life, perhaps the principle is rather better than the practice. I mean, how can you possibly live like that every day of your life? "Oops, sorry…just sat on 50,000 micro-organisms." 'Splat'! "Oh blast, there goes another 30,000!" Mind you, on the plus side, I'm all for people not eating meat. If ever you're in a plane crash and marooned in the desert for weeks without food, a vegetarian will sure as hell taste better than anyone else around. (Next time you're sitting on a plane, take note who orders the pasta!)

I think it would be very difficult for anyone to dispute that colonialism was a terribly wrong thing, and that it caused an incredible amount of grief to a great many people. But if you believe that something positive comes out of every situation, then perhaps this is it; for, after the various European powers had taken over half the world, most, having enjoyed all the spoils of somebody else's lands before cluttering off or being booted out, did at least leave some sort of infrastructure -whether it was wanted or not. Now, one of the more obvious legacies that the British left to the Indian subcontinent was most certainly its railways, where here, the trains have become both famous and infamous. In fact, what remains today is a network of tracks that criss-cross the whole of India, much as they did before 1947 when the British were finally but passively kicked out. (I'm not sure if you can 'passively' kick someone out but if you can, then Gandhi sure as hell did it!) But, not only did the Brits build the railways -with local labour of course- but also most of the trains that run on that track. This meant that up until quite recently, because very little had been replaced, most of the trains were still under steam, so for train buffs India was an absolute paradise. Sadly though -for the train buffs anyway- most of the steam engines have now gone, to be replaced by equally dirty and noisy diesel engines -but minus the romance. Nevertheless, I still found these old diesel trains in India preferable to just about any other form of transport available, and especially when compared to the vintage school bus option. It's just a shame then that you can't use the railways without the bureaucracy which goes with it. As I've said before, anybody who's been told to stand in a certain queue for over an hour and, on finally reaching the ticket counter, been waved away to an equally long queue alongside, will appreciate this. The whole system is just so incredibly frustrating.

On a personal level, the culmination of all this frustration manifested itself when the two boys and I were on a train journey somewhere between Chittaurgarh and Bombay. We'd once again patiently gone through the whole queuing thing and had walked to the appropriate platform, jubilantly clutching our three single tickets for a departure within the hour to somewhere -I don't recall where- several hours down the line. Then we nuzzled our way through the crowd and, when our train pulled in, we duly took up our places in the second class carriage and settled down for the long journey ahead.

After a couple of hours of chuntering through the Indian countryside, a very smart but officious looking ticket inspector slowly made his way through the carriage toward us, clipping away at everyone's tickets as he went...until he came to ours. Well, it transpired that the ticket clerk, from whom we'd quite inadvertently and innocently bought our tickets, had given us tickets not for that day but for the following one. At this juncture I'd like to add three points in our defence: that there were most certainly free seats available; that the price for this journey was the same whichever day you travelled; and the fact that it was the ticket clerk's fault wasn't in dispute. However, in the eyes of this one ticket inspector, we were on the wrong train at the wrong time, and somebody was going to have to pay for it! So, with several interested 'by-sitters' looking on, there followed a rather lengthy discussion between the three of us -and the one of him-which became more and more heated as neither side was willing to back down. And the more we pleaded for reason, the more resolute he became.

It was then, just as the quarrel was reaching its climax, that a scuffle broke out as Steve -the history lecturer- tried to grab our tickets back from the over zealous inspector. The ticket inspector though, was having none of it; he gritted his teeth and held on to them as though they were winning lottery tickets. As far as he was concerned he was in the right, and he certainly wasn't about to be beaten. Well, this led to a sort of animated stalemate between the two parties, with the ticket inspector refusing to hand back the tickets, and us refusing to let the inspector continue with them down the carriage. So all that happened in the end was that we gave up the tussle for the tickets, and our fat and round, resolute little ticket inspector sat down amongst us, a prisoner in his own train; all this, much to the initial concern but then general amusement of all around. For our part, we were of course, relatively happy with this arrangement. As we were due to get off in only four hour's time, we naively assumed that we'd either meet another inspector with a little more compassion and understanding, or at worst, we could 'jump ship' and run off when we'd reached our station.

Eventually though, when we did reach our destination, we did just as planned but when we'd jumped down from the carriage, were immediately and closely followed by Adolf, who shouted out something to an office across the track. The next thing you know, there was a flurry of activity and we were being escorted to the station master's office by a small battalion of baton wielding policemen. Well, once in the office it was quite hopeless; though there followed yet another mammoth session of pleading, we were soon forced to give up the battle. Our high Western principles were by now in tatters for, not only were we ordered to pay for yet another ticket for the journey which we'd already undertaken, but also a fine for riding the train without the correct ticket. In our eyes, of course, all this was totally unreasonable and unjust, but we were left with no choice whatsoever but to give in to this insanity and pay the money.

Now, it would've been rather nice, under the circumstances, if we'd been able to retain just a smidgen of pride in all this, but, you know, we weren't even afforded that. For as hard as I tried to hand the money over to the station master he would have none of it. We were forced to walk along the corridor to another office, and who should be sitting there but...our old friend the ticket inspector. In all of the six hours we'd endured in his company, we hadn't seen so much as a softening of the eyes; but now, as we threw our money onto his desk and were issued with our 'new' tickets for the journey we'd already bloody well completed, a beam of victorious delight came over his podgy little face. We turned and without a word, picked up our packs and left.

NB Since this trip, things have changed markedly for the better. I've found the railways to be far better organised and the majority of attitudes of its workers refreshingly human. So, taking account of all the old bureaucratic hassles would I do it all again?...Of course I would. The Indian railways are an institution, an incredible adventure and...an absolute must!

I'd heard all sorts of stories of crowds of people riding on tops of trains and it seemed to me such a great way to travel. I mean, what better way can there be with all that fresh air, room to spare and uncluttered views of the passing scenery. Unfortunately I never did quite manage to get a ride on top at any time during this journey. Mind you, although at times a common occurrence, I'm told that this is more usually a way of escaping payment rather than for reasons of overcrowding -or for the benefit of fresh air and views. We did however, experience first hand, the delectable delights of third class travel; and as if this wasn't enough of an experience, it was to be third class with 'standing room only'. Granted, on this occasion, it was on a mere thirteen hour journey but, you know, we would have killed for one of the bare wooden benches occupied hip to hip by our numerous fellow passengers.

Now, unsurprisingly, there didn't appear to be any seat

allocation system in operation at the time, so when the very last slat had been bagged by a local, we had no option but to stand for the entire journey, wedged in at chest height by a sea of little brown heads -like three rogue Marshmallows in a box of Maltesers! Though, strictly speaking, even in this position we could have been deemed to be a little hoggy with the space available, being as we were reluctant to put any of our packs down. This wasn't because we thought they might disappear though, but because the whole carriage floor was awash with what appeared to be a soup of cabbage leaves and urine, which ebbed and flowed back and forth with the train's movements like a rhythmic vegetarian tidal sewer.

Now I'm quite sure that at this very point in time, I'd sooner have been French kissing a camel with halitosis than standing in that carriage but well, it's strange what tricks the memory plays, isn't it -or perhaps, the lack of it- and now I can only think back fondly to that journey. I will never forget, especially, the seemingly limitless patience and good humour of our carriage mates, the wall to wall eyes and teeth facing up at us as we passed the considerable amount of time singing old English hymns. What an unusual trio we must have seemed and sounded; but it was always to an appreciative if undiscerning audience.

I had, so far, survived over two months of near continuous travel without so much as losing a bean. Everybody I'd bumped into seemed to have had something stolen on their travels, and I suppose that at the time, I put this down to their general lack of vigilance. My luck however, was about to run out; not once, but twice…in the very same week. The first of these times was whilst dozing on yet another long train journey; my pack stashed below my seat and just a carrier bag of bits and pieces in the rack above. I was sitting next to a squat middle-aged Muslim man who sported the traditional, hand-embroidered 'Thunderbird' style hat, whilst opposite us sat his wife and two young children. After a while, with night drawing in and his family now fast asleep, the man next to me decided to put his feet up along the seat and rest them in my lap. At first this seemed a little odd -not to say rude- for as yet, he hadn't uttered a single word to me. But anyway I thought, "Where's the harm", and so I left things as they were. But then, just as I started to doze, I was suddenly awoken by an inordinate amount of fidgeting going on in my lap. I quickly looked at the man but he appeared to be in a deep sleep, and so I thought no more of it. A little more time passed by and I was soon dozing once again. But then, no sooner had I dropped off a second time, than there was that same sensation, not unlike, in fact...somebody pressing their heels purposefully into your groin. I looked across and yet again the man appeared to be in a deep, deep sleep. It wasn't until the third time of being woken that I was left in absolutely no doubt as to what was going on. I looked down into my lap to see this chubby little brown hand making a grab for my wedding tackle. Well, naturally I was somewhat surprised and under the circumstances it would have been extremely easy to over-react but, do you know -and this is all in total silence of course- I did nothing more than fix him with my sternest of glares and shake my head calmly but disapprovingly. Thankfully, this seemed enough for him to get the message.   He hastily recoiled and returned to sleep bunched up in the foetal position beside the window, his wife and children still totally oblivious to his goings on.

Now all this may seem to have little to do with my losing anything but, bear with me; for as it happens, shortly after this incident I was woken with yet another start when suddenly we pulled into my station. I then rushed off the train and, still wondering whether or not the chubby chap's wife knew about her husband's wandering hand and foot problem...I clean forgot my bag! Fortunately, on this occasion, it was only the plastic carrier-bag up in the luggage rack which I lost, and this actually contained very little, as I'd at least had the sense to carry both money and passport in a money belt strapped around my waist. It did however, contain something of great personal value: namely a small address book containing the names and addresses of fellow travellers I'd bumped into in Europe - ones mostly from my inaugural truck hitching days. "Damn!" I thought. "What an incredible pain in the posterior!" I did try to trace it of course; I even made several quite fruitless phone calls to various station masters up and down the line, but it was quite hopeless. Why, even if it had been handed in by some kind soul, the chances of my being reunited with it were exceedingly slim. In any case, it probably would have been found by my old mate the ticket inspector. I imagined having to make a sizeable donation to his retirement fund because my diary had occupied a luggage rack without a ticket. I cursed my stupidity and felt so helpless; but the moment, like my diary, had gone. Yes, I knew that it would be yet another incident to go on the 'put it down to experience' pile.

My second 'loss' of the week -since I could hardly call the first a robbery- happened shortly after Dave, Steve and I had pulled into Bombay station feeling near to comatose after yet another sleepless night. We'd disembarked from the train and trudged zombie-like into the first available café outside the station, plonking ourselves down around the typically small, metal table -complete with equally typically white and yellow checked plastic sheet. The café was sparse, basic and grubby -like a transport café especially for students but without the transport...or students- and I sat there in silence, gazing into nothingness; thinking how strange it is how you can long for a good sit down having spent all night...sitting!

When the waiter appeared, it was all any of us could do to order three cups of *chai before I was to fall hook, line and sinker -inside of three short minutes- for probably one of the oldest con tricks in the book. Why, before the chai had even arrived, there was a gentle tap on my shoulder; I looked round to see a waiter pointed down to a handful of small coins scattered on the dirt floor beside me. I, of course, thought nothing more of it, assumed they'd fallen from my pocket and bent to retrieve them. Well, within the few seconds that this took me, somehow, my day bag, which had been wedged quite firmly between myself and Dave, was spirited away. I just couldn't believe how they'd managed it but, as sure as eggs is eggs, it was gone. I jumped to my feet and put up all the usual protestations but, of course, nobody had seen or heard a damned thing. I knew very well that all the staff were in on it, but what could I do. My questions were met by nothing but blank, innocent faces, shrugged shoulders and well-rehearsed concern. The whole thing was so bloody, bloody annoying!

You know, it's times like these that can bring out real extremes of emotion. So, whilst feeling both raging anger and frustration, I also felt an incredibly dull sense of stupidity. And if there's one thing worse than feeling angry, it's feeling angry and stupid or more, feeling angry, frustrated and stupid. But do you know though, beyond all that, the one lingering sense that stayed with me was simply one of wonder; not one of wondering how on earth they managed to snatch a bag wedged between two people, but of the expression that must have come across the thief's face as he reached his safe haven and opened my bag to reveal his booty: an empty plastic water bottle, half a pot of strawberry jam and an extremely well used box of Travel Scrabble!

* 'Chai' is the hot and airy, milky, sugary tea found all over India; invariably poured at arms length and flavoured with various herbs, depending on the region.

CHAPTER 12

- SNAKES, COCKROACHES AND MYSTERIOUS BUNDLES -

In Bombay

Bombay was our first major city after the capital, and one that hits you full in the face with its hot, noisy, scurrying, horn-blasting hecticness. This was Delhi with just an added pinch of chilli powder; a city constantly on the go but seemingly nowhere to go to. Its huge and teeming population a melee of madness, like millions of blind mice running around in 'never' decreasing circles; a seething throng shaken vigorously from side to side and around and around, confined within its city limits like a sack full of frantic gerbils. Cars, rickshaws, hawkers and beggars: jostling, remonstrating, cajoling and pleading; nobody waiting for anybody, and everybody busying themselves in masochistic defiance of the searing sun. Here, only the ubiquitous holy cows seem to have the sense to take things easy; but then, theirs is a life of almost unsurpassed privilege, a surreal existence -a life that requires little effort to sustain it. For them, the rat-race is for the rats and for the people of the street. But in these streets, you either stay with the pace or stay in the gutter; and sadly, this is where most of country dwellers coming into town to seek their fortunes are destined to end up.

Just how many can a city like Bombay support? Certainly there's money to be made; the wealth is there for all to see in its Manhattan-esque skyline. But behind every skyscraper, every large and grandiose government building, there is a darker side; a side that can be seen in almost every major city of the world; where once proud rural people now compete with mangy dogs for the scraps of wealthier society. Many people live here in Bombay, but many more just simply...exist!

The three of us were severely travel weary by the time we'd arrived in Bombay, and hadn't the energy, in this heat, to spend time searching for even passable accommodation. We settled on a triple room with blotched, manky walls, highly dubious looking beds and a glassless window, for a little over a pound. Steve and I immediately collapsed onto our beds whilst Dave braved the streets again in order to seek out somewhere where he could report his stolen travellers cheques (these had been 'magic-ed' away recently, though none of us had a clue where). Steve meanwhile, was asleep no sooner had his head hit what masqueraded as a pillow, whilst I lay on my bed staring up at the two tone, white-wash and ochre grime, ceiling.

Despite the glassless window, the room was still unbelievably hot and claustrophobic; like trying to sleep in a microwave only without the pleasant distraction of a giant turntable. The slightest movement caused a small pond of sweat to accumulate in every crevice of the body and, although there was absolute pandemonium down on the street below, nothing moved in the room, not even the air. I lay spread-eagled on my mattress, as motionless as possible and soon fell asleep.

Later, we both awoke and joined Dave out amongst the throng. The heat was still far too oppressive to appreciate anything that the city had to offer, so we made our way through the madness and mayhem and down to the waterfront. It was the first I'd seen of the sea since Istanbul, and as I stood at the shore, even here, in this the most foreign of lands, I was at once awash with that feeling of calm and contentment that comes with the familiar: that feeling of blissful tranquillity that water seems to have on us all. Here, at last, there was light relief from the clawing heat as a gentle breeze blew in off the ocean. It was quite wonderful!

Delhi Gate, that huge stone arch and stoic symbol of an independent India, stood guard at the waterfront, and all around, vendors pestered passers-by, trying to hawk tooth-sized packets of chewing gum. Others toted small, cylindrical paper packs of 'bidis', the ubiquitous little green cigarettes of India. A smart looking man in a grey safari suit approached me with a small Ali Baba basket nestled under one arm.

"Excuse me sir, you are varnting to see snake dance?" he said, "Honest, I tell you, good god, blimey, I am nut varnting any money sir, nutting!"

He obviously did want money, but before I could turn tail and run, the chap was down on his haunches and blowing away, puffy-cheeked, on a sort of flattened recorder. Soon, a woefully sad looking cobra was prodded out from the comfort of his basket, and was standing up and swaying from side to side to his tormentor's movements.

This was the first time I'd seen a snake charming act and I have to confess that, however staged and pathetic it may have been, I couldn't resist photographing it. More annoyingly, I also failed to resist paying the man for the privilege; though this was only after he'd poked the poor wretched creature back into its basket and had chased after me along the waterfront, successfully hounding me to exhaustion. Apparently, there must have been some gross misunderstanding on my part, for it turns out that, actually, he did want payment for this performance (silly me!) I rather begrudgingly handed over a few rupees; he, even more begrudgingly, took it, and then sped on his way off toward some other gullible and weary wanderer.

That evening, we returned to the relative sanctuary of our room. We'd all been a little concerned about how safe our stuff was in this particular place, and so were relieved to find that our packs were still just where we'd left them. We were not quite so pleased however, to have to batter to death a small battalion of almost tortoise-sized cockroaches before we could retire for the night; and as anybody who's tried will testify…these critters certainly do take some battering! Yes okay, so I did feel a little cruel and guilty about splattering the local wildlife all over the concrete floor, but not guilty enough that I wanted to sleep with the things.

Come to think of it, it's a bit tough on the old cockroaches really, that along with rats, mice, snakes, frogs, spiders and the like, they seemed to have joined that illustrious and elitist group of 'most detested animals in the world'. Not that they've necessarily done anything wrong; they just don't enjoy a great press with us humans -and in particular…the female variety of humans. Personally, as I've said before, I don't like to kill anything bar mosquitoes; it's just that cockroaches have to be one of the most difficult things on earth to catch alive, and having already woken one night with a cockroach antennae up my nostril,* I'm damned if I was going to share my room with a whole herd of the creatures.

* In truth, this probing antennae incident was actually on another occasion entirely. I'd woken up with a start one night, feeling this irritating tickle deep inside my right nostril, and quickly sat up to give it a good itch. I then noticed, in the half light, a big blob on my pillow and, assuming it to be blood, went to touch it...only to see the blob scuttle off across the bed. Not really something you'd want a repeat of on a regular basis, and especially if you happen to sleep with your mouth wide open!

After a hot, clammy and near sleepless night, all three of us felt more than ready for a change of room, and so first thing in the morning we were up, not so bright but early, and over the road queuing at the Salvation Army hostel. Thankfully, though extremely popular, we managed here to acquire just about the last three dorm beds available, and these came with 'all meals included' for the princely sum of thirty five rupees (or about 50p) each. The Ritz it certainly wasn't, but it was squeaky clean, cool-ish, delightfully bug-free and a Mecca of a travellers' meeting place. In fact, the place was so umm...tolerable, that we were very nearly seduced into staying on. However, something had happened here which had affected us all. For though only in Bombay a short time, I'd already sampled a whiff of that cool Indian Ocean air. Now, the three of us shared that same anxiousness to leave the city behind us so, no sooner had we settled in than we were off into the centre of town again to book ferry tickets for the twenty-two hour trip down the coast to Goa.

Meanwhile, Dave, after a great deal of donkey work - there's a lot of that goes on round here- had eventually managed to get his traveller's cheques replaced, and so now we were all in buoyant mood, keen to get away from the big city and to hit the beaches down south.

That evening, whilst still in Bombay, I bumped into Simon, a young photographer from London whom I'd met previously in Pushkar. I'd passed him walking up the hill by the lake and, physically at least, he could almost have been another person. He'd been suffering from a bad bout of hepatitis and back then, his face was the colour of the surrounding desert and he shuffled about with a sort of dole-queue-like lethargy. Now, thankfully, he'd regained his full colour but had still been left weakened by the illness. In this respect though, he hardly differed from the rest of us. We'd all either succumbed to various bouts of Delhi Belly somewhere along the way or, even if we hadn't, we'd been slowed to a sloth-like pace by the constant bombardment of a merciless tropical sun.

It was nice to see a familiar face again -albeit a different coloured one- and once Simon had also settled himself into the Salvation Army hostel, we sat on our beds gassing away together like two old Lancashire lasses in a laundrette. You know, I never tired of listening to travellers' tales; and though the stories were often quite similar, the storytellers seldom were -much like the same scene painted by different artists; there was always a slightly different slant on things. Now and again though, I would hear a story that was just that bit more hard hitting, more thought provoking; and the following night was one such time. I heard it on our final evening in Bombay where I got chatting to a Scot called Angus, over our free evening meal at the hostel. If I thought that our previous night's accommodation had left a lot to be desired well, it hardly compared to his; because Angus, a young and softly spoken Glaswegian, had apparently fallen on rather hard times -even by my standards- and as a consequence, had reached the point where his only option was to sleep on the pavement. Well that same evening, as the night was drawing in, he'd decided for security reasons that rather than sleep out alone he'd lie down alongside somebody else; a man whom he assumed to be a local and who was curled up in a blanket against the wall of a building. (This may to some sound an extremely risky strategy, but in a place such as this it can often be a case of better the devil you 'don't know'!) Anyway, it wasn't until first light the following morning that Angus, feeling some sort of empathy towards his bedfellow, had attempted to make contact with him. However, after several attempts at communicating Angus gave up trying to be sociable because, no matter what he said or did, there was absolutely no response. It was only after probing a little deeper that Angus discovered that the poor chap was dead.

When I heard this story, it made me think back to all the odd shaped bundles I'd stepped over in bus and railway stations, or simply passed by along the roadsides in Delhi and Bombay. I sometimes wonder what might have lain amongst all those motionless piles of rag, sacking and blankets. Who knows; I shudder to think!

CHAPTER 13

- TROPICAL FERRIES AND THE BRIDGE
TOO FAR -

Bombay to Goa

At 7.15 the next morning, we were up, had had our 'included in the price' breakfast and were off down to the port to catch the ferry to Goa. It was a sizzling day as usual and it appeared that a large proportion of Bombay's population had also chosen this day to take the very same ferry. (In truth, I suspect that this day was no different from any other and that, in common with all forms of public transport in India, the vessel was carrying its normal quota of people; that is to say: think of a number, double it, then throw in a few more just for good measure.)

Having reached the port in good time it was slightly disheartening to find a small village of people and all their worldly possessions already between us and the boat. However, very soon everyone was on the move and we were being shunted up the gang plank, pushed, pulled and pummelled by the seething throng. I could just about see over the jiggling mass of liquorice-y heads of hair that there didn't yet appear to be a problem with deck space; what we didn't realise was that, although there was still space to be had, we would be very much novices in acquiring it. Granted, we were hardly in pole position at this time anyway, but we did seem nicely placed to at least get 'some' free space. Soon though, just when we'd

180

almost reached the boat, there was a tremendous cacophony of verbal exchanges between those already on deck and those still on the gangplank. The noise was incredible, simply amazing; like the frenzied meeting of two rival football supporters' clubs -without the rivalry- or a giant al fresco stock market trading floor perhaps, just before a crash. Within a few short minutes, bundles of every shape, size and colour were being passed over heads or thrown into waiting arms. Then, as we finally neared the end of the gang plank, the pressure from bodies still pushing from behind reached its crushing climax. I stepped from the end of the gangplank and popped out onto the deck like a cork from a bottle. Immediately, now free from the madding crowd, I wasted no time but ran with Dave and Steve for a space near the back of the boat. Then we hit the deck and quickly closed ranks, forming a tight seated circle, our backpacks a small barrage of wagons against the all surrounding Indians.

Within an hour though, the frenetic fray was over; the tidal wave of people had subsided and families and groups of friends began settling into loose circles amid their belongings. The verbal pandemonium now cooled to an excited chatter and great heaps of rice, chapattis and vegetables were already being enthusiastically consumed. Very soon, the whole boat was just one huge makeshift and mobile open-air restaurant.

I really don't recall seeing any cabins on board the boat, but if there were, you certainly wouldn't have wanted to be in one. Without some form of air-conditioning they would doubtless have acted as little more than large mobile ovens. There was only one place to be in this sort of heat, and that was on deck. Not that the temperature

181

seemed to have any effect on our fellow passengers. They appeared totally immune to the oppressiveness of the heat, the stifling crowds and the overwhelming humidity. In fact they seemed to find our big and flustering white, leaky bodies nothing but a great source of amusement.

At 10.30am though, with everyone on board, the great steel tub finally drifted from a still bustling dockside and out into the Indian Ocean. Even at such a sleepy pace, the gentle breeze afforded by the boat's movement did at least give some relief. And as Bombay slowly passed away into the distance, Dave and I settled down to yet another game of chess -closely attended by a silently watchful sea of faces.

It was a long and tiring journey for us 'three men in a boat', and although a refreshing change from the dusty plains of India, the dull, juddering vibrations from the engines deep below made sleep quite impossible. Sitting in an upright position the sound and vibrations were bearable, but with your head in contact with the deck, albeit through the cushioning of a well-stuffed rucksack, it was like trying to sleep in a suit of armour whilst being attacked by a very large and sadistic woodpecker.
During most of the journey, the land was kept at too far a distance to be of much interest and so, apart from chess games, the time was passed either day dreaming or simply observing our fellow passengers...most of whom, in turn, spent their time observing us.

You know, a fair proportion of young travellers who go to India like to dress in 'ethnic gear' in order to blend in with the locals. The truth is though, that by the time most of us get to see these countries, the locals, or certainly the local men, have already converted to wearing Western dress. It's therefore a rather bizarre paradox in that both cultures have exchanged their traditional costume in order to look like the other. But in any case, as Europeans, we're hardly likely to be taken for Asians are we! Even in full Indian garb and with an exceedingly well honed tan, most travellers I've come across in India look like they've had an invitation to a fancy dress but turned up at the wrong party!

Mind you, who am I to speak; personally, I'm all for dressing up -a mild theatrical interest rather than a perverted streak. And anyway, I rather like to look 'different'. After all it's one of the reasons why we travel isn't it. Well, not to look different, but to see other people looking different to us! But the variations of the wrappings is only half the story; I have on many occasions caused long bouts of raucous laughter simply by having hairy legs and arms, so who am I going to fool; I'm hardly ever likely to be taken for a local. As for Dave, who by now was sporting a full 'out in the wilderness' type beard, amongst the majority of the other young passengers he might as well have come from another planet. But, regarding the dress thing; although there've been numerous occasions when I've joined in with the ethnic costume charade, it certainly hasn't been for the want of trying to blend in; in fact, quite the contrary. But where's the harm in indulging in a little bit of fantasy in what is undeniably a fantastically diverse and interesting world.

By early next morning the distinctive silhouettes of palm trees could be made out lining the distant shore. Within a mere few hundred miles we seemed to have emerged from

183

semi-desert into the luxuriant growth of the tropics. And as the ferry neared the shore, the greenness of the tangle of growth on the bank became evermore clear and vibrant. Soon we were floating alongside a gleaming strip of verdant tropical jungle. It was quite incredible. There was simply nothing but green. Not just the green, green grass of home but green of every conceivable shade: trees, leaves and grasses of every conceivable shape; an unbroken belt of lush, tropical, greener than green vegetation, hugging and overhanging the water's edge. (I think you get the picture…it was green, okay!)

Now, this description may all sound a little over the top, but you have to remember that this was the very first time I'd seen tropical foliage in the flesh, so to speak, and I couldn't help but feel a great sense of excitement. This was something completely new to discover; not just like entering a different country but an entirely different world. Naturally, I'd seen plenty of the stuff on television - usually with David Attenborough buried somewhere in the middle of it- but well, somehow that just wasn't the same. This bit of tropical foliage seemed even bigger, even wilder, even greener than anything I'd ever witnessed; but more importantly than that, I was about to be right in there amongst it.

It was 8.30am when we slowly chugged into the dock at Panaji -or Panjim, as it's known locally- and yet again, the day seemed set to be another hot and cloudless one. Once the ferry had juddered to a halt and those most anxious to leave had left, we slowly hauled on our packs and inched our way back down the plank and onto dry land. It was a strange sensation being on terra firma again, almost as if one of the Hindu gods, feeling a little playful, had temporarily severed the link between my mind and body. The ground still vibrated up through jellied legs in empathy with the snoring giant from which we'd just disembarked; my ears still ringing to the rhythm of the engine.

Yet again there was the familiar hum of excitement and anticipation from the passengers on board; the cheers of recognition from those waiting on shore. But at once, the people here seemed somehow different to the ones we'd left behind in Bombay. They lacked the furrowed brow of the city dweller and seemed to carry with them, just a little more of that Caribbean-type coolness. Not laid back - tropical island style- as to be near horizontal, but with the relaxed air of a people who at least have the means to feed themselves and yet have remained 'fortunate' enough to have little more than this in the way of aspirations. (I realise, of course, that these lack of aspirations are often born out of the lack of means but, having spent most of my life living in a capitalist society, I feel that there's an awful lot we can learn and even gain from simply having less!)

The little state of Goa was, until 1961, still governed by Portugal and, along with Daman and Dui, formed a trio of tiny enclaves within India which the Portuguese had managed to retain a foothold in right up until modern times. Consequently, Goa still displayed a great deal of evidence of its recent colonial past. In fact, if it seemed at all odd to see British architecture in Delhi, then it was even more remarkable here to come across the little white Mediterranean houses of Panaji; where, half-round terracotta clay tiles bedeck every roof and terracotta flower-pots full of blooms brighten every wall and window. In the centre of town, the Catholic church in the square still towers above the surrounding buildings, its high façade of white arches framing a heavy cast iron bell that clanged lazily back and forth against a perfect blue sky. The houses here all looked so terribly neat, so cared for, many even newly painted; the streets refreshingly free of dirt. Though this could be partly due to the fact that, down in the tropics, not only is the dirt and dust largely 'contained' by the surrounding vegetation, but also that the streets get a regular labour-free hosing down from tropical rainstorms.

After a brief stroll in the old town, the three of us looked around and found a hotel that seemed to suit all our needs…well, almost all: it suited Dave and Steve's needs, and all of mine bar the price. This was because -and I openly admit it- by this time my finances were wearing a little thin; and although this room was just a little over £3 between us, for the very first time on this trip, I decided it was necessary to tighten my ethnic belt a little and look elsewhere.

Back in November, I'd left England with the princely sum of £240 -represented two weeks wages minus a £60 debt- but sadly that had now dwindled to the point where even the slightest expenditure had to be taken into consideration. (This dwindling of finances was perhaps largely due to one too many French truckers' banquets back in Europe!) Money aside though, I'd also left home without the foggiest idea of how far I'd get, how I'd get there or how I'd pay for it when I did get there. I suppose in essence it was always going to be one of those 'cross that bridge when I come to it,' sort of trips. After all, if

186

things really did get bad I could always have money sent out to me…couldn't I?

Anyway, having left the others, I set off alone and after a bit of pavement pounding, I did eventually manage to find a room to match my meagre resources. Dave and Steve had already gone off to the town of Vasco de Gama to look for train tickets for their next onward journey down to Bangalore. I, meanwhile, quickly off-loaded my belongings into my new hutch, and then, just as quickly went straight back out in the sunshine again for a good old mooch around town to see what Panaji had to offer.

It was wonderfully tranquil walking alone around the narrow little streets of the old town, but before long my peace was rudely shattered by a hail of rock music reverberating from one of the windows above. A handful of well-turned out Portuguese/Indian men were chatting casually on the step below the open window, and after a brief conversation with them I was invited upstairs. Well, soon I found myself laughing, drinking and dancing the night away at an exceedingly nice little Portuguese wedding reception...in the middle of India; and all to the greatest hits of those old Portuguese favourites: Elvis, and The Beatles.

You know, it was lovely to be included in such a happy occasion and Terence, the newly wedded groom, made me feel, not only like a good friend, but like a part of his considerably extended family. However, by 10.30pm, unaccustomed now to all things energetic, I decided it was time to leave the family to their revelries, and Terence to his stunningly beautiful bride -lucky bugger- and then, with a spring in my step and sporting a well-lubricated smile, I hummed my way back all through the alleyways and off to my room.

The house containing my little room was in total darkness by the time I got back. In fact it was so deathly quiet I could've been forgiven for thinking it had been deserted. However, this seemed pretty unlikely given that I was expected back that night -plus the fact that all my belongings were inside. But well, after trying for over half an hour to gain access or at least raise some kind of response from the house, I was forced to give up; it was absolutely hopeless; the house was clearly emptier than a tax inspector's social diary. There was nothing for it but to totally abandon the idea of staying at my 'budget saving' accommodation. I walked back through the streets and across town -my step decidedly spring-less; then, with tail stuck more firmly between my legs than a chastised whippets, I gratefully accepted a piece of floor space with Dave and Steve.

The following morning I was up with the larks -well I would've been had there been any- and was showered and dressed well before old Panaji had even thought about coming to life. Which reminds me, talking of showers…do you know, one of the delights of travelling further south in this part of the world, is not having to check and double check that there's hot water available when booking a room. You see, up north -even in sub-tropical India- this is still quite a consideration, as nights can be surprisingly on the chilly side. Down here in Goa however, not only was there less need of hot water because of the warmer nights and evenings, but any water that did appear out of either hot or cold tap was likely to be of one temperature anyway: that is to say, tepid -which, because of the warmer outside temperature, is actually quite acceptable. Somewhat bizarrely though, this is one advantage the cheaper places have over the slightly more expensive hotels in that, because they haven't splashed out on insulation, most of the pipe work coming into the house is completely un-insulated and therefore 'solar' heated. By contrast, when going for something just a little more upmarket, it's quite likely that you'll end up having the luxury of two taps, but both of them will be cold. The reason being, that your lower to mid-range hotel may well have splashed out on pipe lagging, but they probably won't be so keen on paying for the upkeep of their boiler (are you with me so far?) On the other hand, the downside to the cheapies is that the hot water that you've been so enthusiastically and emphatically promised by the hotel proprietor, though perhaps a tad warmer, will almost certainly be one of three things: guaranteed only until you've parted up front with your money; extremely erratic or just plain non-existent. In fact, on many occasions when I've received such a promise of hot water, I've ended up with a bathroom whose pipe-work provided nothing but extremely noisy, solar-heated air!

Anyway, as I was about to say…my first job the following morning was to write letters to both the Delhi GPO and Khandwa railway station: the GPO, for them to forward to Goa any mail that I might yet receive in Delhi; and Khandwa station, in the vain hope that my lost address book just might still show up somewhere 'along the line'. To be perfectly honest, I felt the chances of a positive result on either front somewhat slim. Still, any hope, I thought, was better than none at all; especially as the only investment required on my part was two letters and a little time.

In the event though, I received exactly what I'd expected...absolutely nothing! I suppose I'd always thought there was a fair chance of receiving both my letters from Delhi and my diary, for the simple reason that neither of them could possibly have any value to anyone intercepting them. What I failed to take into account though was, that in order to have any chance whatsoever of retrieving either, I had to post something of value along with my letters; namely, a stamp. Now this may sound pathetically petty to think that I might lose something for the price of a stamp, as indeed in the West it would be; but when you consider that a single postage stamp here can have the value of several hours local wages, you begin to understand just why so much mail goes missing; either that or countries such as this have rather more than their fair share of philatelists. Either way, it's a savvy traveller who always sees his letters franked at the post office before they disappear into the 'to be posted' pile. (Of course, this advice comes having already made the non-franked stamp mistake. You know, I really must go to more of those, wise 'before' the event classes.)

At noon, having posted my freshly franked letters, I left the Goan capital and caught a local bus all the way through the gently undulating wooded hills and palm forests to Colva beach. I couldn't help noticing that there didn't appear to be any scheduled stops on this route; the local people just hopped on and off willy-nilly whenever they felt like it. And so it came as quite a surprise when we squeaked to a halt at a sizeable river and, without so much as a single word being uttered, the whole bus emptied out onto the road and all the passengers started to walk across the bridge up ahead. "Had we misunderstood about the bus's destination," I wondered? "Was this bus perhaps even more 'local' than we'd thought?" There was nothing for it but to find out. I got up, walked down to the front of the bus and began a slightly animated conversation in flagless semaphore with the driver. Well, this was quite hopeless, of course; it proved about as fruitful as a coconut crop in Peckham. Not only was there a total lack of understanding on both our parts, but it became all the more exasperating because of this chap's apparent neck problem. For whilst it was frustrating enough trying to understand what little he said, mostly all he did was waggle his head from side to side, before eventually waving us off his bus.

Well, somewhat bemused, there was clearly no choice but to follow the other passengers, hoping that surely there must be some other form of transport waiting for us on the other side. Suffice to say... there wasn't! But what became even more puzzling was that, before we'd even reached the far side of the bridge, I turned around to see the bus, the very bus which we'd just got off, slowly trundling up behind us. "Bloody hell" I thought, "would you credit it. The times I've envied all these overpaid pop stars being hotly pursued by hundreds of screaming, scantily-clad teenage girls; what do I get stalked by...a battered bus with a waggly-headed driver in the window"! The local people though, were as nonchalant as we were perplexed. It was then that I noticed the plaque on the bridge. Apparently, in 1961, this bridge had been severely weakened; not by some great natural catastrophe but by the patter of tiny feet; namely, those of the fleeing

Portuguese troops when they were finally being ousted by the Indian army. Strangely, after all these years, it had now been deemed safe enough for a bus to cross, or indeed a bus load of passengers; but not, unfortunately, the two together.

CHAPTER 14

- FLAT BROKE IN PARADISE -

Colva Beach

Colva, when we arrived, was everything I'd hoped it would be: a lazy little fishing village with a picture postcard beach of soft white sand, fringed with tall swaying palms. It had long been discovered by hippies during the sixties of course, but far from being spoilt, there seemed to be a special kind of atmosphere; a tranquillity; an easy going tolerance and attitude between both Europeans and Goans towards one another. Everything and everybody here seemed so wonderfully relaxed and I couldn't wait to be a part of it. Dave, Steve and I wasted no time but wandered off from the small village centre and checked into one of the many fishermen's cottages that lay back from the beach. There were plenty to choose from of course, the majority of families here had already taken to letting out rooms to supplement their meagre incomes; incomes that were almost certainly derived from fishing. Not that there were any obvious signs of this -there wasn't a net, lobster pot or Aran sweater in sight- it's just that here in Colva, there was clearly very little else to do.

The room that we rented occupied the rear half of a small square detached cottage which, like virtually all of its neighbours, was a simple block-built bungalow, rendered on the outside and painted in either white, or one of those 'hint of white' mellow pastel shades of slightly yellow, almost blue or nearly pink. To the front, a wide palm-fringed beach ran alluringly down to a vibrantly blue sea, and to the rear, just beyond our bedroom window, stretched a brochure-cover panorama of impossibly fresh, green paddy fields divided by little raised earth walkways and dotted with yet more palms. Around the rice field margins, half naked children ran about laughing, catching frogs from the shallow water and conjuring adventure from bamboo canes and discarded plastic bags. Overhead, busy flycatchers performed mid-air aerobatics in pursuit of invisible prey, flitting about this way and that, before returning to a favourite perch. High above, buzzards drew slow and lazy spirals way up in the wispy clouds.

As night fell, we went and sat in the aptly named 'Sunset Restaurant' and watched a glowing tropical sun disappear into a quiet and tranquil sea. I ate fish curry and rice and took moonlit photos of palm trees. It was simply idyllic; many a daydream come true. But I knew that to wake up every morning in this heavenly haven just wasn't enough. Pretty soon now I would have no money and would be forced to face some realities…yes, even here in paradise. I went to bed that night, happy but thoughtful.

The following morning I woke early to the muffled bark of a distant dog and the snuffling of pigs just outside the bedroom window. I dressed quickly, anxious to be out in the open air. Hidden amongst all the pastelly bungalows there was a single communal well with a small wall surrounding it, and just alongside, a rope and bucket to bring the water up. I joined a couple of teenage boys, who were kitted out in football shorts and performing their morning ablutions. I watched closely and then followed their lead as they hauled up buckets of water, lathered themselves from head to foot and showered themselves under the upturned bucket. Then, each in turn briskly cleaned already perfect sets of gleaming white teeth with nothing more than a squeaky index finger before loping off together, happily chatting away, ready to start their day.

Today, I felt in particularly buoyant mood because I had a date in Panaji. I'd previously written home asking my family that, as I was rapidly approaching destitution, "Would they please send some money out to me". Thankfully, my elder sister Dawn had agreed to come to my rescue, and it seemed that the best option available was to have the money sent out to the State Bank of India in Panaji; alright so far. Unfortunately for me, my sister's bank back in England had been not so reliably informed by somebody high up -apparently so high up that his fat head must have been in the clouds- that no State Bank of India existed in Goa. Well, they were right about one thing; there wasn't a State Bank of India in Goa…there were at least three! So anyway, this chap, in all his wisdom, had given the go-ahead to the State Bank of India to issue traveller's cheques to me, not in Goa but…in Bombay. This, of course, was about as useful as a pair of chocolate sunglasses, as it not only meant that I'd have to splash out on yet another bus fare to Panaji, but also on a telex to the Bank in Bombay in order to have the money transferred down to Goa (remembering, of course, that this was all before the advent of email.)

Now, this may all sound a rather long-winded way of getting hold of some cash, but at the time, I was told that this was actually the only way to do so. I have since learnt that even back then there were far easier methods of obtaining money. Nowadays, of course, to have access to cash almost anywhere in the world -at any time- is mind numbingly simple.

The journey from Colva to the capital, though on this occasion absolutely necessary, was at least always beautiful and always an adventure. To get there, there were two half sensible ways to go: either the long and scenic option, heading inland over the dodgy Portuguese bridge; or the more direct, but slightly less exciting route running parallel to the coast. The first, given a great deal of time, was undoubtedly the loveliest way to go but, because mine was more a journey with a purpose, I decided this time to take the shorter route. Mind you, this route too had its eccentricities; it may well have gone pretty much directly as the brahminy kite flies, but even on this, a relatively short journey, it still involved a ferry crossing. So actually, neither option can really be said to be straight forward.

Of course, for the people living in Goa, or indeed anywhere else in India for that matter, any journey of more than a day's walk was something of a rarity, so even if the local government had had the funds to upgrade the roads and transport system, it was hardly ever likely to figure as a number one priority. As a consequence, all routes to Panaji, whether direct or not, were always more the scenic expeditionary variety rather than purely for getting from 'a' to 'b'; reserved perhaps for odd family visits, or for fortnightly forays into the big city to shop for tinned foods and household goods, rather than for casual jollies.

By this time, I'd already been forced into cadging a little money from both of my room mates whilst waiting for my sister to come to my rescue, and so, when that too had gone, I felt somewhat reluctant to impose on Dave and Steve further. I realise of course, if indeed it's necessary to borrow money at all, it would seem more sensible to scrounge from a single source. Personally though, I found it a just a teeny bit less embarrassing to borrow a little from many; and especially as most of my fellow travellers were on fairly meagre budgets anyway. Sort of 'damage limitation' if you like, to both their pockets and my pride! But well, whatever the rights and wrongs of the whole thing, I was now down to a total sum -in English money- of four pence; and even here in Colva, I knew full well that this wasn't going to go far. No, the time had come for more drastic measures. I decided, albeit extremely reluctantly, that I'd have to walk down to my local beach bar and offer my camera lens up as collateral, "if only they'd provide me with a few meals to keep me going until my money came through". Now obviously this was pretty much a last resort, but I really felt I had little option. (What an annoying thought; having to resort to my last resort in my first resort!) Happily though, I wasn't to make it as far as my local, for as I neared the beach, a rather stocky, crop-haired figure in an exceedingly loud and flowery Hawaiian shirt and shorts, came pedalling up the dirt track towards me. It wasn't until he'd ridden a good ten yards past that he suddenly squealed to a halt and both our heads spun round in unison.

"Mark!" I shouted,

"Gary!" he cried. He dropped his bike onto the dusty track, ran over and we threw our arms around each other. It was Canadian Mark, the real estate agent.

"Of all the...well I'm blowed!" We hadn't set eyes on one another since our all singing, all dancing Westside Story nights back in the streets of old Istanbul. It was so lovely to see such a friendly familiar face again -albeit temporarily disguised by unfamiliar tropical trimmings- I just couldn't believe my eyes!

Now just to recap, you may remember that Mark had told me in Istanbul that he was on his way home back to Canada, and so it seemed pretty near impossible that our paths would cross again so soon, if at all. However, something had happened -I don't remember quite what- to make him change his plans; and instead of sitting cooped up in a high-tech office in the middle of the Canadian winter, here he was casually cycling along in a sleepy little fishing village on the west coast of India. What an exceedingly small world...or rather, what a pretty damned gigantic world, but with lots and lots of small co-incidences in it.

Well, we spent the rest of the day and well into the evening gassing away like a couple of house-wives at a coffee morning; catching up on old memories and laughing about all our respective experiences. Then, when midnight came and the Colva beach bars were preparing to eject the last of their hippies, we found ourselves still sat on that very same patch of beach, chatting away and looking out across the dark ocean. And, as we did so, an almost full moon flooded the sand around us with a soft bluey light. Way out to sea, lonely crests of foam were illuminated like tiny drifts of snow on crumpled velvet; they tumbled about on a softly undulating ocean and then scurried toward the shore only to be swallowed up in the blackness before they could reach us. Just beyond our feet, gentle waves rolled up the slope and sighed back down again; spilling their frothy whiteness and leaving the sand sparkling like tiny diamonds. Surely though, this was no ordinary night. Back home, I'd often watched the waves crashing down onto the beach under a full moon, it was a wonderful sight. But here, here on this little beach, the whiteness of the surf was simply beyond belief: not just snowy white, or the white of fresh cotton sheets, but one which was positively luminous. We decided we had to go for a midnight swim. We dropped our clothes where we stood and ran down the beach leaping into the warm and inky sea, and as we did so, with every single movement of our bodies, a million tiny lights lit up in the water around us. I stood up, waist deep in the Indian Ocean, and the whole of my body sparkled under the moonlight as if alive with an orgy of miniature glow worms. Then, as droplets of water ran from my skin the lights simply disappeared, slipping back somewhere into the ocean. It was a truly magical experience and an experience that, to this day, I have never known since.

Rather sadly this magical illumination is actually caused by nothing more than millions of light producing plankton. It was, nevertheless, both an incredible experience and an unbelievably romantic one. Just a shame then really that, rather than share it with a stunningly gorgeous, sylph-like naked female...I was joined by a fat, white Canadian male. Still, you can't have everything in life can you!

Aside from my passport, I had only three things with me that could possibly be of any value to anyone. By far the most expensive of these was my trusty camera, which I knew I'd only ever part with as a matter of life or death. (Though, in truth, I'd already checked in Panaji and was assured that I could get what I'd originally paid for it...so much for life or death!)

The other two items in my luggage, of considerably less value, were both pairs of jeans. Now I'd been told sometime during the oh so murky past that good quality English or American jeans were 'hot property' in countries like India and so, since I was stony broke, now seemed a good time to put this theory to the test. My only slight reservation however, was that, being as these two pairs of jeans were the only trousers I possessed, they'd been worn in rotation pretty much ever since the day I left. Therefore, although still in 'reasonable' condition, they did have a few miles on the clock. So anyway, I decided that if I were to try to raise some much needed cash by selling them, then I'd better let them be seen in as good a light as possible. Yes, that's right; what they needed was a jolly good clean.

Now, I'd already observed, on many occasions, the groups of women washing their clothes at the well or down by the river, and the whole washing process all seemed simple enough really. Basically, you just get hold of your garment, dunk it in water, add a bit of soap powder, whack the item soundly and repeatedly against a handy rock, then rinse and dry. How hard is that! Well, the theory was great; the practice, umm...I don't know, maybe I left something out or perhaps was just a little over zealous with the 'whacking on a rock' bit. Anyway, whatever the ins and outs of it, by the time I'd finished the washing session, both my precious pairs of jeans were severely streaked with white and looked decidedly dishevelled. I have to say, it was a bit of a shock really. Still, there was no going back; I held them out to study them at arms length feeling somewhat dispirited. "Ah well" I thought, "I'm sure once they've dried they'll be different"...they were; they were much worse! Having left them out in the sun for a good couple of hours -as per Indian drying instructions- I came back to find two big, blue rashers of very streaky and very crispy bacon! What a complete bummer! Mind you, trying to look on the bright side, though hardly in mint condition, the fact remained that they were still 'quality' Western jeans and therefore the envy of every teenage Indian…surely?

On my very next trip into the capital, I slung my rashers over one arm and, wearing my only pair of shorts, I once again went to check for mail. This was to be my eleventh hour, my very last chance to see if I'd received any money before having to part with my precious jeans (ironically perhaps, before having to sell my streaky jeans to save my bacon). I half skipped into the post office, half expectantly…there was 'whole-ly' nothing! The time had come to play my penultimate card -my camera being the ultimate- I wandered aimlessly around town, not really knowing what to do or where to go; waiting to be approached by a jeans enthusiast.

Well, strangely, but thankfully, this didn't actually take all that long. Within less than an hour of arriving in town, I was standing there in the street trying my best-est ever sales patter. The trouble was that to my prospective buyer, it must have been blindingly obvious by my get-up and demeanour that I wasn't really in the best of positions to negotiate. I did try hard to push the fact that my jeans bore a Western label of course, I even tried to convince him that the streaks were the very latest in fashion, but well, my heart just wasn't in it. Back in Colva, I'd heard that brand name jeans could fetch as much as £20 a pair in India, and yes, okay, I suspected that I might have to settle for a little less. And the end result? After a good old haggle, we finally reached an agreement...I sold both of them to him for the princely sum of £2 a piece!

You know, it was rather a disappointing return for selling half my wardrobe. Clearly, I had a lot to learn about 'flogging' jeans, and I would undoubtedly have flogged them for more if I'd flogged them less. Still, the money did at least allow me to cancel a few debts. Dave however -my biggest sponsor to date- would have to wait. Both he and Steve were keen to leave Goa now and to continue on their travels down to Bangalore. When they did leave though, it was sad to see them go; but I assured them both that I would catch up with them again just as soon as I got my money through. (In the event, my money took so long to come through that I never came close to catching either of them. I finally paid Dave back -with interest I might add- a full eleven years later after mislaying his address somewhere in one of many house moves.)

Though my prowess as a jeans salesman had proved somewhat limited, whilst there in Panaji, I did at least get to witness, first-hand, a brief moment of Goan political history in the making. You see, not far from where I stood, a large crowd of very noisy and animated men were gathered in the main square with an even noisier and more animated little man at their head. This man was standing there shouting incomprehensibly to his flock and waving his arms about like a demented weatherman; and the more the crowd responded to him by joggling their banners up and down approvingly, the louder and more animated he became. This went on and on with the one encouraging the other, until the whole gathered crowd was almost pogo-ing with excitement.

I couldn't understand any of what was going on of course; and besides, what could there possibly be in Goa to rebel against? Perhaps they were all Hindus, I thought, and were rebelling against the fact that their lives were so idyllic here they'd have nothing better to look forward to in their next lives, I don't know; I just had to find out.

I darted into a small tailor's shop and found an English speaking tailor, who explained to me that these people were all local fishermen and they were protesting that the government had allowed the big trawlers to come too close into shore, thereby threatening their livelihoods. (Apparently, this was a dispute that came to a head quite frequently here, and as virtually everyone back on Colva beach was either a fisherman or was married to one, the fishermen surely had a point.)

Anyway, as I stepped back out of the tailors, it was just in time to see the little band of banner-toting fishermen march down the street and round the corner. They were heading for the Mayor's house, and although obviously aggrieved by their predicament, they were surprisingly orderly; excitable perhaps; agitated...maybe, but hardly threatening. However, before they could get anywhere even near the Mayor's house, marching in from the opposite direction towards them came a khaki-clad, mini-platoon of soldiers armed with four foot bamboo batons. Well, things weren't looking great for the little fishermen; but still I assumed that, as this was quite a regular event, it would all probably come to nothing; the fishermen would simply shout about a bit to make their point and the soldiers would just stand their ground and look menacing; and then, everyone would leave. It wasn't to be. Before you could say, "red lorry, yellow lorry, red lorry, yellow lorry, red lorry, yellow lorry" very, very fast; around the corner came a couple of army vans and, before you knew it, everyone was running about all over the place; the little fishermen scattering in all directions hotly pursued by bamboo baton-wielding soldiers. A few die-hard fishermen tried vehemently to make a stand and were whacked and herded into the vans for their troubles. I meanwhile, dived into a crowded shop doorway and quickly tried to change over to a telephoto lens in order to capture the event from afar. Seeing my camera, two local Indians eagerly egged me on, encouraging me to get back out there into the thick of things; to shoot some pictures of the beatings to help the fishermen's cause. I tried desperately hard to explain that I needed to change my lens in order to keep at a safe distance, but it was hopeless. The next thing I knew I was bustled out into the street by the Fishermen's Supporters' Club. I quickly ran to another place of safety but by now, every single bystander and his dog had wedged himself into a shop doorway just beyond baton wielding range -but still well within view of the action. By the time I'd found a place off the street with enough elbow room to move, had fiddled about with my camera and was pushed back, yet again, onto the street...that was it; the worst was pretty well over. I did tentatively take a few photos of what action remained, but was just too unsure of the consequences of being caught with a camera to risk too much 'exposure'. Annoyingly, I hadn't managed to capture on film so much as a single sadistic 'thwack'; just the odd little fisherman or two being herded into a van; better than nothing perhaps, but scant reward for a face full of tear gas.

It had all been a rare piece of action for the local community here, this fish fight, and whoever's side they may have been on, everybody was abuzz with chatter about the day's main event. Okay, it may have lasted less than half an hour in total, but it was nothing if not exciting; or exciting that is but for the one remaining soldier. This soldier, having hardly broken sweat, obviously thought the whole thing had ended in a bit of an anti-climax; so, before returning to his khaki van, he exchanged a few words with a physically impaired beggar and then promptly gave him a few deft whacks about the body with his baton before retiring for the day. Yes, life can be tough on the streets, and especially, if that's where you happen to live.

When I returned to Colva I decided to move into Mark's beach hut. He'd been renting it from a local chap for the equivalent of thirty pence a night. This price wasn't for the whole hut of course -good heavens no- it was the price for one room of four within that hut. It was however, the total price for the room and not per person, which meant that the more people we could cram into the room, the cheaper it became. In the event I was to stay in this hut for several weeks and at one time shared the room with no fewer than five others -quite a bargain at five pence a head!

Our little hut was situated in about as perfect a location as you could possibly dream of. It sat on a beautiful stretch of fine white sand just two hundred metres back from the ocean, and all around stood clusters of tall mature palm trees providing both shade from the fierce tropical sun and which cooled the sand outside my bedroom door, very handily, to walking temperature. But if my front garden was beautiful brochure-esque sand and sea; then the back yard, for me, was no less idyllic. For not a Pooh-stick's throw away from the hut, a small brook babbled cheerfully by, whilst beyond it laid a backdrop of sumptuously green paddy fields.

Our particular room faced eastwards and so had wonderfully rural rather than beach views. This meant that every day I could open my door and watch the early morning sun creeping up through the trees behind the paddy fields, slowly lighting up and warming my perfect and very private little garden. Then, as the sun rose higher and higher in the pale morning sky, it glinted blindingly off the patches of water missed by the rice grower's hand. A pair of strikingly beautiful pied kingfishers stopped and started up and down the small brook in front of me, periodically pausing motionless on low branches to scour the shallow water below. Sometimes they would bound on down the stream to try their luck elsewhere, but often I would watch as, almost within touching distance, they would torpedo into the water and return to their perches, glistening and triumphant with a small silvery prize.

Over the next few weeks -after Mark had moved on- I was to have quite an assortment of room mates in my little hut. The ideal number of occupants, I suppose, was probably three or four: this being a good compromise between having enough room to stretch out a little but, at the same time, having enough people to keep the price down. I had long since established a routine by now and would wander down into the village centre to meet the early morning bus coming in from Panaji. Then, when the bus had pulled to a halt, I'd wait there by the bus door and try to convince anyone getting off -or anyone remotely resembling a backpacker- that my hut was "undoubtedly the best place in town to stay." Though, in this, I had no need to lie, as I truly believed it was. Okay, so I didn't have such luxuries as electricity and running water, but for me, it was a little piece of heaven. And anyway, what do you want for the price of a box of matches!

For their part, most who stepped down from the bus were clearly a little surprised to be hustled, not by a local, but by a fellow traveller. Though once I'd extolled the virtues of my own little private paradise, many of them did come along and join me. Consequently, over the following weeks, there were some interesting and varied combinations of numbers, sexes and nationalities. The numbers, varying from an extremely cheap but sardine-esque six, right through to the occasional night spent totally alone. But, you know, there was also just about every combination in between.

Now, obviously during this time, I managed to strike up quite a few short term relationships; unfortunately, none of them of the sexual kind. Though, it has to be said, I did spend one whole night with two Swedish sisters which, on paper at least, sounds pretty damned good. Unfortunately for me it 'was' only good on paper; not necessarily because of their lack of interest, but because they were more of the Eastern European shot putting variety than exotic glamour models; and as such, even if there had been any other sports on offer I feel sure that I would've had to decline.

Still, there were the odd faint rays of hope; like the night that I spent with a rather luscious young French girl for example. Now she most definitely went in and out in all the right places and couldn't have been less of a field events type. Sadly though, my amorous advances on that one and only occasion didn't quite yield the results I'd hoped for. Why, I even tried the old 'rolling over in my sleep' trick, but somehow there always seemed just enough room in the hut for her to do exactly the same...but in the opposite direction!

Mind you, I wasn't alone in my apparent ability to repel girls of every nationality. Jeff, a one time room-mate and annoyingly handsome Canadian, undoubtedly had the edge on me in the subtlety stakes, but the result would almost invariably end up the same. You see, Jeff had decided to join me in my small thatched palace for quite a few nights and, between the two of us, we'd tried just about every conceivable trick in the book to entice various members of the opposite sex into bed -or more correctly, entice them 'onto mat'- none of which seemed to work. But, you know, a lot of the time our home and surroundings were just so idyllic that the idea of sex didn't even enter our heads. (Though, being in our early twenties as we were, during the other twenty-three and a half hours a day, vivid and vibrant thoughts of scantily-clad bronzed fillies were never too far from our minds.)

Colva Beach was never crowded at this time and there would normally be, on average, about half a dozen sunbathing Westerners to the beach mile. It was, I suppose, in that sort of transitional period caught somewhere midway between being occupied by true hippies and over-run by tourists; or put more plainly, a few years after being discovered by adventurous young Westerners but still before entering the glossy brochures that would inevitably lure the hoards.

Actually, most of the time the beach was remarkably free of not only 'whites' but also local people; and so, only two or three hundred meters away from the only road into the village, Colva beach had become something of a naturists' haven -that is to say, people lying, sitting or walking around 'in the buff' as opposed to ones looking at nature.

Now, whatever the rights or wrongs of lying about totally starkers, in this, such a very different and foreign land, the idea of it did have a certain appeal to me at the time -and, I confess, still does. Also, I can't deny that walking up and down a beautiful tropical beach dotted here and there with the odd naked female, did come pretty close to pole position on my list of pastimes. (I was going to say that it always put 'me' in pole position, but well…that would just be immature and smutty!) It wasn't just that though; okay, so I may have spent more than my fair share of time wandering about and thinking carnal thoughts; but also, I found that lying alone on a sandy beach dozing to the sound of the surf, totally unencumbered by clothes, was such a remarkable and liberating feeling. I never did it quite as blatantly as others mind, and when the mood took me I was always discreet enough to walk some distance away from the main village; but this was for the benefit of both the villagers and indeed, myself. After all, flashing my bits about in public was still rather new to me. I'd been quite unaccustomed to displaying such freedom of expression in Goring-by-sea and, wonderfully liberating though it was, I found that I still couldn't quite fully relax for more than a couple of minutes without having to scan the beach for intruders with my one squinty eye. (A habit clearly inherited from the Turks.) And, as if the possible intrusion of others wasn't enough to make me a little on edge, annoyingly, I also found myself having to continually turn over, not in the vain attempt to get an all over tan you understand, but simply because it was evident that one particular part of my body appreciated the warmth of the tropical sun even more than the rest did. Indeed I tried just about everything I could to remain on my back for longer than a few seconds, ranging from total lack of movement to thinking bizarrely dull thoughts, but it was absolutely hopeless. Even the most mundane of conjured pictures seemed to become somehow erotic. At other times I'd just get settled and gather enough concentration to remain motionless, and then suddenly the whole thing would go to pot as a wonderfully warm breeze teased between my thighs. Of course, turning over on my front hardly helped matters either, as it was impossible to lay face down without coming into contact with a crutch-ful of warm and soft caressing sand. The outcome of all this was: that any time I wanted to experience total unabashed freedom down on the beach -heavenly though it was- I felt compelled to constantly change from back to front and front to back, every few seconds, going through a strange and erratic non-stop flipping routine, like some giant pink floundering fish in its last throws of life.

Naturally, I was far from alone in my admiration of the bronzed, naked females that lined the beach. For the most part though, all that these girls had to put up with was the odd drooling Westerner such as myself. I'd walk slowly toward them in my rather fetching technicolour sarong, feigning nonchalance; then all of a sudden show an eager interest in an old broken boat or fallen palm frond which just happened to be beyond where the girls lay. Not that they were ever taken in by my shenanigans; I'd even occasionally try the old 'flat hand over the eyes' ploy, as if trying to peer through the harsh sunlight at a distant object. I needn't have bothered; whatever I did my ill concealed lustful gaze was invariably met by 'that look'!

Still, at least I did make some attempt at subtlety; for the Indian men visiting the beach though, there was never any such attempt to hide the real reason why they were there. As if Scandinavian porn films hadn't already done enough to sour Western women's reputations abroad, then the sight of seeing these young females strewn about the beach, quite literally 'in the flesh', was clearly too much to bear. The local Goan men, with wives well within shirt-tugging distance, did at least manage to exercise a soupçon of subtlety, but for the hoards of holidaying Indian men who'd occasionally turn up in their droves, this was definitely a sight not to be missed: this, to such an extent that all male coach -party away-days to Colva Beach had become uncharacteristically but extremely popular for this very reason. In fact, quite regularly I'd see large stag parties turn up at the village, saunter along the beach and then, egged-on by a bit of group bravado, slowly surround their unsuspecting prey like a pride of young lions around a sleeping wildebeest.

Now admittedly, I never once saw any physical contact between these 'tourists' and the naked Western girls, but there's little doubt by the reactions I witnessed, that some of these girls endured a number of insults and frighteningly lurid suggestions. Of course, it may seem narrow minded or even ignorant for Indian men to see all white women as Scandinavian porn stars, but on the other hand, is it not equally ignorant or foolhardy for a Western girl to go to a place such as India and not take into account that country's culture and standards? As for myself, well yes, I suppose I was doing exactly the same thing as these girls were; but, you know, not once was I ever surrounded by a single coach party of drooling young Indian girls.

211

Still...I live in hope!

Jeff, meanwhile, handsome as he may have been, never did get even close to having sex with any girl of any description. In fact the nearest he ever got to physical contact with a female was when he went out of the hut one night to do a 'number two' round the corner of the hut. He'd let down his trousers, crouched down beside a low bush and, before the remains of yesterday's dinner had time to even hit the ground, he was butted up the backside from behind by a very large and hungry sow. Well, I've seen pigs back home eat some things alright, but I've never ever seen one quite so anxious for a hot meal. We'd been warned not to eat pork around here, now we knew why!

Funnily enough, pigs in Colva, for the most part, seemed to have quite a pleasant existence. They may not have appreciated their surroundings in quite the same way as we did, but they always looked fat and snorkingly healthy and appeared to have the whole run of the village, happily vacuuming up anything in their paths that remotely resembled food; a sort of rotund and bristly free-range Hoover. Thankfully, human excrement seemed to make up only a small part of their diets -a weekend treat perhaps- and the only bane in the pigs' lives here seemed to be the occasional prod with a pointy stick by some bored young child. These casual proddings though would invariably provoke a prolonged high-pitched squeal from each and every pig as if they'd been punched by a branding iron, perhaps giving rise to over-acting actors being known as 'hams'; for there has surely never been such hams as these Colva pigs.

So generally speaking, a pig's lot in Goa, I'd say, was quite a happy one. Dogs, on the other hand, were most definitely at the very bottom of the pecking order (ironically even lower than chickens). It was clear to me that all dogs in Colva obviously came from the same gene pool, for every single one of them was half hairless, had a set of ribs you could park several bikes in, and had absolutely repulsive and revoltingly scabby skin that hung off them like it had been borrowed from a dog twice its size. Not only that, but they all seemed to be homeless and lived totally by their wits, scavenging anything they could at any opportunity and always sleeping in a sunny spot with one eye very much open…rather like a Turk or a first time nude sunbather.

Now, these dogs must have done something pretty awful in a previous life for they were picked on mercilessly by just about everyone and everything. Every single day of their wretched lives they ran a gauntlet of thrown stones, wielded sticks and hurled handfuls of dirt: in fact any missile that happened to be handy. The kids were the worst of course; the adult inhabitants here occasionally found a reason to pick on the dogs if they were after the family food, but the children appeared to bully these creatures out of nothing but sheer sadistic pleasure. In fact, come to think of it, the only time I ever saw one of these mangy mongrels get the better of anything else, it was when picking a fight with an even more hapless and mangy mongrel.

In true British animal loving fashion I once befriended one of these 'underdogs,' but then found that, unaccustomed to any compassion at all, it quickly latched on to me like a four-legged limpet and took up residence outside my hut.

213

This was fine for a while and breakfasting by the river each morning I was quite willing, happy even, to share a few scraps with my new mate. My compassion though would never quite run to stroking the poor thing; I'm afraid that its lumps, scabs and sores were just too grotesque for words -or indeed, any caring actions; it would've been like running your hand across a doormat encrusted with yesterday's porridge, only blindfold. Then sadly, one day my friend didn't show up for breakfast and I assumed the worst. For this God-forsaken creature though, it was probably...for the best.

Had the pigs not been a source of food they would undoubtedly have shared a similar existence to the dogs. Happily for them though, their lives were infinitely more preferable -if a tiny bit shorter. In fact, I'll never forget the very first time I saw a small pig trussed up with string on a rack at the back of a bicycle. It was squealing for all its worth with every hump and bump over the paddy field pathway. Bizarrely, it conjured up all the happy sounds of children on fairground rides. I strongly suspect though, that this particular squealing wasn't an expression of joy; and that for this poor little porker, it would almost certainly be his last ride.

I had originally only intended staying in Goa for a week or so. Beautiful though the beach may have been, I still had a long way to go if I were to make it round the world. Not that this was necessarily my original intention, but having come this far I'd become excited by the possibility of going the whole hog (no pig pun intended!) In the end I stayed in Colva for over five weeks. This wasn't, as you might expect, due to not being able to prise myself away, but simply because I was still out and out flat broke.

By this time I'd had no end of communications with home, the local banks and the post office, but there was still no sign of any money coming my way. Borrowing, of course, was always the very last resort and so, before actually reaching the 'bread-line', the first thing to be struck off my menu was the numerous egg-curries which I'd been gorging my way through. These were then closely followed by both the lunchtime tomatoes and boiled eggs, which I regularly bought from the local shack. This left me literally -and yes, I do mean literally- trying to exist on nothing but bread rolls and bananas.

Now, as luck would have it, banana sandwiches had always been one of my most favourite things back in England but, here in Goa, after ten days of existing on nothing but banana butties, do you know, I'd very, very nearly had enough. Actually, come to think of it, that's not strictly true about only eating bread and bananas for ten days, as I also ended up eating rather a lot of 'ants'. Not intentionally mind, it's just that there always appeared to be a small colony of them in every bread roll. God knows how they got there, for as hard as I tried, I could never ever see any point of entry into the roll, but somehow...they were just always there. Now admittedly, there were times when I would have killed for fresh meat but well, there's fresh and fresh!

Do you know, during my ant-roll period, I seemed to acquire, amongst my fellow travellers, a bit of a reputation for eating a lot of bread; which of course, I was; but not necessarily by choice. As a consequence of this, one day a big square-jawed, fair haired and freckly Australian chap called Doug, who happened to be around at the time, decided he'd challenge me to a bread eating contest. It was an unusual request to make, but being as I didn't have any other pressing engagements that week I decided to take him up on it. It was decided that we should meet that same evening, just before sunset, and go down to the local beach bar equipped with twenty bread rolls a piece -all complete with soft ant-centres. And so it was... the scene was set!

Now, in the centre of this particular restaurant was a large round wooden table. Doug and I approached and sat ourselves down on opposite sides of it and, with that, a great posse of other travellers -most of whom we knew- gathered round in anticipation. A mound of rolls, the size of a small family saloon, was stacked up in the centre. At our sides, men stood like boxing seconds, towels draped round their necks. Another stood to one side holding a watch. There was an air of tension. The restaurant went silent. Doug and I stared at each other over the bread mountain like a couple of nervous gunslingers. Then, with everything and everybody in place, the referee holding the watch called...

"Go!" And we were off. One, two, three bread rolls; easy. Four, five and six; still both chomping away like there's no tomorrow and still level pegging. Then seven and eight, both of us just beginning to slow to a manageable pace; there was absolutely nothing in it. Nine, ten, eleven; we were matching each other roll for roll; the bread mound was diminishing alright but we were starting to struggle. Twelve and thirteen, and I was now chewing away at tortoise tempo. Supporters on both sides shouted and encouraged; we were both nearing the end and yet still we munched on. And then...at fourteen rolls, like a marathon

216

runner approaching his nineteenth mile, that was it; I'd hit the wall. My jaw muscles felt tired and tender and my mouth as dry as a Bolivian salt flat; I just had to stop.

Now, our rules dictated that any other substances we cared to use were allowed to be consumed in order to ease the swallowing process...the time had come! I went for the soda water; Doug reached for his ample supply of exceedingly squishy tomatoes. Game on, but still little in it. Then, after a few more minutes and with the referee's watch just about to reach the allotted thirty minute mark...it was all over! As Doug slowly munched his way through his sixteenth roll, he could take no more. He squinted at me across a cat litter of breadcrumbs and tomato pips, and then...his head hit the table with a loud 'thoomp'; mouth still dribbling tomato juice and bulging with the remains of his final roll. A cheer rang out around the crowd. Tired but triumphant, I slowly swallowed my sixteenth roll aided by a last swig of soda; then, with big Doug still lying in a pool of juice, I went on to complete my metaphorical victory lap, a jaw-straining but glorious 'seventeenth' bread roll. I'd done it! Do you know, I hadn't the heart to tell poor Doug that, between breakfast and lunch, I'd already eaten twelve bread rolls!

CHAPTER 15

- DRUGGED UP HIPPIES AND DEADLY PRAWNS -

Stuck in Colva

After a few weeks, I did eventually manage to get hold of some money. It was sent to me in the form of a postal order from my sister Dawn. The trouble is, it had been such a long time coming that the £50 which I received had largely been already accounted for in small debts to a variety of people. Still, things were beginning to look up a bit and even after settling my debts -bar to a couple of friends who'd already moved on- I at least had a little money in my pocket. Yes, I was back on the egg and fish curries down by the beach and what's more could even afford to join my friends for an occasional beer at sunset.

One day I decided to hire a push bike and ride into Panaji. It was a good couple of hours ride away and so I stopped off before leaving the village at one of the roadside shacks selling samosas. (For anyone interested, these are crispy triangular pasty type things found all over India and usually filled with meat, vegetables or both, and would generally range from quite bland to 'blow your head off' spicy.) Anyway, when I arrived at this shack there was a large pyramid of freshly cooked samosas sitting on top of the wooden counter and so I walked up and said jovially,
"Excuse me; can I have two samosas please?"
"Sorry, no samosas" came the chirpy reply.

"Then what are those?" I said, pointing to the pyramid. "Samosas" he said, without so much as batting an eyelid or changing tone. I looked at his exceedingly smiley face a little perplexed, bought two and left.

It was a beautiful ride to Panaji; a little hilly, but incredibly lush and tropical. Goa, at this time, possessed neither the traffic nor the totally manic drivers of other parts of India, and it was lovely to be able to gaze out across the fields whilst cycling along; trying to identify the many different birds without losing your right elbow to a passing truck. Nevertheless, I still exercised a little caution on this trip and made a habit of swerving off the tarmac surface every time a bus or truck approached. This wasn't due to an ultra-nervous disposition but because, you can bet your old boots, at the very moment that a truck was approaching from up ahead, there would be another truck or bus approaching from behind; and if I didn't pay heed to the 'size really does matter' mentality around these parts, then I would almost certainly be taking an even closer look at the surrounding scenery than I'd bargained for.

When I got to Panaji, I thought it a good idea to do a little homework on the price of beer. You see, there were a growing number of travellers staying in Colva now and it seemed to me that, if nothing else, there might well be a good market there for alcohol. I worked out that by buying the stuff by the crate in Panaji, I could actually sell it on to other Westerners cheaper than they could buy it themselves in Colva, and still make myself a small profit. So that's exactly what I did. Now, I'm not talking about taking on Whitbreads here; in fact, when all's said and done, I actually ended up only doing the one trip. I simply bussed in a couple of crates of beer and shared them around the beach one night as the sun went down. Hardly an entrepreneurial masterstroke I know, but still, it seemed to go down rather well -both metaphorically and literally. And, at the end of the day -both metaphorically and literally- I'd made enough money for two or three more egg curries. As for my fellow travellers well, they got a good night out drinking cut-priced beer and so, all in all, everyone was happy!

For us tourists, of course, the possibilities of making any money here were severely limited. I did once try to get a job as a waiter in one of the local beach bars but it was pretty hopeless. These jobs were invariably much sought after by lean-budgeted backpackers which, considering the fact that they were unpaid positions, was a little surprising. What you did get though, as a member of staff, was three free meals a day and so, consequently, several Westerners who passed through Colva spent their time in beach cafés, both dishing out and consuming a great deal of egg curries and the like.

There didn't appear to be much free time though if you were employed as one of these waiters, but then, I suppose, as the cafés were often built directly onto the beach it didn't really matter; you were slap bang in the middle of Colva's very limited but stunningly beautiful amenities: namely its sun, sea and sand.

One day whilst down on the beach, I watched one of these cafés being constructed. I was sitting on the sand one bright and sunny morning when eight or nine local men walked down the beach in a sort of procession, each carrying a straight, stout pole of about three metres in length. At first I couldn't begin to guess what they were up to; perhaps they were out for a quick saltwater punt or maybe they were members of the Colva rustic-javelin team, I don't know. It wasn't until they stopped at a particular point on the beach that it started to become clearer. These poles were to be the main structure for yet another beach café. The surprising thing is though, that there was absolutely no ground preparation, footing or foundations; six of the men just laid their poles out in two parallel lines, another chap bound cross members to all the poles to form 'goals', and the three goals were held in an upright position. Then, with each goalpost held rigid, yet another chap shinned up each upright in turn and bound the whole thing together with homemade string before going on to gradually add more and more cross-members. Finally, huge palm fronds were laid on the structure and tied across the several horizontals to form a roof. The entire construction was so very quick and simple; every man knew his job and did his bit, and by the time the sun had mellowed to a warm orange glow, the whole thing was all done and dusted. The café was up and ready to go. How marvellous I thought, how simply marvellous; and how bleedin' obvious that no Western architect had been anywhere near this project. Okay, so ramshackle and cheap it may have been; but it was on time, totally in harmony with its surroundings and quite, quite beautiful.

You know, it felt lovely to be part of a village community. I'd been around quite a while now, and on my daily excursions into the village I was on speaking terms to at least a handful of stall holders and on waving terms to almost everyone. I, especially had developed a great

221

rapport with a couple of young dogs'-bodies who ran around looking after the whims of wealthy guests in Colva's only hotel that boasted any stars. It was a smart hotel but had I wanted to be one of its clients -which I didn't- I couldn't have afforded it anyway. However, what this hotel did possess was something of far greater interest to me, and that was the village's only reliably clean supply of water. So, because of this, I began making daily visits to the gents' toilets there to fill my water bottle and, on occasion, to have a quick strip wash at the basins. The boys at the hotel knew full well what I was up to of course but, far from complain, simply found it all amusing. Perhaps they were more able to relate to my meagre needs than to those of their usual guests who, every day, would casually hand over the equivalent of the staff's daily wages for nothing more than a cup of tea and a round of lightly buttered toast.

Life wasn't terribly hectic for me in Colva. Sometimes I'd wander into the village to do some shopping -after checking the morning bus for backpackers of course- other times I would just…wander. A couple of American backpackers who'd moved on to pastures new had left me two old cooking pots -which in turn had previously been left to them- and so I now had the means to be wonderfully self sufficient; able to knock up a homemade campfire casserole in the tranquillity of my own back yard. Here it was so beautifully quiet, so totally uncluttered by the sound of human voices; I could be totally alone with only the cattle egrets across the river and the busy kingfishers for company.

I have to confess, the meat in the local market had never

tempted me before; it hung there pale and limp in the searing tropical sun, attracting more flies than a whole herd of cows' bums. Now though, armed as I was with my own cooking facilities, I looked at this warm and dishevelled meat through new eyes. It now presented me with a whole new proposition. Regardless of how many hundreds of flies eggs were sitting in there waiting to turn into nice, big, fat, juicy maggots, I could simply hack the meat up into chunks, throw in a couple of handfuls of fresh vegetables and boil the whole thing to death. Not necessarily what I'd choose to do under normal circumstances but, I thought, by giving my stew a good half an hour over the campfire it would at least lessen the chances of giving me a severe bout of the 'Calcutta Quickstep'. And, that's exactly what I did; and do you know, though I say so myself, it all tasted rather good. So good in fact, that for a while there, whilst I remained on Colva beach, campfire casserole became my standard daily winter menu-del-dia. Granted, I may not have been terribly discerning at the time and my memories of those dishes were no doubt more than a little coloured by the setting in which they were cooked, but well, given what I'd been used to living off, to me this was really something quite special. What a crying shame then, I thought, that my scabby little four-legged friend wasn't still around; I'm sure he'd have absolutely delighted in my new culinary skills…provided, of course, I kept those evil bullying chickens at bay.

Very few people tended to wander up my end of the beach except for those who were either staying at my hut or one of the few others like it. Just occasionally though, a young Goan chap would call by on his rounds to harvest the coconuts from the surrounding palm trees. I'd always marvelled at how the local people here seem to be able to run up a near vertical palm tree with such apparent ease. It wasn't until living right amongst the palms myself though that I noticed that neat little steps had been cut into each and every one of these trunks, right the way up, from bottom to top. Well, I thought, no wonder it's so easy; that explains it! So, one day, encouraged by my local coconut picker, I decided to give it a go. I kicked off my shoes and started to climb up just like I'd seen him do. Aaaaaaaah! God, it was agony, my poor, poor feet. It was like walking on broken glass; unbelievable; absolutely excruciating! After several determined attempts under the ever watchful eye of a smirking young coconut farmer, I could bear it no longer. I was forced to give up. I'd barely scaled a third of the way up the blessed trunk but already my feet felt as though they'd been savaged by a shoal of ravenous piranha. I gingerly retreated back down and hobbled over to my breakfast log. Then I sat there wincing and feeling slightly dispirited, my calves recovering from an over-anxious grip and the soft Western soles of my feet looking like somebody had gone totally berserk with a Spyrograph. "From now on that's it" I thought, "there's no way I'm going to subject my feet to such torture ever again; I'm definitely leaving it to the locals." The palm tree man, meanwhile, smiled on noticeably smugly and then sprinted up yet another palm trunk. I looked on a little enviously, nursing my poor shredded feet.

"The next time I buy a pair of shoes" I said, muttering under my breath, "I know exactly what I'd like the soles to be made out of; and the material won't be from anything four-legged!" Still, he's probably useless at football and can't hang a door to save his life. You know what…I bet he can't even curl his tongue and make owl noises!

One evening, on yet another trip down to the beach bar to join a few friends and watch the sun go down, I decided to take the long way round. I jumped the river and cut up through the paddy fields to another part of the village. Back away from the seafront there were small clusters of wooden bungalows, each with their own little front garden all neatly fenced off from the others, and with little well worn pathways running between each property. It was an unusual scene to come across here in India, more akin perhaps to a small hamlet of seaside holiday homes back home.

The sun was still up when I passed through, and so old men busied themselves in their gardens whilst care-free young children chased amongst the trees, grubbed about in patches of dirt or ran after hapless dogs wielding weapons of bamboo. A little further on, some slightly older children returned from the well with water filled plastic buckets weighing heavily on their little heads, their faces held in concentration until their eyes met mine and then they'd break into heart warming smiles. Then each of them, still grinning away, would hurry by with tiny barefoot steps, hardly spilling a drop, always maintaining their poise like diminutive cat-walk models.

A while later I watched a small group of boys kicking a slightly withered and deflated plastic football about. The ball was of the black and white, almost opaquely lightweight variety found hanging outside a thousand tacky seaside shops in English resorts; the ones displayed alongside 'Made in Hong Kong' bucket and spade sets, rock pool nets and blow-up dolphins; footballs that, back home, would be quickly relegated to the back of the garden shed somewhere having been speared during their first week on next-door's rose bush. Here though it was different; this football clearly hadn't been bought on a whim or as a bribe to keep the kids quiet, it was a closely guarded and much treasured possession. It didn't matter that, by now, the thing had turned into a two-tone plastic blancmange; this excuse for a ball was a key part of these children's lives, a means to a tremendous amount of fun and bonding. However, though it was certainly wonderful to see them at play, it was also interesting to note that actually, children -if indeed they are allowed a childhood- are pretty much the same wherever you go. For, halfway through the game I witnessed a sort of ritual being carried out by a young boy that I've since observed the world over. I couldn't understand what was being said, of course, but I didn't need to. Mid-game, this one small boy -clearly the ball's owner- picked up the football, stuck it resolutely under his armpit, uttered a few words through pouted lips and then stomped off leaving all the others a little lost and bewildered. Quite obviously, if these boys weren't going to play the game the way he wanted them to…then he was taking his ball home (this sentence, in any language, invariably followed by the internationally recognised phrase of, "Ner, ner, ner-nerrr ner!")

A little further on in the same part of the village, I came across a very fat and jolly looking woman in an 'extra large' floral blouse. She looked like she'd mothered at least a couple of dozen children and was heavily into sampling her own cooking. Well, that afternoon, she was hanging out the washing and, as I passed by not thirty feet in front of her, she surely couldn't have helped but notice me. However, without batting an eyelid or so much as pausing for a single second from pegging out her bright white bed sheets, she proceeded to open her legs slightly and, from an upright position, wee onto the garden. This, I swear, is the absolute truth; it plainly didn't matter a jot to her that there was anyone around to witness this. And then, when she'd finished, she just kept right on pegging away as if nothing had happened and no-one had been there to see it. I was quite astonished. In fact, it reminded me of how I'd seen all those men get off the bus and 'crouch down' to wee in the Pakistani desert; and now, here I was, in Goa, watching a woman relieving herself standing up. What a very strange and diverse world we live in!

Down on Colva beach meanwhile, it was business as usual. The evening was quickly drawing in and all the local men had gone home to their families and were no doubt tucking into their Himalayan-like mounds of rice topped with thimblefuls of fiery sauce. The travellers, of course, were already sat around at their favourite beach bars or scattered along the seashore in their couples, heady with dope, romance or both. I took up a favourite position on an old fallen palm trunk to catch the last of the sun. Dusk here was always such a beautiful part of the day and, as the light dimmed, so thousands upon thousands of tiny crabs would venture out of their burrows to see what the day's wind and tide had brought them. It was an incredible daily spectacle, and from a low vantage point, at this particular time of the evening, there'd often seem to be more crab than beach; there were simply millions of them; just a seething, silhouetted mass of movement hurrying and scurrying to and fro on tiny clockwork legs.

227

Sometimes earlier in the evening I'd try to catch a crab before it made for the safety of its burrow. It was usually pretty hopeless in a straight race because, if pursued, they'd tear across the sand at such an amazing speed, as if propelled by rocket-fuel -presumably supplied by Shell! However, they never actually ventured far from safety and I discovered, by trial and error, that if you went for the burrow rather than the burrow's owner, then they didn't know quite where to retreat to, and it would invariably panic them into diving into somebody else's hole. Then, of course, this poor little terrified fleeing crab would quickly be booted out of the hole by the hole's rightful owner. And so, just twice, I actually managed to trap one of the evicted crabs by hand before it had the chance to sprint off and find yet another refuge. Now I know that, to some, this may all seem a bit cruel, and perhaps it was, but I just thought it would be an interesting experiment. And in any case, we are only talking about a minor hassling of a crab or two. I don't normally make a habit out of bullying crustaceans.

Some mornings I would wake before it was even light - provided I hadn't spent half the night trying to roll onto a female lodger. Naturally, there was no electricity anywhere in or around the hut and so, usually, it was very much a case of early to bed and early to rise. However, regardless of the time of night, it was never completely dark outside, for the night sky was invariably cloudless and so, even with only a fine sliver of moon, there would always be enough light to half illuminate the surroundings. It was during this time that the local fishermen would fish out at sea and so, by early morning, they'd already be hauling their boats into the shallows and carting handwoven basketfuls of fish up onto the beach. If ever I was up early enough, it was nice to be able to go down and meet them before the fish had been sorted and taken to market. Occasionally, if I was feeling a little flush financially, I'd pay a few rupees to sample some of that night's catch. I never knew what it was I was buying of course, for there was always quite a variety of fish, but none which I could either recognise or name. Sadly though, however many different varieties there may have been, there was seldom very many of them quantity-wise. (This, probably due to the 'not so offshore' trawlers)

Of course, the local fishermen, like their rivals, the trawler fishermen, also used nets, though on a far smaller and more sustainable scale. Well, sustainable that is, up to a point; for there seemed to be few regulations here and the nets used were of a mesh size that would ensnare just about anything and everything that lived in the ocean. I suppose the problem is that, as in Europe before the Second World War, it must have seemed to the Goans that the sea's bounty was endless, and so, anything to them -be it shark or minnow- was more than fair game. One thing you can be sure of though; almost nothing caught here would be wasted. For the most part, somewhat bizarrely, the fishermen could hardly afford to even eat their own catch and the vast majority of it had to be sold on to others in order to sustain the fishermen's happy but humble lives. Indeed, the only time I ever saw fish on a fisherman's plate here it was an absolute apology of a thing the size of your average angler's bait, looking like a rather sad and withered autumnal leaf balancing a top a mountainous mound of boiled rice. But always, whether for breakfast, lunch or dinner, this would be accompanied by that ubiquitous condiment: a dribble of super-fiery, tongue searing chilli sauce.

Now just occasionally, amongst the daily catch brought in by the locals, there were some things that weren't terribly welcome. Though to be fair, the only regular unwanted casualty of the fishing industry here were normally just sea-snakes. These would invariably end up in the same nets as the fish and so, everyday after a busy morning's sorting, the fishing families would eventually leave the beach and there would be three or four of these poor wretched creatures tossed aside and left to slowly fry to death on the sand. Well, I really had no idea whether these snakes were harmful or not, but it seemed to me such an awful and tragic death that I just couldn't bring myself to leave them like that. So, each morning I'd walk along the beach, seek out the snakes, grab them by their tails and fling them back into the sea. I hadn't a clue how these snakes would react of course; many of them were still sufficiently 'un-fried' and lively enough to turn on me, and so just in case they were at all venomous, each time I ran down to the water's edge with a snake, I'd repeatedly shake it…just to make sure that the dangerous end stayed down long enough for me to hurl the poor thing into the sea. This may not have been great for the snake in the short term, but then sometimes, as they say, there's just no gain without pain is there; and I certainly didn't want the pain to be mine. And besides, whilst the sea snakes might well have been a bit shaken up by being a bit shaken down, surely I thought, it's got to be a whole lot better than being fried alive! I later discovered, of course, that these creatures were all highly venomous and so I was rather glad that I'd taken the precaution of keeping the head at the bottom...A wonderful but slightly hazardous thing, naivety!

You know I was never quite sure why but, apart from the regular night fishermen, there was sometimes also a small group of fishermen who fished from the beach by day. This always seemed to me more like fishing as a hobby rather than for their livelihoods because, although it would involve upwards of twenty men and boys, there would scarcely be enough in their net to fill a plastic bag at a fairground, let alone sustain several families. They did, however, always appear amazingly happy in their 'work', and this is how they went about it...

Firstly, the whole group of them would wade out into the sea with their net -which would probably be about sixty metres long by a couple of metres deep- and then, when they'd got as far out as their heights would allow without drowning, they'd form themselves into a large semi-circle arcing out from the beach, with everybody spaced evenly along the net. Then, holding the net so that the top of it was just barely below the water surface, when everyone was ready, the two groups holding the arms of the semicircle would walk up into the shallows and up the beach until only the bottom of the arc was left in the water. Next, the two lines of men, now on the beach, would close in towards each other until they met, and then the whole thing would be pulled out clear of the water bringing with it 'the catch'.

It was a fascinating spectacle and one which I really enjoyed witnessing but, you know, it didn't matter how many times I watched this, I never once saw enough silvery flickerings in the net to fill so much as a carpenter's lunchbox (I know this because I was one...a carpenter, that is, not a lunchbox). I can only sensibly assume that all this had either become an age old ritual - thereby not necessarily requiring any justifiable reward- or that it was more for sport or a male bonding exercise perhaps. Whatever the case, all of the participants seemed to thoroughly enjoy the whole thing and, when you think of it, compared to sitting all day on a riverbank in an English drizzle, stooped under a green umbrella and staring at the end of a length of fibreglass; this, as hobbies go, does have a certain appeal.

On the fish front meanwhile, when it comes to actually eating it, I have to say, this is exactly what I like to do…eat it! Now, the fish that these locals were catching were all pretty miniscule and so, unless I had a severe case of banana boredom, I usually didn't bother buying any. The reason being -and this may just be a personal thing- but well, I just can't be doing with picking about on a plate or gingerly feeling round your mouth to extract pin sized fish bones. I don't know, perhaps I've been spoilt or maybe I'm just plain 'bone-idle', but really I simply can't be bothered. In fact, while we're at it; neither am I into prizing pea-sized morsels of seafood from their shells; especially the likes of winkles, which I find are not only eye-strainingly tiny but seem to come complete with a small lorry load of aggregate inside every one!

So anyway, the main point of all this is that when it comes to shellfish and here, prawns in particular, unless they are monstrously huge, I'll normally give them a miss. The problem I have is that I love the things so much that I quickly forget the amount of fiddling and faffing around involved until the second they're put before me -having already gleefully ordered them. Thus it was -more or less-one morning on Colva Beach. I'd bought a small cereal bowl sized portion of tiny prawns from the fishermen and returned back to camp to boil them up in my faithful pan. Then, that done, I walked over to sit by the sea and was joined by a couple of English girls from a neighbouring hut for a sumptuous seaside picnic of home cooked prawns and ant rolls. Well, it wasn't long after we'd sat down that, as usual, I suddenly remembered just how frustrating prawns can be, and especially when they're the size of Bonsai baked beans. So within five minutes of sitting there, I'd already had enough of trying to shell the things. I thought, "sod it" and ate the lot, shells and all! Decidedly crunchy, they may have been, but as far as I was concerned it was that or nothing.

Well, not long after this, I would pay dearly. For over the next few days I started to develop slight stomach cramps which, as time went by, got progressively worse and worse. To add to this I was staying in the hut on my own at the time and so, not wanting to be ill alone -if only someone else could be ill with me- I went to stay with a couple of Swiss hippies whom I'd met earlier (needless to say, unfortunately by now, the two girls had left). The trouble is that both of these hippies were on a permanent high from the ultra-cheap local wacky-backy and, under normal circumstances, they most certainly wouldn't have been my room mates of choice. But I felt so ill and weak by now and so craved any sort of company, I'd have happily slept alongside the scabby village dogs.

You know, at times like this, there is nothing quite like your own bed is there! But, being as my bed was several thousand miles away there really wasn't a lot of choice.

No, for the time being, the Swiss hippy hut would just have to do. "At least I had some company" I thought, "and that has to be better than none at all...doesn't it?" As things turned out, by my fourth night in the 'company' of these new-age hippies, I would have given almost anything to be alone again. The problem is that I was growing considerably weaker and weaker by the minute and was, by now, totally confined to bed. Not that this seemed to affect my room mates at all; they simply carried on with their daily routine as if I wasn't there. They'd get up every day at the crack of lunchtime, wander dreamily outside -presumably only to replenish their pot supplies- and then return again within two or three hours to start yet another mammoth smoking session. Now this was sort of okay I suppose, except for the fact that, by mid-afternoon, they'd both be totally horizontal; silently levitating in a billowing cloud of sweet smelling haziness. "God, what an existence" I thought; "what a complete and utter waste of life!" You know, I never ever once saw either of them eat, drink or come to think of it, wash; but whatever their failings, the one thing they did seem was: supremely happy. All that these two appeared to live on was the heady combination of marijuana and music. A combination that may sound fine for an evening, but after four days and nights?...No thanks! It may have been nirvana to them, but to me...I was slowly being driven stark raving bonkers! If that wasn't enough, the Walkman they had, equipped as it was with two extremely able external speakers, would be blaring out their mystical, hippie-type music all day and all night to an attentive audience of absolutely no-one bar me. And invariably, it would be me who'd have to stagger from my sickbed and turn the bloody thing off before fighting the fug back to my mattress. No, having endured yet another night of exactly the same I decided that this definitely wasn't the place to be ill in. My two room mates certainly weren't any company at all; they were hardly more comforting awake than asleep, and mostly, I couldn't even tell the difference!

After four days of living in a small wooden chimneyless crematorium with two Swiss corpses for company, I'd had enough; I just had to get out of there. I dragged myself off to the only local doctor in the village, entered a small waiting room and slumped into a chair, a decidedly weak and limp lump.

Now, to his credit, the doctor saw me straight away, and when I told him of my symptoms, he had a bit of a feel around my abdomen, uttered a few suggestions in broken English, waggled his head about a bit in that characteristic fashion and pointed to a poster on the wall indicating, yes you guessed it, a 'prawn'. Well, it was a remarkably quick diagnosis but, after my seaside snack, I had little doubt that it was probably a correct one. Apparently, or so I've since been told, there's a certain species of fungus that lives on the shells of prawns in the Indian ocean and well, I don't know what it does exactly but, it doesn't do you an awful lot of good when you eat it. In fact, I was told that if left untreated, this fungus, or the result of consuming it, would gradually eat away the inside of my large intestine. This didn't sound terribly nice to me but anyway, over the next few days I was given a course of jabs and remarkably quickly, started to feel almost back to normal; or at least…normal-ish!

Before leaving the doctor he told me that I was to stay off

anything even remotely spicy -which I thought rather limiting here in India- and for the moment at least, to stick to dry crackers. Then, perhaps a little later, "if I was very good" I could move on to an apple. So that's exactly what I did. After four days of eating absolutely nothing, my very first meal consisted of precisely four Jacob's Cream Crackers. (Strangely, I'd managed to find these in a local shack-cum-shop just outside the village; like the railways perhaps, yet another colonial legacy.) These dry crackers were all I had to look forward to for another three whole days; yum! Although...come to think of it, that's not strictly true; for after a couple of these hearty 'square meals', I soon realised that plain dry Jacob's Cream Crackers, boring as they are, could be made infinitely more exciting simply by adding salt.(Levels of excitement, of course, are always...relative.)

Then, after the three days were finally up, I could contain myself no longer; I threw caution to the wind and rewarded myself with one whole apple. But by now, bolstered by my 'Jacobs', I felt a hundred times better anyway, and soon I was pretty well back to full strength.

In the event it actually took me a whole two years to recover properly. This may sound like either hell or a hell of an exaggeration and, to some extent, it's a little of both; for whilst I was unable to eat either spices or onions for the whole of that period, I could only find this out by periodically trying them. So consequently, though I initially had to endure food-poisoning like pains almost daily for the first six months after having eaten the infamous fungi-infested prawns; gradually, little by little, the gaps between pains did become longer. Then, and only then, just occasionally I'd try something that wasn't ultra-bland, but would usually suffer a short but painful setback. And so it was indeed two whole years before the pains finally went altogether and I was back happily tucking into Indian takeaways and raw onion and cheese sandwiches. A long awaited delight for me, if not my girlfriend!

My hippie Swiss friends meanwhile, were almost certainly totally unaware of all this; they just carried on with their own little lives in their own little world; a world of short sunny days and long, smoky, dreamy nights; a stress free but strange existence. As I've said before, I'd heard so many of these young and not so young travellers say that they'd come to India 'to find themselves'; well, living like this strikes me as rather an odd way in which to do it. And in any case, how on earth can they ever hope to find themselves or anybody else, amongst all that fug!

Mind you, when it comes to smoking dope, it has to be said that I was hardly the Pope either. (Though perhaps that's not the best analogy; haven't you ever wondered about all that celebratory smoke that pours from the Vatican every time a new Pope's chosen?)

Now generally, as mentioned before, I like to have a go at just about anything in life, and so I felt that whilst I was here, I had to at least sample a bit of the local ganja. The ideal place for this was at a bar in the village called 'The Boomshanker Bar'. Now I daresay that this wasn't actually its proper name, but that's what it was known as by every Westerner in the area. The name presumably had something to do with smoking joints but well, I never did quite work out what that something was.

Anyway, every evening the bar would be packed to the gunnels with mostly, very young Europeans, sitting about in relaxed and happy circles. On first impressions, there didn't really seem the need to smoke anything as you could just as easily inhale from the communal cloud that sat curling thickly and sweetly at nostril height. But this smoking business appeared to put everyone in such a good mood that it seemed crazy not to at least give it a go.

So, 'give it a go' is exactly what I did, and during the first few nights of my hippie inauguration, I keenly joined in with a good many games of pass the parcel. But, you know, for some reason these 'spliffs' didn't appear to have much effect on me. Sure, it was a nice smell and all that, but this somehow didn't seem to be enough to put the whole bar in a semi-torpor of glassy-eyed grins. There definitely had to be more to it.

So a couple of nights later I really gave it my very best shot and, when the over-sized rollies were handed round the circle, I have to admit, I did take rather more than my fair share! Well, this certainly seemed to do the trick. What an incredibly odd sensation! I'd be happily chatting away to a dozen or so people, and then halfway through a sentence...I'd pause...for what, to me...seemed like hours, whilst the whole crowd looked at me in anticipation, waiting for me to continue except...they weren't...because...the 'long pause' didn't really exist! Then, I'd simply continue the sentence as if nothing had happened which, most of the time...it hadn't! Either that or, mid-sentence, I'd completely and totally forget what the hell I was talking about, in which case there would most certainly be a pause, shortly followed by fits of laughter...usually my own!

Now, to the uninitiated, this may sound all pretty bizarre but I'm sure that most people who have sampled some

238

'stuff' will know exactly what I'm talking about. For the rest, well, you'll just have to take my word for it. It's quite an extraordinary thing though isn't it; that, for some unexplainable reason, smoking hash in any sort of quantity seems to deprive the smoker of any sense of time, or is it just 'any sense'? I don't know.

Of course, all of these so called 'soft drugs' are still illegal back at home, which might seem strange considering the passive nature they create compared to that of alcohol. But also, you have to ask, does making a substance illegal actually deter those who want to indulge, from using it anyway? On the contrary, when you consider the age of the majority of people taking these soft drugs, the illegality of it might even be an incentive! As the quote attributed to Elvis goes; "What are you rebelling against?"...Answer: "What have you got?"

Anyway, for me personally, the culmination of all this sampling of new substances was to be 'the red party'; so called because everybody who turned up at the party had to be dressed, funnily enough, in red!

Well, a few days before the due date, I excitedly thumbed through my wardrobe only to discover that nothing I possessed was the right colour -even though recently, I'd quite unknowingly come extremely close by acquiring a rather fetching pair of bright purple, tie-up-at-the-ankles cotton trousers. The main problem was, I wasn't just lacking in red items but...lacking in items of clothing generally. This was largely on account of my selling off my jeans; and so my entire wardrobe now consisted of: a pair of white shorts; two T-shirts -one white, one yellow- a well ventilated pair of bumper-boots and a motley collection of 'seasoned' underwear (and the purple trousers). So anyway, it occurred to me that if I was going to make this party, then clearly something had to be done. My saviour came in a somewhat unusual form; for, though lacking the correct attire for the forthcoming event, I soon discovered that someone staying on the other side of the village had had the forethought to set up a huge cauldron of red dye especially for the purpose of kitting out party-goers in the appropriately coloured gear. Consequently, hoards of people started visiting this cauldron over the next few days with an amazing array of clothes, and all with the view of making them look pretty much identical.

So, come party night, it was early-ish in the evening and we were once again all sat around in The Boomshanker Bar; heads in the cloud, pathetically smiling at one another, and smoking a few hors d'oeuvres. Then, much later, as the bar started to empty, various straggly groups started to drift off and make their way across the paddy fields towards the party venue. I followed on just behind a group of five or six others.

Well, what happened next was quite extraordinary for, you know...I'm not quite sure whether I'd smoked rather too much that evening or that my group of friends had become unbelievably indecisive about their party wear, but somehow, as I followed along behind the others, every time I looked up from the narrow walkway in front of me - the path leading between the paddy fields- my friends would magically be wearing something totally different from what they started out in. One minute I'd be following somebody in T-shirt and trousers, then suddenly he would change into a Red Indian Chief; and then another, into a spaceman. How very peculiar, I thought. In an effort to gain some sort of self-control, I tried repeatedly scrunching my eyes up and looking again, but it was hopeless; my friends appeared more indecisive than ever. Well, I found all this incredibly strange of course but, for the moment, I had little choice but to go with it. And anyway, I couldn't help but find it all quite amusing. In fact, a short while later and I really couldn't have cared less. I eventually arrived at the party -via an extremely 'unmemorable' route- a very red and giggling wreck. Yes, just me, Neil Armstrong and virtually all of The Village People.

The party, when we arrived, was like no other I'd been to before, or indeed since. It looked as though I'd inadvertently walked in on the Valencia tomato fiesta. Not only were the many young party-goers kitted out in nothing but red, but so too were all the trees. Somebody had gone absolutely berserk with an abundance of red crepe paper and the whole scene now looked like a huge open-air brothel; a nuclear explosion in a ketchup factory; like somebody's view, quite literally, through spectacularly rose-tinted spectacles (I'm sure by now you get the picture, okay, it was red!)

Anyway, by the time we'd arrived, most of the people there were already in a trance-like state, varying in intensity from slow motion dance to horizontal and totally comatose. Some stood in random, loose circles chatting and laughing, almost like normal party-goers -were it not for their appearance. I went and sat myself down on a grassy bank as far as possible from Deep Purple, Pink Floyd, Santana or whoever it was yelling at the tops of their voices from a violently vibrating speaker through the open window of the house. They seemed a very agreeable crowd though. Everyone was obviously heavily into this kind of music; many sat cross-legged on the grass, nodding to each other in unison like a convention for 'dogs that sit in the back of car windows'. The trouble is, this sort of dance may just have looked vaguely cool in the late sixties perhaps, but now, here in the eighties and without the accompanying yo-yoing chest-length hair, it just looked a bit ridiculous really, even in my state.

To be fair to the party hosts though, it wasn't all dodgy substances going round. I do vaguely remember a few paper-plate loads of rice and various other titbits appearing now and then. Also, though not totally in a switched on state, I had actually managed to display some sort of normality by remembering to bring a few beers along, which I thought, quite remarkable. This, as it happens, was just as well because, having sampled the punch, I wasn't entirely sure they didn't have an excess of red dye. Mind you, neither was I terribly sure about what else was on offer either. There seemed to be a constant stream of people wandering past me offering plates or bag loads of the most unusual party nibbles. These ranged from 'hash' browns and 'chocolate chip' cookies, to an eclectic assortment of rather special mushroom vol-au-vents without the vol-au-vent! Then, within a couple of hours things began to get decidedly hazy, and though I did manage to decline most of what was offered me, it would have seemed terribly rude not to at least 'try' the odd biscuit or mushroom wouldn't it!

And so, well I don't know, but sometime later that same evening I guess I must have developed some sort of fungi or chocolate chip cookie allergy, for the next thing I knew, I was waking up back in my hut with the sun seeping under the door and with a tongue that felt like a rancid slug in an old football sock.

And the end result of all this? Do you know, I can't say overall that getting stoned to that extent -or anything like it- was really my cup of tea; though...I enjoyed the experimenting.

I suppose some hash aficionados would say that my reaction to taking all these substances was a little over the top, but well, I can only say what I truly saw and felt like at the time. I guess that, as with over consumption of just about anything, we all react differently to it, whether consciously, subconsciously, or indeed, unconsciously! But if nothing else, at least I'd had the opportunity to temporarily enter the 'outer-world' of the fully paid up hippy; an eye-opener –no, most definitely not- I mean, 'an education' in itself. And this also included the sampling of some of their more unusual tools or trappings. You see, quite apart from the varied party food going around and the rather plump cigarettes floating around the Boomshanker Bar beforehand, I confess that I did also sample a fair assortment of bongs and chillums. (And no, this isn't the name of the local Indian solicitors, by the way, but simply names of containers for smoking hash or grass.) But before we go any further, for the uninitiated, I'll explain a little:

Now, chillums come in various shapes and sizes and are sort of pipe-like contraptions, tapering down at the bottom, like a sort of wooden, stone or bone ice-cream cone with the bottom end nibbled off, and are filled usually with a mixture of tobacco and...some other dodgy ingredient, depending on the user. You can smoke these things in much the same way as a traditional pipe, only chillums differ in that they're often intricately carved and have the capacity of the average family's weekly shopping. Bongs, on the other hand, are constructed far more along the lines of the hookahs or hubble-bubble pipes of the Middle East because they rely on water as a filter which, I'm told, is far better for the smoker. Though, whether this is because of the quality of the health or the 'high', I never quite established. But in any case, although they may lack the finesse of a traditional hubble-bubble, here in Goa, they did have a sort of rustic charm. This is because, more often than not, these bongs were made from the very coconuts which fell amongst us. All you had to do in order to make one was: take one coconut, de-husk it, bore a couple of holes, half fill the coconut with water, poke a straw to below water level in one hole and a well packed chillum in the other, light the chillum and suck! Now, in the interest of science, I must confess to having tried this a number of times and found that smoking from a bong, unlike from a conventional spliff, always seemed to give, how can I say, the 'desired effect'. But, you know, the one thing I'll never ever fathom is: how on earth anyone can even begin to think they look cool, whilst sounding like an elephant farting under water.

After four or five nights on the trot down at the Boomshanker Bar, I'd just about had enough of all this. I'd finally come to the conclusion that, although I enjoyed the flirtation, it just wasn't for me. No, long term, I decided that as far as I was concerned, grass was something you either sat or played football on. Real dope was only for real dopes, and they can keep it! Okay, so Colva wasn't huge on other forms of night entertainment, but to sit on the beach with a beer and watch the sun go down was enough for me. The truth is I suppose, I really didn't like the feeling of not being in control and anyway, as corny as it may sound, I simply didn't feel the need for any high other than that given me by my quite wonderful and natural surroundings.

CHAPTER 16

- THE GREAT SOCCER MISMATCH AND THE GOAN MAFIA -

Still stuck in Colva

In my view there are two mediums in particular through which you can unite people of every race, who don't possess a common language, and they are both music and sport. Regarding the former, I've always envied enormously anybody who has mastered a musical instrument, especially the guitar, and this is because there surely can be no better instrument to travel with. Okay, so a harmonica is a damned sight easier to stick in a rucksack, but have you ever tried playing one and singing along at the same time? No, for me, the guitar has to be not only the instrument of choice, but the ultimate musical language barrier breaker. Why, I've lost count of the times I've sat and watched as so many faces from so many different places have lit up at the sound of singing and strumming; and, you know, it never ever fails to give me that 'good to be alive' feeling to see it. Not only that, but whenever I've been with a group of people and there happens to be a guitar around, I'm constantly amazed at just how many ethnically diverse people can pick the thing up and actually play it. Granted, most of the people I'm talking about come from the so called, 'developing' world and so don't have the modern day distractions of TVs and computers; but well, they do still have to get down and do it, don't they! It maybe begs the question: which of us is it who lives in the developing world?

Unfortunately, from a personal perspective, my musical period was somewhat short lived. Yes, I did play a pretty mean glockenspiel at junior school -having already mastered 'London's Burning' on the descant recorder- but come senior school, when I progressed to the flugelhorn well, it really wasn't for me. I did stick with it for a couple of terms but all that my particular horn seemed to produce was flat notes and sore lips. So when I eventually had to give it the elbow due to my family's lack of finances, it was probably no bad thing.

As for sport however, now that's an entirely different matter. I'd always been a keen footballer, and if there's one single language more global than English or music, then surely this is it; not merely as an excuse to get a bunch of mates together, but as a way to unite people from virtually every culture and background around the globe - or certainly most of the males, at least. Well, I'd already arranged a few games within Europe in the past, but how nice it would be, I thought, to be able to do the same in other countries, and more especially, here in India.

Anyway, there were, as I've said, several people now staying in Colva, and so I decided that if I was going to be stuck here anyway, then this was the ideal place to try to get a team of travellers together for a match. Earlier, I'd watched the local Goan team practising on the village ground and had already approached the manager about the possibility of their playing a game against an 'international' team. To my surprise he absolutely loved the idea, and so off I went and spent the next day and a half scouring the beach for likely team members. Now, obviously my choice of players was always going to be somewhat limited as, for the moment at least, I was trying my very best to avoid selecting either girls or hard-core hippies. (Yes I know, it's all very sexist and hippy-ist). Unfortunately, it didn't take me long to realise that if it were to be a footballers only team, we'd probably be talking two-a-side; so, whilst doing my recruiting, I thought it wise to at least give the benefit of the doubt to any male who was still 'of this world'. I also thought it prudent to include rather more players than I actually needed for the team in order to allow for those that might just be temporarily out of this world when it came to kick-off time. And so, with this in mind, I went about trawling the beach and bars -it seemed the thing to do in a fishing village- and I eventually finished up with a list of at least two dozen mostly coherent males.

And so...the stage was set. Everything was ready for 'the big match'! I'd already arranged to meet up with the Goan team late one afternoon and so, as the allotted time approached, I walked over to the pitch closely followed by my enthusiastic team...of four. The Goan players of course, were already out there on their patchy pitch kicking a ball about, and so now, at the eleventh hour, I dearly hoped that the rest of my makeshift team wasn't going to let me down. Well, with only minutes to go before kick off, there was still no sign of the others so I had a brief tactical chat to my small and motley crew, mostly along the lines of "you've got a heck of a lot of running to do" and "let's try to keep it to single figures", then, we took up our positions. Meanwhile, up at the far end of the pitch, the Goan team had just finished with all their Brazil-like ball juggling and were gathered together in a huddle to collectively don a freshly laundered soccer strip. Things so far just weren't looking great. But then, just when all seemed lost, just when the ref' was about to signal the start of the annihilation...very slowly but surely, and to my great relief, a raggle-taggle assortment of wanderers moseyed in from various parts of the beach and came over to join us. Well, best dressed, as fit as fleas and professional...we weren't; but, hoorah; we were now, at least a complete team!

There were just two people on our side who'd actually played the game at some time in their lives; as for the rest well; I guess that sport just wasn't something that you normally participated in. Mercifully though, we did have Matt, who'd agreed -because he didn't know any better- to take up position in goal. Now Matt was very much your sort of 'home-baked apple pie' American -sweet and innocent but with a thick crust between his ears- but, whilst he may not have quite grasped the intricacies of the English game, he did, nevertheless, have the considerable advantage of being built like several very substantial brick shithouses which, I figured, could come in jolly handy.

Of course, if I was pushed for players, I was also hardly in a position to be picky as far as kit was concerned either. We were, after all, a random bunch of beach bum backpackers and so, even though I did ask them all to at least try to turn up in white T-shirts, our final soccer strip was, let's say, a tad unusual. Not so much a strip as such; more a sort of selection of 'designer label' type outfits - from the Stevie Wonder spring collection perhaps? To be fair though, I suppose that all our outfits did at least have one thing in common...they were all, every one of them, completely different!

Well anyway, as I say, everything was set, the match kicked off and umm...look, I won't go into detail but, suffice to say, it was one of the greatest football 'mismatches' I've ever played in. But you know, after the final whistle had been blown, one thing was beyond doubt; a really great time had been had by all. The Boomshanker Babas -a name we'd rather appropriately given ourselves- had actually only lost out to the Goans by an exceedingly respectable 4-1. A minor miracle! Mind you, had the Goan team worn football boots or indeed any form of footwear, we might well be talking rugby scores here. As it was we were probably saved total humiliation by this fact alone. And us? well, because our own footwear had ranged from junior school type plimsolls right through to tractor type soled hiking boots, perversely, this had evened things up a bit. Not skill-wise mind, and in truth, if some of our slightly more over-zealous defenders had even been capable of catching their counterparts, it may not have been the friendliest of friendlies. Thankfully, the young and agile Goans proved more than athletic enough to hurdle just about every dubious scything tackle that the Boomshanker Babas could swing at them, and it all ended both bloodless and happily.

After the match everyone went away in good spirits and agreed that the whole thing had been a great success. The Goans returned jubilantly to their homes, whilst we, in equally buoyant -if jaded- mood, retired to the nearest beach bar to celebrate our coming second.

It was a fun and memorable evening (or rather just 'fun', as later, a slight over-indulgence in the local beer prevented it from being too memorable.) There was much chatter and laughter and male-bonding type stuff; and by the time we had to leave the bar, our table was heaving with empty bottles and glasses. Then, to round off the evening, goalkeeper Matt, normally a teetotaller until now, rose to his feet to propose a toast to the team. He stood there in silence for a good few seconds, and then promptly toppled forward like a felled giant Californian redwood, totally clearing the table with his massive frame. Unbelievably, as we picked him up and plopped him back in his chair, he still wore that same all-American smile, and though even more bemused than usual, no damage was done; or rather, no damage to him that is. As for the beach café; it now had a deep and shiny, thick pile carpet of broken glass that extended wall to wall, (or it would have, had there been any walls.) Still, if the café staff were in the slightest bit annoyed by all this, they certainly didn't show it. Surely they can't have been used to wreckage on such a grand scale -unless accustomed to staging Greek theme nights- but their attitude was both pleasant and remarkable. Of course, after that, the least we could do was to help with the clearing up, so, for those still sober enough to remain upright, it was all hands on deck with the brushes and brooms and then we quickly chipped in a little for the breakages and left.

A few days later and word had spread up and down the beach about our soccer match. Soon people were asking about when it was all going to happen again and, of the original players, all were keen for revenge. So, the following week we were at it again. This time though, we'd managed to acquire just a few more players who could not only kick the ball in roughly the intended direction, but who could also break into a canter without the need for oxygen. Yes; this time we were ready for them! Hundreds of fans lined the pitch. (Or was it a handful of hippies who'd got lost on the way back from the beach? I forget now.) Anyway; the match got underway and in no time at all Colva had put the ball in the back of the net. But then, within five minutes, and quite unbelievably, we equalized. This was more like it. There was a buzz around the ground; the crowd started to get so excited that they almost stayed awake. The score quickly went back and forth: 1-1, 2-1, 2-2, 3-2, there was nothing in it. Then, by the time the final whistle had been sounded, half the Boomshanker Babas were strewn about the pitch horizontally; we were completely and utterly 'done in': pooped, poleaxed and paralysed but above all else....supremely jubilant! We'd gone down '6-5' to the home side but to us, it was an indefatigable, indisputable victory. The whole team rushed, limped and staggered down to the sea and plunged in for a much deserved dip. God, what heaven! Oh how deliciously, coolingly wonderful! After ninety minutes of tearing around, manically chasing a ball under the fierce tropical sun, water had never felt so good. I lay back floating on the Indian Ocean, looking up at the sky. "Sure, I love football", I thought, "but never again in this heat...perhaps I'll take up swimming...you never see fish sweat like this, do you!"

After half an hour of cooling off, I felt like a different person. There was only one thing left to complete a near perfect afternoon; the whole team hit the bar again for a few celebratory beers. All that is, except for big Matt, who for some reason, seemed to have become teetotal again!

Just along from the Boomshanker Bar was another similar bar but one which attracted a slightly different clientele. For some reason it seemed to appeal to a rather younger crowd. Well, by now I'd grown a little tired of the type of conversations I always seemed to get into up the road: "So how long have you been in Colva?" "How long? Man, I live here!" type of thing. So I took to frequenting this other hip but 'not so hippie' bar. Now one thing that made this bar a little bit different was that, out in a kind of car port thing behind the bar area, there was a table tennis table. Well, I soon realised that it was a whole lot better spending an evening round the table tennis table than lounging about with my head in a cloud, talking some bizarre drivel with a load of Worzel Gummidge look-a-likes.

The people who I met in this bar, although younger in years, at least had something intelligible to say, and so it soon became my 'local'. Now, in all honesty, I don't remember an awful lot about this place except that it was the only place I ever came across in the whole of India, where I was actually treated to a beer by an Indian. But my surprise wasn't that I didn't get treated more often but, because of the vast difference in our potential incomes, that I was ever treated to a beer at all. This one occasion came about simply because of a casual bet between me and a local chap who happened to be watching a bit of table tennis one night. Now apparently, according to his quite substantial entourage, the man in question happened to be a 'professional' table tennis player -or so I was told. Anyway, when somehow, I just about managed to get the better of him in a hard fought match, my prize was not only an awful lot of backslapping but one bottle of the local brew. And very nice it was too! (At this point I must offer my most humble apologies; I may have been rubbish on the flugelhorn but one does occasionally have to blow one's own trumpet; especially when there's no-one around to blow it for you!)

On my second evening out at the non-hippy bar, the table tennis table was occupied and so I began chatting away to an Israeli man who'd come away travelling, having just finished his National Service stint. He seemed a nice enough chap but, as with most Israelis, when it came to politics, he could talk the hind leg off Joseph's donkey. You know, having subsequently bumped into quite a number whilst travelling, I can honestly say that I've never met a more politically aware nation. Maybe not surprising perhaps when you consider the amount of turmoil they've been through in their short history as a newly formed nation. (They may well be a very 'oldly formed' nation in their eyes, but let's not go into that here!) The one thing though that this Israeli most liked to talk about, were his two years spent in the army and, more specifically, about the absolutely tyrannical captain whose orders he was bound to follow during that period.

Of course I can't possibly vouch for what this particular captain was like, but, whilst we're on the subject…you know I've always been in favour of some kind of National Service. Not necessarily for quite so long a period as the Israelis perhaps, but surely a six month spell in one of the British armed forces can't be bad, can it? Even if simply to give young male lives, in particular, a little discipline and direction; and wouldn't all the learning and social bonding prove to be the icing on a sadly neglected cake!

Anyway, the picture that this Israeli painted was far from

rosy. Okay, the fact that he enjoyed talking about his experiences wasn't in doubt but, do you know, he physically grimaced as he told me of the things he had to go through during this enforced period of service. But however tough things may have been for him and however much I sympathised, I found it hard to agree with all of this man's political opinions -of which there were many. It just seemed that there was no capacity to see things from the other side or from a slightly different angle; there were no 'shades of grey' whatsoever. And I'm not sure why exactly, but he was rather surprised that someone should disagree with him. Though surprised only in a relative way; for that very same evening, who should stroll into the bar but his old friend, the captain; the very same man who'd supposedly just given him two whole years of hell. I never saw my Israeli mate again.

I began to return nightly to the table-tennis bar but, although quite enjoyable, nothing else much happened there that's worth recalling. Indeed, the only other occurrence of note was my first ever meeting with a Russian. Well, okay, not the very first, as I'd previously spent an evening amongst a gaggle of Soviet truckers - accompanied by raucous rock music and fast flowing vodka- back in the Paris truck park. Still, that was hardly a revelation as none of us could understand a single word that either party was saying. This young Russian chap however, could at least speak some English.

Now, Russia was still very much part of the USSR at this time and so, away from their homeland, it was difficult for Russian nationals to either walk or talk freely without a 'Big Brother' chaperone well within hearing range. True to form, this Russian was no exception. So although he stood alone, he also had his own personal minder in tow, who was busy in conversation with somebody else at the time, but never quite far enough away that he couldn't at least keep a sneaky eye and an ear on his younger mate.

They were a handsome duo, these two -in an Eastern bloc sort of way; both tallish with fair skin and hair, and with typically finely chiselled cheekbones. The only difference really, being in their build. In fact they looked so very similar that they could easily have been older and younger brother, rather like well, Russian dolls. The two of them were apparently working on a *H.E.P. project just south of here which was being funded by the Soviet Union, and they'd come up here for a bit of R&R.
*(Hydro-electric power)

Anyway, that evening, the younger of the Russians was leaning against a post in the bar watching as we played table tennis. He appeared fairly relaxed most of the time but I couldn't help noticing that he would always keep one eye slightly nervously on his more senior mate who lurked in the background. But he'd obviously been paying attention to the brief bits of banter going on around the table tennis table because, when we'd finished the game, he straight away approached me,

"You are English?" he asked.

"Yes" I replied.

"Then you are the first Englishman I have ever spoken to," he said rather slowly and deliberately.

"And you're the first Russian I have ever spoken to," I replied again. He took a quick glance over one shoulder towards his comrade, then turned to me and said in a slightly hushed and secretive voice,

256

"There is one thing I have always wanted to ask an Englishman".

Well, I had no idea what was coming of course, but I eagerly awaited his poignant question that would undoubtedly lead to a good old cultural or political debate, but the question came as a bit of a surprise...

"What do you think of Bob Dylan?"

Do you know, I didn't know quite what so say? In any case I never did get the opportunity to voice my opinion about old Bob before Mikhail was quickly whisked away by his burly minder.

For those living in Colva but not involved in tourism - which at this time was still in its infancy- men appeared to have little option but to become fishermen. Now, the fishing industry here, in its own small way, had been going on virtually unchanged since long before hippies were 'invented'; and that's how it now continued. And largely, because of this one small industry, Colva still very much retained its own identity and flavour and had yet to become just another Western playground. Sure, there were plenty of young Europeans around, but still it required just a little effort to get to and so hadn't completed its transformation by way of the usual stages, namely: discovered by explorers: adopted by hippies: put on the global map by travellers and finally, transformed -usually for the worse- by the presence of hoards of tourists into an international resort. (Though of course, these stages are seldom clearly defined.) Thankfully, Colva at this time had only 'progressed' to stage three in its sad but inevitable destiny to becoming a full blown resort. That is to say, it still appeared a happy-go-lucky teenager with a sense of adventure; just about earning enough pocket money to get by, but without the responsibilities and incumbency of adulthood. (You could perhaps liken this 'metamorphosis' to that of a caterpillar turning into a butterfly, but ironically, in terms of beauty, the transformation is all too often…quite the reverse.)

Now, as previously mentioned, for reasons best known to fishermen, most of the fishing in Colva, apart from the daily small-time beach trawling, was done at night. All the fishing boats would go out each evening, stay at sea all night and return at around five the following morning. Although the exact timing of the morning return is only hearsay for, though always full of good intentions, I never did quite make it down to the beach in time to discover this for myself.

Of course, I've already mentioned about the times when I'd limber up on the beach with a spot of snake hurling, but just occasionally, these fishermen would come across something rather larger; something more 'prestigious' in their nets. This may well have been purely accidental but just once or twice a year, attracted by an abundance of captive fish, dolphins would also get caught up in the nets. Well, it just so happened that whilst I was staying in Colva, this was one of those rare occasions.

Uncharacteristically, that particular morning, I hadn't actually made it along the beach when the fishermen drew up and so had missed the moment that the poor creatures had been brought in. In fact, the first I saw of the two dolphins -or rather black finless porpoises, I think they were- was when they were being held captive in a small natural lagoon just two or three hundred metres up the beach away from the sea. But as I stood there watching, it became obvious that this was indeed a fairly rare event in the calendar, not least because the whole thing was causing such commotion, and it seemed by now, that every fisherman and every fisherman's friend had gathered in the village to celebrate. I could see that there was a great deal of drinking and back-slapping going on at the nearby bar whilst, down at the lagoon edge, others laughed raucously and egged on one of their red and bleary-eyed fishermates as he splashed drunkenly about in the water, thrashing around and occasionally managing to grab hold of one of the poor creatures. He'd then pick it up clear of the water before throwing it back in again, all to great cheers from the bank.

These two animals, of course, were extremely distressed by this and desperately tried to swim away from their tormentor, but it was futile; there was simply nowhere for them to go. I noticed that one of the dolphins had an open wound on its head -presumably from its original capture- and was beginning to flag badly, getting weaker and weaker by the minute. Valiantly the other one swam alongside it in the lagoon in a desperate attempt to support its mate's rapidly tiring body. It was so hard to watch; such an incredibly sad and pitiful sight. I looked on helplessly and, as I did, was joined by a handful of other foreigners. Then, when I could stand it no longer, I went to the fishermen down by the lagoon and tried to reason with them. It was quite hopeless. By now, most of the fishermen were drunk beyond reason and our concern for the creatures only seemed to encourage these men to step up their tormenting. We felt pathetic and inadequate but there seemed little we could do...or was there?

Now, by and large I'd be the first to say that, when with

people of a different culture, it's pretty ignorant to try to apply your own culture's rules i.e. when in Rome do as the Romans! However, on this occasion I'd been informed by a number of local people that eating dolphins, and in particular this species, is strictly illegal here in India. Well, whether or not that is true I wasn't in a position to verify, but anyway, seeing as 'being eaten' seemed likely to be these particular dolphins' fates, the possibility that it was true was more than enough incentive for me to want to do something about it. (Even though obviously, the main objection was to their treatment rather than their eventual fate.) Now, my reasoning for assuming they would eventually end up on a plate was this: that if indeed it was illegal for dolphins to be on the menu here in Goa, then they were unlikely to be sold to anyone for fear of the catchers being caught in the act. On the other hand, these two creatures represented an awful lot of meat to a relatively poor community, and so I thought it equally unlikely that they'd be released back into the sea. No, I decided that of all the options, the most likely one was that they were secretly destined for the local pot. After all, up till now the best I'd ever seen here to supplement a rice-mountain diet was the occasional cornflake-sized dried fish and, even then perhaps, only as a weekend treat!

Anyway, the morning passed slowly and by mid-afternoon the fishermen were still there milling about around the lagoon. By now, the celebrations had subsided somewhat but the alcohol up at the nearby bar was still very much in full flow. I suppose the only upside to all this drinking is that it seemed to render the taunting fishermen even more tired than the dolphins were and so, for now at least, there was a slight lull about the place; a few minutes respite in which the creatures could catch their breath. The majority of the fishermen were now either gathered at the bar nearest to the lagoon or in loosely scattered groups in the village square animatedly regaling other fishy tales.

Whilst all this was going on, I'd had a bit of a meeting with a few gringo friends who'd also witnessed the morning's events. This group consisted of: Andy the Ozzie, Canada Jeff the pig fancier, and Jim and Margot, a young couple from the States. It appeared that we all felt much the same way about what had happened; and so, we decided to formulate a rescue plan. This was it:

With all the fishermen now otherwise engaged in raucous revelry and conversation, Andy and I would sneak down to the lagoon and try to gently coax a dolphin into the shallows. Then, with the fishermen's backs still turned, we'd carefully pass my towel underneath its stomach and Andy would hand the dolphin over to me; and then, finally, simple...I'd run down the beach and release the animal back into the sea! Well, that was the plan at least; beyond that, we hadn't really thought too much. Now, whether the plan would work or not was anyone's guess. It did just occur to us however, that at some point in proceedings I might just get noticed by thirty-odd fishermen if I was to hare off down the beach with their dolphin under my arm. And so, as a precaution, I asked Jeff and Jim to run behind me and to hold back any trouble, should there be any, until I could at least get the creature into the sea. As for dolphin number two well, we'd vaguely hoped somehow to return for it and set it free in much the same way as the first but, for now, that wasn't the priority. Then, after all this, we'd all simply run off down the beach out of harm's way and eh...disappear!

Not that we really expected any trouble; why should we? For some naïve and bizarre reason we thought that once the fishermen had lost their brace of dolphins they would just lose interest; that they would simply shrug their brawny shoulders and give up as if to say "Oh well, it was good while it lasted and those dolphins there would have fed the village for the next two months but, ho hum, win some, lose some." In truth, I suppose there were certain flaws to the plan; flaws that in reality should have slapped us all full in the face like a sadistic fisherman would have with a particularly large and wet kipper; but well, it just didn't. This is what actually happened:

As per plan, the four of us boys, Andy, Jim, Jeff and myself, sneaked down to the lagoon, keeping as low a profile as possible and partly camouflaged by the dappled shade of the surrounding palms. Then, Jim and Jeff held back a bit whilst Andy and I, under the cover of a small bridge spanning the lagoon, waded knee deep into the water. The fishermen up at the bar appeared to have all but lost interest by this time, and so we had enough time to coax one of the dolphins to the side of the lagoon and pass the towel underneath its belly. Then together, we carefully lifted the creature clear of the water and Andy the Aussie, passed it over to me wrapped up in my wet towel; so far so good. Then, as soon as I'd adjusted myself and got a decent grip; that was it…I was off! I broke from the cover of the bridge, quickly went into a kind of stooped canter, gathered momentum and sprinted out of the shade and down the beach towards the sea, as fast as a dolphin laden man could possibly run. Well, I must have run all of ten feet before the alarm went up. From over at the bar a cry rang out across the village and almost in unison, thirty drunken heads span round in my direction. I briefly looked back at where the cry had come from; then turned to face the sea...and ran and ran and ran. Within seconds I was a third of the way down the beach, gasping like an asthmatic, heart thumping in my chest, kicking up sand like a demented meerkat. I could hear the cacophony of angry shouting from behind me but I daren't look back; and the louder the shouting got, the faster and faster I ran. I knew that Jim and Jeff were close behind, just over my shoulder, but then, somewhere behind them was a whole herd of angry fishermen tearing down the beach like a pack of drunk and disgruntled soccer fans. If only I could make the sea then it would all be alright. Still they chased and still I ran; the poor puzzled dolphin wobbling and flapping about in my arms like a giant epileptic frankfurter. The sea got closer and closer; the shouting got nearer and nearer, then suddenly...I was there! I splashed breathlessly through the surf and waded in up to my waist before releasing my grip on the towel. The dolphin, freshly unwrapped, hesitated for just a second and then, with a flick of its tail, swam off out to sea and disappeared amongst the waves. I stood there motionless; the ocean splashing around me, my heart pounding and pounding with adrenalin and exhilaration. Somewhere behind a giant palm tree a huge orchestra struck up a rousing rendition of Born Free and my eyes welled up with the sheer emotion of it all. It was unbelievable; such a wonderful, wonderful feeling. (Actually you'll be surprised to know that I made up the bit about the orchestra but...I think you get my drift!)

I watched for a moment after the dolphin had gone and then turned to wade back to shore. A young Indian chap was walking away clasping his head. It was difficult to comprehend what could have happened to him, but then it suddenly dawned on me: he'd been the only one of the chasing pack to get close to me before I'd released the dolphin, but had paid for his running prowess by being hit on the back of the head by a badly aimed rock…a rock that had been meant for me. This was rather more serious than we'd thought!

Andy the Aussie meanwhile, obviously realising this, had ran off along the beach away from the trouble and was already disappearing into the distance. Jim and Jeff though were still with me and joined me at the water's edge. We looked at one another, panting heavily, and then looked back up the beach from whence we'd come, awaiting the grisly consequences of our actions. We fully expected the fishermen to be there; right there behind us ready to mash us to a pulp. But no; for some inexplicable reason they had stopped just short of reaching us and had already turned and were heading back toward the lagoon. Perhaps it was ok. Perhaps we'd be alright after all! Unfortunately…it wasn't to be. We looked back further towards the lagoon, and even from a distance could see that several of the fishermen had already encircled Jim's girlfriend, Margot. She was understandably near hysterical. Any hopes or thoughts of running away from here or being let off were quickly dashed. There was absolutely no choice; we would have to go back and face the music; though sadly…not that of my romantic imaginary orchestra.

Initially, when the three of us returned to Margot and the surrounding fishermen, we didn't really know what to expect, except that it was unlikely to be a vote of thanks. Jim, of course, immediately put a comforting arm around

Margot and, with that, the fishermen's focus switched from her to us. We were, by now, totally surrounded by a largely drunken and very aggressive circle of men and couldn't understand a single word that was being shouted at us. Though actually, to be fair to them, a little of it may even have been in English, but it was shouted with such venom and aggression as to be rendered incomprehensible in any language!

I tried my level best, of course, to calm the situation. Not that I had a tremendous reputation in the diplomacy department -as yet I was still too young, naïve and 'honest' to be a diplomat- but, I thought, if ever there was a time for a clear head then this was surely it! Anyway, mostly what followed was just an awful lot of finger wagging and shouting; but then, when both Jim and Jeff started to get pushed and kicked about a bit, things weren't looking too good. In fact they were beginning to get a little out of hand. This thought was further reinforced when, through a gap between the fishermen, I spotted two uniformed policemen standing not fifty yards away. They looked directly towards me -catching my eye- and then...slowly turned their backs. Yes, things were definitely getting a little worrying.

Just then, beyond the crowd on the far side of the lagoon, a white van raced into the village, tore round in a tight circle outside the bar and crunched to a halt in a cloud of dust and grit. There was a slight pause -just like the one when Pinkerton's posse are hiding in a train carriage ready to jump out on Butch Cassidy and the Sundance Kid. Then, suddenly...the doors slid ominously open! A handful of exceedingly beefy and well-dressed men calmly stepped down from the van and strode towards us. It was...'The

United Seven Brothers'! (I knew that because it said 'United Seven Brothers' on the van.) They approached us calmly and confidently with a certain air of foreboding; and as they did…so the circle parted. As 'The Brothers' waded into the centre of the circle they looked as cool as cucumber raithas, but I could see that, underneath those calm exteriors, they were no less angry than the fishermen. I thought, "That's all we need; it's one thing coming up against the mob, but quite another taking on the local mafia"! The lead man stormed up to me and jabbed a pointy accusing finger in my face.

"Why you steal our dolphin?" he said aggressively.

Well, at least he spoke our language. It was blatantly clear that for some reason I'd been singled out as the spokesman and ringleader (possibly because I happened to be doing most of the talking for our side; coupled with the fact that I'd not long since been seen sprinting down the beach with a dolphin under my arm!) Anyway, I tried my best to calmly explain the situation, but he didn't seem at all interested in an answer to his question.

"You must pay," he said.

By now the shouting, kicking and pushing had stopped, by the way; the mob obviously had a great deal of respect for these men and it appeared that we were now just a little more officially on trial for our 'crime'. I ignored his demand for money but kept up with the reasoning.

"You must pay!" He repeated even more aggressively.

Again, I did my utmost to explain that we were only doing what we thought was right, adding, at my absolute diplomatic best, that he may just recall that, "It is indeed illegal to eat dolphins in his country". Well, this might not have been the best thing to come up with under the circumstances but, remarkably, it seemed to hit a nerve.

Miraculously, he stopped his furious prodding for a moment and turned to the other United 'Six' Brothers for a brief consultation. (I'd assumed, by this time, that the other Brothers weren't quite up to giving me a good roasting in English and, understandably, I could almost appreciate their frustration at having to rant and rave through an interpreter.) He then turned back to me and still snorting through flared, demerara-brown nostrils, said something none too convincing about catching the dolphins for the local zoo.

Well, I'd never heard mention of a zoo anywhere in the area and anyway, even if there was one, it seemed a highly implausible story. Still, whatever else their version of what the dolphins' fate would be, this did at least give me the excuse I needed to try and change the mood a bit, and to act um, sort of apologetically. Now this tactic, though hardly sincere, definitely helped cool the situation and began to make me feel in just a teensy bit safer a position. But, you know, whatever the truth, the more time that went by, the less likely it seemed we were going to get off the hook (oops, sorry) without forking out at least some compensation. In fact, as things turned out, what the Brothers were asking, no 'demanding' of us, was for the rupee equivalent of over £300! Well, this seemed an unbelievable amount of money to me at this time, and particularly when you consider that I was short by about...£300. Jim, Jeff and I just stood there, looking open-mouthed at one another; then I feebly tried to explain to the Brothers that, "we just didn't have that sort of money." To this, the Brothers all leaned forward as one; it obviously wasn't quite what they wanted to hear. I suddenly started to feel very alone and wondered if I might end my days tied to a block of concrete at the bottom of the Indian Ocean. Then I tried to picture my poor mum's puzzled face weeks later as she'd open a parcel from Colva containing two exceedingly small dried fish wrapped in a waistcoat.

For the moment there was a brief stalemate. The spokes-Brother did some more ranting; I did some more pleading; and there then followed a good twenty minutes of ranting and pleading; but as yet...still no physical violence. Then, something happened; something that I was quite unprepared for. The interpreter, all of a sudden, seemed to have had enough of all this talk. He looked to his team, took a deep breath and, still with blood boiling and teeth gnashing like a demented pit-bull, he came in with just a 'slightly' lower demand. Not much mind, but to me this couldn't have been more significant. It meant that the whole thing, the whole caboose, was actually 'negotiable'. Whatever morals may have been involved before; whatever the rights or wrongs of keeping or releasing these animals; it had all vanished in a wonderfully sweet smelling puff of smoke. It was now down to plain, good old fashioned bargaining: the same rules for a pair of dolphins as it was for say, a pair of tie-up-at-the-ankle purple trousers.

Well, without going into more detail, the upshot of it all was, that after nearly two and a half hours of non-stop negotiation and without so much as a single fist, foot or finger being laid on any one of us -by the Brothers, anyway- I'd somehow managed to get him down to the equivalent of just £27. This, I was assured, was the absolute rock bottom price that they would accept; a totally non-negotiable payment. And though I did try to

268

lower the 'fine' further still, I was left in no doubt whatsoever that he really did mean what he said. The negotiator spoke one last time to the Brothers and then looked me perfectly straight in the eye. His voice now as calm and controlled as a Bond villain…

"You either pay the money or we break your legs".

We decided to pay the money!

So, that was that. Fortunately, both Jim and Jeff agreed to go thirds with me on the compensation payment and so, between us, we just about managed to rake enough cash together to pay off the 'United Seven Brothers.' (In truth, Jim very kindly lent me my share of the money as I was yet again down to my last few rupees.) It was though, probably the happiest I've ever been in my life to be both in debt and indebted; I was just glad that we could make the payment and were all in one piece. And after all, £9 is a pretty small price to pay for a third of a dolphin. Okay, so the deal may have put me back on the banana butties for the foreseeable future but well, at least I still had two functioning legs in order to go and buy them.

Over the following few days I tried to keep a low profile on my visits to the village. Of course it's easy to make light of it all now, but at the time, my brush with the local fishing community was a frightening experience; and so, shortly after this incident, I tended to avoid the village centre when banana shopping, for fear of bumping into one of the Brothers. The trouble is, I was still waiting for money to come through from England and so really I had little choice but to stay put in Colva for the time being. There were a couple of occasions, of course, when I did come across some of the fishermen in the village -hardly surprising when they formed the bulk of the community-but they would do nothing more than look across at me and then their faces would inevitably break into wry smiles. But, you know, I never quite knew what was going on in their minds. There certainly didn't appear to be any hostility there but, all the same, I felt far happier keeping my distance.

Do you know, sadly, I never got to know the fate of the second dolphin; the one we'd failed to come back for. In fact, the last I ever saw of it was as it bounced off down the road in the back of a pick-up truck suspended in a plastic hammock. As it disappeared into the distance I couldn't help wondering…maybe, just maybe the zoo story was true after all. Who knows…I, for one, probably never will.

PS Incidentally, the young boy who caught the rock in the back of the head was fine and lived to run another day.

As I've said, all the time these various goings on were going on, I was still desperately trying to get hold of some money from home. Now, not to have found some way to get this money sent out to me may seem incredibly naïve or disorganised. However, you have to bear in mind that I was merely acting on the information given me at the time (plus the fact that I may have been a little naïve and disorganised!) There was no e-mail at this time of course, and both telephones and telegrams were prohibitively expensive; so any communication with the UK had to be by mail. This was incredibly time consuming -if indeed, it got there at all. There had already been several letters flitting between myself and home -and undoubtedly some, to this day, flitting somewhere in between- and although at long last, I'd received the fifty pound postal order, this had long since been used up. It had now been five weeks since

I'd first tried to get money sent to me in Goa. True, there was money sitting there waiting for me in Bombay, courtesy of my elder sister, but by now I'd lost count of the amount of times I'd tried to get the State Bank of India in Bombay to send it down to me -or more correctly perhaps, to give authority to the Bank in Panaji to issue me with the money. But well, it just seemed hopeless. Every time I made contact with the blessed Bombay bank, I'd either speak to someone who'd say that, "It's impossible to make the transfer", or else I'd speak to someone who'd tell me, "It's absolutely no problem to make the transfer," and then...it still wouldn't arrive anyway. In the meantime, I'd been here so long now and seen so many people come and go through Colva, I'd become absolutely pig sick of waiting. (Sorry again pigs!) I was also severely fed up with being under-fed and of being continuously down on the banana and bread line. In short, I was becoming more and more anxious to get out of Colva and to be on my way again. There was nothing for it; it was time for some last-ditch action. If I couldn't collect the money here in Goa, there was simply no other option...I was going to have to go all the way back to Bombay to get it myself.

Because I had to borrow the fare in order to get to Bombay, I thought it only right, on this occasion, to take the cheapest form of transport available. Sadly for me this was the local bus. So, the following morning I was up early, left what little possessions I had in the beach hut - bar my camera- and set off for Panaji. Here, I could catch a non-stop bus all the way back up to Bombay.

You know, I remember little about the journey there other than it was long, hot, sticky, claustrophobic, boring

271

and above all so bloody, bloody, bloody frustratingly unnecessary; this, a feeling I found hard to shake off for most of the journey. In fact my state of mind, regrettably, was probably all too obvious to my fellow passengers as I sat there like a hormonal teenager moodily stewing in my own pent up juices. Hardly a way to conduct yourself in a foreign country I know, though even engulfed in such a black cloud as I was, it did appear to me mildly amusing that, as I was on a bus, I should have to conduct myself at all! It's just that I so hated backtracking like this. However, there was one thing I had to focus on: soon, at last, I would have my money, everything would be okay and I'd be back on the road again, heading south.

The next morning in Bombay, as soon as was physically possible, I was standing at the counter of the main branch of the State Bank of India. There was the usual protracted wait of course, and then I'd give all my personal details to every single bank employee and his collective dog, before being directed to a different counter only to repeat the whole thing yet again. And each time, the chap at that particular desk would painstakingly note down all of my details: Name; address in UK; address in India; next of kin; next of next of kin; colour of hair and eyes; last bowel movement...but then, after some considerable time, I did actually manage to speak to someone whom I presumed to be just a little higher up the postal pecking order. This man listened intently as I told him the whole story of all the ins and outs and ups and downs, and how I came to be there standing in front of him. Then, he sauntered over to a pile of papers somewhere behind him and began flicking through them. Well, I could scarcely believe my eyes and ears but, lo and behold, miracle of miracles, he actually had a record of the money transaction from England. Great! Fantastic!

"So, can I have the money?" I said excitedly.

There was a pause. The clerk looked up slowly from his papers....

"I'm afraid not", he said, "We have received a request from our main branch in Panaji, Goa, asking that the money be issued from there."

I looked at the clerk dumbfounded, momentarily speechless.

"Ah-ah well yes, that's true; I 'did' ask to collect it from there (about sixteen years ago) but, but, but...I'm here now; I can collect it from here...can't I?" I gibbered.

"I'm sorry sir, the request was confirmed this morning, you must collect the money in Panaji".

I turned and left the bank in silence.

Do you know it was touch and go whether to save my remaining money for the long trip back to Goa or to go to the nearest bar and get absolutely legless. At that very moment in time, I have to say that the latter definitely had the most appeal. But thankfully, on this occasion, what little sense I still possessed did prevail and I shortly caught yet another hot, sticky, claustrophobic, smelly, dirty and even more bloody boring bus all the way back to Goa.

The next day I found myself, once more, back in Panaji and, within minutes, had been to the bank and at long, long, long last collected my money. Then, back on the beach in Colva, I quickly packed up my meagre belongings, donated my inherited pots and pans to a nice neighbouring Goan family and, without so much as a cursory wave to even one of the United Seven Brothers, caught the first bus out of Goa heading south.

CHAPTER 17

- DIVAS, BACKWATERS AND PEANUT BUTTER MAKERS -

Goa to Kerala

The bus from Margao in Goa departed at 5.30pm and didn't arrive in Mangalore until 3.30am the next morning, so I had plenty of time to reminisce about all the goings on during the past few weeks. Goa had given me such exciting memories, and now that it was all behind me, it was nice to be able just to sit back on the bus, gaze out of the window and reflect. Not that all the memories were good ones of course, they certainly weren't; but somehow, after a time, the thought of even the bad ones made me smile. Such is life!

By now though, despite having been away from home for over three months, there was one thing I was quite sure of: I wasn't going to make it to Australia. Not for financial reasons mind, but because I knew that over the past few weeks I'd caused my Mum so much stress, so much anguish; it just simply wouldn't be fair. The last letter I'd received from her had obviously been written in tears (it would've been a damned sight easier to read if it had been written in ink) and so I'd decided that, whatever else happened, I would soon be on my way home again; well…via Sri Lanka.

Now, for all I know, Mangalore may well be a very nice place to visit but, even after having to endure an all night bus journey, I was still keen to put some more miles under my belt. For however nice Goa had been, it felt great to be moving on down the map again. I was now anxious to reach that little lump at the bottom of India and to catch up with all the transient friends who'd come and gone through Colva. So when I discovered that Mangalore had a railway station there was simply no contest, it was an easy choice to make; within an hour of arriving I was on the first train out of there and bound for Cochin.

You know, I've never been very good at sleeping on public transport at night which, on long journeys, is both terribly frustrating and incredibly boring. Frustrating, because it's such an ideal opportunity to catch up on some much needed sleep -and you know darned well that if you don't, you're going to pay for it later- and boring, quite obviously, because at night, there's not a whole lot to see. By contrast, stick me on a bus or in a train by day and I'll be fighting to stay awake before my bum hits the seat. This is perhaps even more frustrating than at night, because by day, there's...so much to see.

So invariably -especially after a sleepless overnight bus journey- if I then continue to travel by day, I'm battling hard to keep my eyes open and take in the scenery, but end up drifting in and out of consciousness for much of the route. Of course, with this in mind, it would seem perfectly logical to sit down on the train and say to yourself, "Okay, I don't want to miss 'all' the scenery by fighting to stay awake the whole journey so, I'll totally give in to sleep and get a few quality hours in first, then I can at least enjoy the rest of the journey fully awake." Does it work? Does it heck! Because as sure as eggs is eggs, as soon as you give yourself totally over to the idea of sleep...you don't feel tired enough!

The first couple of hours out of Mangalore was just such a time. I was absolutely determined to stay awake, but within minutes of settling down, the scenery started blurring and I began drifting in and out of consciousness. (A bit like being hurtled in a wheelchair through a gallery of Monet's interspersed with dark tunnels). This time though it was different; for though I did fight to keep the scenery in focus, within a short time my tunnels soon became longer and longer, the Monet's smudged to a dark pea soup and, before I knew it, I was totally out for the count. How wonderful! How snoozingly blissful! Do you know, I probably only slept for an hour, but it was just enough to give me a new lease of life -or if not a lease, then at least a short term rental.

After I'd woken, on this particular occasion I decided that if I were to have any real chance of continuing to enjoy the scenery, then I'd have to resort to standing up at the open carriage doorway. This proved to be the perfect solution, for not only could I stand on the step with all the room I wanted, but to feel the wind on my face, to both hear and smell all the sounds and scents that came my way, was simply sublime. And not only that, but I'd have a totally unobstructed view of all that passed by. This, as opposed to the usual views from the carriage windows where, inevitably, everything is partially obscured by the horizontal metal bars characteristically put across all Indian train windows to prevent people from boarding the train without a ticket. (An interesting idea, these bars, given that so many of the passengers still ride on the outside of the train anyway; and, paradoxically, should the train crash, the roof may well be the safest place to be.) But, in my experience, half the locals that do enter via the door don't bother with a ticket anyway. After all, it would seem that in India, it's not an offence to ride without a ticket, only to be caught without one. Strange how so many don't pay for a seat but use one; whilst I, rebel that I am, do pay…but don't!

Anyway, I decided that if it is indeed permitted, then for me at least, the best possible place to be on a train journey, is right there on the carriage doorstep. Consequently, I ended up spending more time half out of trains in India than I did actually sitting within them. Admittedly though, standing on a doorstep which happens to be travelling at 50mph can have its drawbacks. Not least when, at times, there is upwards of seven or eight other bodies fighting to join you on your few square inches of foot polished metal because the carriage is full. Things then can start to get a little hairy. Add to this, that nobody standing inside the train can see what's happening to those on the outside; well, when the pushing and shoving starts, as it surely will do, that's when it becomes all too easy to leave the train before you're quite ready to; especially when you only have a two finger hold on one of the two metal handles outside the doorway, and that this handle has been liberally lubricated by the grease of a thousand fingers. Now that really is exciting!

The last few hours before reaching Cochin were quite beautiful; not in a terribly dramatic way, but one which was wonderfully warm, simple, green and rural. The train had emptied a lot by now -mostly I gathered, of people who did actually want to get off- and so by the time I'd arrived I was in a quiet and mellow mood, and would have been quite happy to continue in the same vein for another few hours.

Unfortunately though, on this occasion, perhaps I'd become just that bit too mellow, for I didn't actually notice that we'd arrived at Cochin until after the train had started to pull away again. I'd been gazing dreamily out of the window and assumed that this was simply one of the many stops en route south, and it wasn't until seeing the words 'COCHIN' glide slowly by that I realised where we were. Well, to be honest, it gave me quite a start; I didn't really know quite what to do. So, without thinking too much, I jumped to my feet, grabbed my rucksack, stuck it on my back and started off down the carriage as fast as I possibly could; parting and scattering the 'standing room only' passengers as I went. Then, by the time I'd reached the door at the end I was already in full panic mode and sweating profusely. The train, meanwhile, was rapidly gathering speed and, as I rounded the corner into the entrance area, I was horrified to see that the step was already blocked by a hoard of bodies. I had no choice; it was now or never. I barged my way through the small crowd and found myself teetering on the edge of the step; half in, half out; rucksack still on my back but facing in totally the opposite way to the direction of travel. There was nothing for it; I couldn't go back; I'd passed the point of no return. I leapt for the platform, hit it with both feet together and was promptly catapulted violently backwards, doing a complete back somersault before landing face down on the platform.

Several waiting passengers witnessed this of course, but were stood back slightly bemused and serious looking, as if I'd done it on purpose. I almost expected them to suddenly produce score cards for my attempted 'triple salchow…with pike'.

Shortly though, as the train disappeared off down the line, I managed to catch my breath a little and was helped to my feet by a couple of concerned onlookers. Then I dusted myself down, thanked them for their 'belated' concern and walked, slightly bruised and embarrassed, out of the station.

It had been an unusual way to arrive in Cochin and one which I felt in no hurry to repeat. Still, it's nice to make a bit of an entrance sometimes and I'm sure it's not every day the locals see an Englishman parachuting from a train. (Diary note: If you really must jump backwards from a moving train, make sure you're wearing a helmet and carrying an exceedingly well stuffed rucksack!)
Do you know, despite the unorthodox introduction, it felt good to be this far south. And then, as soon as I'd gathered my composure, I found myself a local bus going over to Fort Cochin.

When I arrived, as usual, I had a quick look at the available accommodation and then checked into the Excel Hotel for the princely sum of seven rupees a night. It was an interesting sort of place, the Excel; maybe sometime in the distant past the hotel had been the 'Excellent' but by now was, at the very least, a 'lent' short.

I'd come a long way over the past couple of days and was a little too weary to do a lot of sight seeing, so I opted for a quick shower and an early-ish night. Well, that was the intention. As things turned out, the shower was neither quick nor the night early. The main reason being, that the shower controls were clearly operated by a sadistic peeping Tom. It worked fine until you were well and truly lathered up with soap but, the minute you stepped under the shower for a rinse-off, there was absolutely nothing but a vacuous glugging. Then, after ten minutes of jumping up and down stark naked, head to foot in soap and screaming various phrases to do with copulation...at a steel pipe; the thing would cough and splutter into action, allowing just enough water through to rinse a leg. Next, the shower would glug to a complete halt and the whole process would be repeated over and over again; waiting, cursing and rinsing until finally, after I'd stood there with a fully shampooed mop of hair for half an hour without a single drop of water issuing from the spout, it really was the last straw. I screamed at the pipe and gave it a hefty whack with the side of my fist. The shower gurgled and gargled, belched and burbled and spat out an indignant egg cupful of water...and I gave up.

By the end of my shower, I was considerably more hot and bothered than when I got into the bloody thing, so I decided that what I badly needed was a calming tonic in the form of a couple of beers before bedtime. This had always seemed to do the trick for me as far as stress-busting was concerned. Perhaps it harps back to my memories as a young teenager when, for some reason, I was given a miniature of Cointreau in my Christmas stocking. Every time I was sent to my room -which wasn't often I hasten to add- I'd sit on my bed and take a quick swig in defiance of my parents, as if to say, "There, that'll teach you!" Though actually, what it was supposed to teach them I'm not quite sure. I suppose it's just that, as much as I loved and respected my dad, I used to get so incredibly frustrated because he wasn't really one for listening to two sides of an argument; and this absolutely infuriated my sense of fair play, even at such a tender age.

Anyway, where was I? Oh yes…After I'd dried off a bit, and still with shampoo caked hair, I was in no mood to go out and so I settled on having a couple of beers in front of the hotel reception television. This, I thought, would surely be preferable to sitting alone, but after less than half an hour of listening to some obese and obsessively smiley Indian girl wailing Hindi songs at me, I retired to my room. Now, I'm not normally one to moan but well, when I say room, I do mean this in the loosest possible sense of the word. It was actually more a large open-topped grocery box with a bed in it. In fact the 'hardboard' walls here were so short of the ceiling that, had the hotelier been a little more on the ball, he could easily have fitted another whole storey on top. This meant that, although I was two rooms away from reception, the TV was still painfully well within earshot. Not only that, but it also meant that the clouds of exceedingly large and voracious mosquitoes in the area had the whole run of the place...and of me!

So, all in all, it was one 'hell' of a memorable night at The Excel, most of it spent wide awake of course; but I did eventually manage to slap myself to sleep; rhythmically splatting mosquitoes about my body like a horizontal, Bavarian folk dancer; and all to the accompaniment of that fat gyrating woman shrilling from the reception TV: the body of an Eastern European shot-putter and a voice like dragged fingernails on a blackboard.

To add to all this, the air was incredibly still that night which meant of course, that I wasn't. In fact the

281

temperature in Cochin, even during the night time, was such that the slightest movement produced half a gallon of sweat, and this combination of both heat and mosquitoes here was enough to drive the insane, insane. It didn't seem to matter how hard I tried to lie absolutely still; spreading out every leg, arm, finger and toe; all through that long, long night, beads of sweat would quickly form on my forehead, gather together into large globules, and then slowly run down either temple before dripping down onto the pillow. And as if that wasn't annoying enough, I could never be absolutely sure whether every little running trickle was simply sweat or the tiny pattering feet of yet another pesky mosquito; so just in case, I'd whack myself in the temple every few seconds, splashing sweat everywhere in the process and making myself even more hot and even more bothered.

Like all bad nights though, morning did eventually and mercifully arrive and, refreshed from my full hour of sleep, I padded along to the shower to see if I could coax some water from the pipe before the evil Water Fairy woke up.

In truth, I expected little in the way of water and well...I wasn't disappointed. But, you know, I felt far too tired today to have a slanging match with a shower pipe. I stood there in the cubicle, hunched and baggy-eyed, contenting myself with a refreshing dribble of water on my forehead. Then, I towelled off the night's sweat before packing and leaving the hotel.

The one feature here in Cochin that makes the town quite unique within India, and one which I was keen to see, are its Chinese fishing nets. They're strange contraptions really, rather like an outsized medieval ducking stool, only instead of an accused witch in a chair at the wet end, there's a net. But, whilst they're certainly very photogenic things, it did appear to me to be an awful lot of trouble to go to, in order to catch a few fish. These contraptions are just so massive; so huge in fact, that they appear to be fashioned from old telegraph poles, and yet, the net at the other end is hardly bigger than a family table cloth or the nets I'd seen chucked into the sea by loan fishermen. I suppose, by the simple fact that there are a number of them here, they must do the trick, but I can't help wondering. I don't know, perhaps they've been erected merely as a talking point. And if that's the case well, they've certainly done their job (as verified here!) Anyway, whether they work or not...they're quite fascinating.

The second reason that I needed to go to Cochin was to collect mail, or more correctly, film. You see, on my route down through India, it had seemed impossible to buy anything other than 100 ASA print film, and even then it was unlikely to be very useful (for "store in a cool dry place" read, "roast under glass for several months and serve hot an' crispy").

What I particularly wanted was a couple of rolls of Kodachrome 64 (a specific type of colour negative or slide film) and so, when I'd first reached India, I'd written home for my Mum to send some out to me. But as I'd only expected to be in Goa for a week or so, it seemed good sense to have the films sent to my next definite port of call -that being Cochin. However, even with over a month's delay back in Colva -waiting for money- I still managed, not only to reach Cochin before my special film arrived, but also to leave it. The problem was, I had no way of knowing just how long I'd have to wait for the film or indeed if it would arrive at all; which left me in a quandary as to whether I should wait or move on.

It was annoying to think that the films might arrive shortly after I'd left only to sit there and be served up hot and crispy to somebody else months later. Fortunately though, unbeknown to me; my mother -bless her short and baggy cotton socks- had had the foresight to send the two films by registered post, in the 'unlikely' event that they might go astray. This proved to be rather a good move because, although I wasn't able to wait for them to arrive in Cochin, at least the staff at the GPO there were on the ball and duly returned the package to the sender - not that I had any doubt of course. They arrived back in England just one week short of....two years later!

That afternoon, I took the short ferry ride back to Ernakulam on the mainland. I was keen to get rid of my pack again and so forked out a whole 10 rupees on a 'room with fan' at the Basoto Hotel. I'd decided by now that a fan here was most definitely a necessary luxury -if you can have such a thing! But this wasn't just because of the oppressive heat in these parts but for the bloody hummingbird sized mosquitoes which, mercifully, happen to have a distinct dislike of any moving air -or maybe they do like it, but at least the buggers can't fly in it. It was a horrible little room though. It may have had a fan and four solid-ish walls that actually reached the ceiling, but it was awfully depressing. More like a cell built specifically for solitary confinement than a hotel room. I couldn't help feeling I was in a scene from Midnight Express; I had to get out of there fast. I grabbed a uniform that was ten sizes too big for me (not really) and quickly went out onto the street. I then spent the remainder of the day wandering around the town, hugging the narrow shadows outside the shops and houses.

Later, I came across a woodcarver's and had a leisurely browse around his premises. I seriously toyed with the idea of buying and sending one of his gargantuan elephants back to England. They were incredibly beautiful things, each the size of a coffee table, highly polished and with a richly coloured and varied grain accentuating the contours of the elephant's body. There were no joins whatsoever, so that every one of them can only have been hewn from a single tree. But as much as I admired and dearly wanted one, it did seem rather an unnecessary extravagance. And anyway, after my experience with the Kodachrome, it did occur to me that even if I did send one home, I may not live long enough to receive it!

That evening I went to the local cinema where 'Jaws II' was being advertised. It may not have been my first choice in films, but I rather liked the idea of seeing an English speaking film dubbed into Hindi. In the event though, it wasn't to be. The whole film was shown -to an Indian audience and one English visitor- in American-English with Hindi sub-titles. Though, to tell the truth, I wasn't particularly bothered either way; just as long as there wasn't some fat gyrating Indian woman wailing in it. Besides, whatever the language of the film, it was every bit as entertaining watching the audience as it was the screen. Why, they appeared to have as much interest in the Hindi sub-titles as I did. Blow the plot, the important thing for them was just how many people Jaws could munch his way through. Every time that distinctive cello preceded the appearance of the shark there were excited whispers of anticipation from all over the auditorium; and then, shortly afterwards, Jaws would pop up and chew some poor chap completely in half, the sea would turn to bright red and a great collective shriek of delight would rise up from the audience. What a macabre lot! I left the cinema both amused and bemused, and was jostled out onto the street by an excited chattering army of shark fans.

Outside, the night was still as warm and sticky as a sauna and so, not wanting to return to my cell, I grabbed a roadside snack and went for a stroll. The snack was a sort of deep fried coconut and banana flavoured ball of dough thing called an unniyappam (I believe); one of the few things in fact which I could buy on the street that I knew wouldn't be laden with chillies. There seemed little to do around here at night -other than eat or watch people being eaten- so after I'd finished my dough ball I went back to the hotel. Then, after a quick shower in which I actually managed a wet wash, I lay on my sheet in my sauna; spread-eagled in the 'maximum surface area' position pondering, "I wonder if Jaws ever thinks to himself...'think I'll just pop out for an Indian'!" Then, with this thought in mind, I was shortly hypnotised to sleep by the clunk-clunk-clunking of the overhead fan.

I was woken at some time during the middle of the night with pains in the kidney region. But being as I was alone, it was night time and I was in India, there wasn't a whole lot I could do for the moment. I did try hard to think of other things to take my mind off the pain, but it didn't seem to work. I even tried shallow breathing in order to ease it a little, but this didn't help much either. There was nothing I could do for now but grin and bear it. I curled up in the foetal position and hoped that the morning would come round soon. Then, at some point I must have managed to drift off to sleep; and when I woke to see the early morning light, the pain was gone.

The third and final reason for wanting to visit Cochin was for the so called, backwater trips. You see, a couple of hours by bus from Ernakulam lies the small town of Allepey, and it's from here that a beautiful network of canals spreads out south allowing yet another glimpse into the very different lives of the people in this little corner of India. Here, it's a far, far cry from the great desert of Rajasthan to the north; and if you're able to venture this far south it truly makes you appreciate just what a tremendously diverse country India really is. But its staggering diversity doesn't lie only in its incredible range of habitats -from desert to jungle to the foothills of the world's highest mountains- but also in the vast variety of people who live within those places. Indeed, in spite of all the bureaucratic hassles, of which there are many, I find it a country immensely difficult to dislike. If indeed you can call India 'a country'; for in many ways, like Africa, it's far more a continent full of several very different countries: each with its own climate, customs, food, language and people.

At first light, I packed my things and walked down to the canal. It was beautifully tranquil down by the water; hardly a person in sight. I strolled along the bank a bit and came across a friendly faced woman, perhaps in her forties, sitting alone. She hardly spoke any English at all but I decided to leave my bag with her. Now this might, to many, seem stark raving bonkers but well, sometimes you just get a feeling don't you. The thing is, I like to think that 'most' of the people in the world are basically good; that nobody is born bad and it's only other people and the incidents in your life which shape you as a person.

Now obviously, I'm only too aware that in a relatively poor country such as India, it may appear to Westerners that rather too many people here have been 'shaped' in the wrong way. But, not only is that terribly unfair -and untrue- but it also certainly doesn't change my philosophy. In fact, I find that it's the simplest thing in the world to sort the good from the not so good, because those who are trying to extract something will invariably come to you; and this, of course, leaves the rest: that vast, vast majority out there who, in all likelihood, will be exceedingly good and nice people. In other words, as I've said before, it really can be a case of, 'better the devil you don't know'! If you want to find a good and decent person pretty well anywhere in the world, do just that, go and find them; don't let them find you! Anyway, enough philosophising; where was I? Oh yes...

It was a beautiful morning in Allepey and so I went for a stroll along the canal (all the nicer for not being encumbered by a rucksack). People along the water were still beginning to stir here, and as the sunlight shone weakly through the bottom of the palm trees, the only audible sound was the soft and gentle wafting of egret wings as they flew up and down the canals. I jumped into the only boat showing any signs of life and sat with a lone boatman whilst he patiently awaited his first passengers. The two of us smiled and nodded at one another, then just sat there in perfect silence, bathed in the early morning stillness before the start of another day. What a wonderful contrast, I thought, to the busy, dusty streets not an hour from where we now sat. What a far cry from the hasslers and hustlers of the nearby town; the hot and sticky, sleepless, mosquito-ridden nights. We sat in silence a while longer, both lost in thought. Then I left the boatman for a while and went off to fetch my things.

When I arrived, my rucksack was exactly where I'd left it beside the little lady. She was still sitting on the bank, still smiling. I thanked her and returned to the boat. By now, other passengers had begun to board and the small boat was already rocking and rolling with large rounded women, skinny husbands and their wide-eyed offspring as they walked the narrow plank; all of them weighed down by packages from town. Then, everyone took up their places on the wooden slatted benches, and I took up mine. Shortly, the motor spluttered to life and we were chugging off slowly down a cool, green glassy canal, sending tiny ripples scurrying to the banks and causing the snowy white egrets to take flight just ahead of us.

As the sun rose further through the trees, the banks gradually started to come to life. Over on the far side, a couple of young heads bobbed by, their bodies partly obscured by the lush vegetation. A scraggy cow, head down and tethered to a short rustic post, munched away contentedly. Occasionally a lone hut would come into view, cut off from the outside world were it not for this small canal. A woman in a colourful and ample dress was stooped at the water's edge cleaning blackened cooking pots; others walked along the banks, their heads heavily laden with buckets, fruits or firewood. And just down from their ever-watchful mothers, small children washed and played in the water, breaking the near silence with their high-pitched squeals of laughter.

It was as near perfect a picture as you could possibly paint and, all too soon, it was over. After just a few hours of this serene heaven, I arrived in Kottayam feeling de-toxed, de-stressed and de...liciously mellow. Such a shame then that, as I stepped from the boat, I completely missed the gangplank and very narrowly avoided being 'de-bagged'! But, having recovered my composure, I then decided to hop onto a bus -albeit gingerly- and went on to Kumiley, way up in the Kerala hills.

The road up to the village was little more than a farm track but, once again, it was a stunningly beautiful journey. At one time, of course, all this would have been thick, thick jungle, but now the trees stood isolated in outcrops: lonely islands in a sea of tea bushes.
.
There was just one other Western traveller on the bus. He was wearing his 'I'm trying to blend in' hippy gear. I didn't notice him at first -clearly it works- but then, at a second glance, I noticed the waist-length greying hair and matching beard. This man wasn't just a new-age hippie, I thought, but about the closest I'd seen yet to the real McCoy! I tottered down the aisle and plonked myself next to him. It turns out his name was Trevor, an Aussie; and though he looked a great deal older was probably no more than in his late forties. Now, apparently, Trevor lived for most of the year up in the mountains of Nepal, scratching a living by making his own peanut butter and selling it to homesick Westerners. He'd been up there now for over six and a half years; but I wondered how on earth a person can survive up in the Himalayas for so long on nothing but the proceeds from peanut-butter sales. It must be a pretty meagre existence surely, even by Indian standards. Trevor

however, had another string to his bow. He may well have been paid peanuts for his peanut butter, but in order to live in relative comfort up in the mountains, he relied on the sales of something rather 'different', rather more lucrative. Apparently, every winter Trevor would shut up shop and head down south to the hills of Kerala. But this wasn't an annual migration or holiday in order to avoid the harsh Nepalese winter, but purely a business trip.

Now, according to sources -namely, the reliable and extensive travellers' grapevine- a certain area in the hills of Kerala had just started producing marijuana; and by all accounts it was reported to be absolutely 'top class ganja'. Consequently, Trevor would come down by train each year and return a couple of weeks later with as much grass as he could possibly carry. This, as it happens, amounted to two whacking great sackfuls of the stuff. I asked him if he didn't think it just a bit dodgy humping two sackfuls of illegal substances the length of India; but he assured me that, compared to the rewards, the risk was almost negligible. Well, that may or may not be the case, but I found it hard to believe the local police could ever be taken in by his 'ethnic wear'. I don't know, perhaps he just always managed to avoid contact with them. But anyway, in a little over six years of grass smuggling, there'd only been one single occasion when Trevor had been confronted by an official. Apparently, he'd been approached by this train guard who'd shown more than a passing interest in his 'luggage', and this had forced Trevor to jump ship -or rather, train- mid-journey. Luckily for Trevor, on this occasion he was unhurt, and they hadn't bothered interrupting the train's schedule simply for one overboard hippy, and so he'd lived to smuggle another day.

That evening we left the bus at Kumiley and checked into a place called, The Mini-lodge. As was usual, away from the more tourist frequented areas, the place was less than salubrious. I gave the sheets the usual bedbug and stain check -as if there were any other choice in town- and paid for the room. Actually, to be honest, this bed check was hardly worth the trouble as it was always extremely hard to spot bedbugs -though easy to feel them- and most of the sheets I ever came across had at least one or two sinister looking, pub-ceiling coloured stains on them, so what was the point! To be on the safe side though, I'd now taken to using my own trusty sheet sleeping bag every night as a rather thin but reassuring barrier between me and the hotel sheets. Mind you, at times I'm not so sure my own sheet was anymore wholesome as it rarely saw things such as soap or washing powder; but well, at least the dirt was of my own making.

NB.   Whilst on the subject of sheet sleeping bags, I personally have always travelled with a 'homemade' variety. The reason being, that the ones you buy in shops are almost invariably too short to allow for a pillow unless you happen to sleep with knees bent and your toes all scrunched up in the bottom. And for those of us who don't sleep with knees bent and toes scrunched: using a bought bag invariably means that, whilst your body is safely cocooned away from all sorts of nasties from the neck down, your head -or more importantly your face- will poke out of the top and may spend the whole of the night squashed up against a motley patchwork of dried spittle, hair grease and earwax; umm, lovely.   No, if you're anything over five foot...make your own!

Within half an hour of arriving at our hotel, Trevor was deep in concentration and busily fashioning a dozen or so rollies on the bedside table. These, he informed me, would be just enough to see him through the evening. Not that he was a particularly heavy smoker mind; it's just that his homemade cigarettes were the thickness of anorexic matchsticks, as seems the fashion amongst 'roll your own' types. This certainly wasn't for me though, and so I left Trevor to it and went out to have a look around town. Now, Kumiley wasn't exactly big on sights...or big on anything really; but then part of its charm lay in this very fact. However, it wasn't only that it was comfortably small, simple and relaxed; it also just happened to sit at as near perfect an altitude as you could wish for; still warm of course, but just high enough in the hills to counteract the ferocity of the sun and to make things well, more pleasant.

I wandered off down the main street looking for somewhere to sit and eat; then, although enjoying the peace and quiet, I somehow felt compelled to seek out the source of a distant drumbeat. After ten minutes of inquisitive honing in, I eventually arrived at a small café blasting heavy rock from every open orifice. Inside, a small posse of Westerners were sat round the far table nursing small glasses of milky tea, but when I entered, disappointingly, hardly one of them managed so much as a glance in my direction. It seemed they were all far too lost in the music to care about anything or anybody else; yet again, calmly marinating in that unmistakable and sweet-smelling cloud of ganja smoke. I thought it sadly ironic really; they had all the time in the world but...no time for anyone. I turned, feeling a little disillusioned, and left.

No sooner had I rejoined the quiet little streets though, when I was greeted by two exceedingly rosy and smiling faces. It was Katie and Julie, the couple of young English girls whom I'd spent time with back in Goa. "What a lovely surprise" I thought, and especially after my recent rebuff. And so I immediately invited them to join me, and a short while later we found ourselves chattering away the balmy evening together in a serenely quiet café far away from the sex 'n' drugs and rock 'n' roll. Well, for me it was potentially very close indeed to the sex, but alas, only geographically!

Of course, at one time, Katie and Julie had been my beach hut neighbours back in Colva, and, in actual fact, had been there on that very beach with me when I'd munched my way through all those fully-clothed prawns. Thankfully though, on that occasion, neither of the girls had fancied my crunchy-coated crustaceans and so had been spared the same fate as me -alas, they didn't seem to fancy anything else either. Although…come to think of it, being a friendly neighbour as I was, I did actually get to spend one whole night in the girls' hut, which is fairly remarkable isn't it? After all, it's got to be every young man's dream surely: a night in a beach hut with two young, free and single girls! Well, in theory, yes! Sadly, on this occasion, it was indeed a 'remarkable' night but only because I don't recall having a single carnal thought the whole time I was there. Not that these girls weren't nice you understand; they were. I don't know; I can't really explain it! I guess that, even normally rampant hormones have to have a day off sometimes, even if you are in your early 20's.

CHAPTER 18

- YOU CAN'T SEE THE GRASS FOR THE TREES -

In Kerala

The next day we were off on our separate ways again. Katie and Julie were pressing on down south, and though it was sorely tempting to join them, I was still keen to see how Trevor would get on at the marijuana plantation further up in the hills. And so, I said goodbye to the girls and then Trevor and I boarded yet another bus and started on the long and winding road leading ever upwards through the jungle.

It had never occurred to me before but, after a time, I asked Trevor where we were heading,

"A place called Double Cutting", he replied. I thought for a moment...

"Double Cutting" ? I said quizzically. I wasn't sure why but, for some reason I couldn't quite put my finger on, the name instantly rang a bell. I sat there pensively gazing out of the window, racking my brains. Then, all of a sudden the rupee dropped! I reached into my pocket, rummaged through my wallet and pulled out a dog-eared scrap of paper with the words, 'Double Cutting' scrawled across it. It had been given to me by the young Swiss chap I'd met way, way back in Lahore in Northern Pakistan. Now, Christ knows how but, there had obviously been some kind of mind-boggling misunderstanding or language breakdown on one of our parts because, the one and only occasion I'd ever spent time with this Swiss chap was when discussing the possibility of buying gemstones in Sri Lanka. Well somehow, extraordinary as it may seem, by the end of that conversation I'd ended up with a small scrap of paper which would lead me to a tiny hamlet up in the Kerala hills; unmarked on any map and without so much as a single signpost. It was an incredible and unlikely coincidence. There I was, an Englishman, asking for an address to buy gems in Sri Lanka but, quite unknowingly, had been directed by a Swiss chap in Northern Pakistan...to a ganja plantation in Southern India. A strange life, isn't it!

Anyway, after slowly zigzagging our way up through the jungle, we eventually arrived at what the bus driver assured Trevor was the place we wanted. How on earth anybody could know this I'm not sure, for there was neither a sign, nor sign of life; whilst all around us there were green, green hills as far as the eye could see. I'd had no idea what to expect when we'd arrived, except maybe a community of some sort or other. But there appeared to be nothing; nothing at all but the tagliatelle thin ribbon of tarmac on which we stood, snaking its way up ahead and then...trees, trees and more trees.

We got down and walked off up the hill, slowly following behind the bus as it gradually pulled further and further away. Then, we watched as it rounded the bend ahead and disappeared. All went quiet; the huge surrounding vegetation absorbing all sound like a giant primeval sponge. A few short minutes later though and a distant baritone purring broke the silence. I looked up to see our little matchbox bus reappear around yet another bend way off in the distance; but then, just as quickly, it vanished again; finally engulfed by the thick, all enveloping green of the forest.

It was Trevor who spotted the small wooden shack hidden in the undergrowth just up ahead. We approached and saw a man grubbing about in the dirt outside, and so Trevor struck up a sort of stilted conversation with him - interspersed with exaggerated sign language- and mentioning someone called josé. The man -who proved equally eloquent in the arm department- gabbled something unrecognisable back, but also occasionally threw in a few 'Josés' and so we set off in the direction he indicated.

Shortly, yet another well camouflaged shack came into view, nestled up amongst the trees just back from the road. (Having said that there was nothing here, for all I know, there could have been a whole town of exceedingly well camouflaged huts.) But before we could even get close, a man appeared from around the side of the hut and Trevor called out to him,

"José?" He shouted hopefully. This time there was little to decipher. The man smiled and enthusiastically beckoned, and so we followed him up the little hill away from the road.

The light was already dimming by now and so, when we arrived at josé's shack, we were warmly welcomed then offered a bowl of hot soup and a rattan mat for the night. There was no electricity here of course and the only light in the hut came from two small stubby candles. And so, by 8pm, having finished our soup and with little in the way of conversation, we were shown to our rattan mats which were screened off from the living area by a heavily patterned curtain at the far end of the hut. Well, we may have not travelled far, but it was wonderfully cool and blissfully mosquito free that night. Up here in the hills it was 'unfortunately' just too high for the darling little creatures to survive -though, inevitably, there's always the one rogue mozzie who hasn't read the guide book- so I quickly settled down on the near bare concrete floor and fell asleep dreaming of deeply sprung rattan mats.

NB Whilst I think of it...for most of the people in the world, of course, electricity is still very much an unattainable luxury, and so they simply 'live by the light'. And this, after all, is surely the sensible way to live. It doesn't necessarily mean that their days or nights are either longer or shorter than ours though, just that they are structured differently. So, whilst we in the West rely heavily on the electric light bulb, the far more sensible majority of people on this planet, rise with the sun and then, when it becomes night...they call it a day!

Anyway, up here in Double Cutting was no exception. By 5am we were all up and dressed. Well 'up' at least, as it was far too cold at night to get out of our clothes, and so there was no dressing to be done. José, predictably had risen before us and had already prepared a small wood fire which was smoking and crackling away at the kitchen end of the hut. Meanwhile, José's wife chopped alien looking vegetables in the half light before throwing them into a couple of blackened pans along with a few handfuls of rice and little chunks of meat. In the corner, their young child sat in the gloom of the room, quietly amusing itself with nothing in particular. Shortly, the stew was ready and we were tucking into what can only be described as rather an odd breakfast, or maybe an exceptionally early lunch. Whatever it was though, it was good, natural, wholesome and above all, extremely welcome. Then, when we'd finished, I thanked José's wife, left the two men trying their best to converse, and walked off down to the road and out from the trees.

The whole place still seemed devoid of life at this time. Out in the open there was an eerie half light and a chill pervading the air; the scene set perfectly perhaps for a 'baddy' to enter stage left. I stood there in silence for a while and then, as the morning light started to grow ever stronger, so a broad panorama of heavily forested and rolling hills slowly but surely began to unfold before my very eyes. It changed with every second that passed; lightening from a dark grey-brown, through pale grey and then gradually to an ever more vibrant conglomeration of greens. There were mounds and swathes of jungle-cloaked forms, like wave after wave of fields of giant broccoli, undulating away; down and away into the distant valleys. It was like nothing I'd ever set eyes on before. I watched transfixed; trying to bottle up this magical moment.

When I got back, Trevor had obviously made a little headway linguistically, because I was just in time to join him and follow José up behind the hut to look at his allotment of marijuana plants. After one look though, I realised that, actually, I'd already seen plenty of these plants sprouting up all over the place. They didn't really seem to need any propagating; in fact they appeared to grow in absolute abundance quite naturally here, even without José's help. Not that I'd have known what they were myself mind, but Trevor; now he most definitely seemed a bit of a keen horticulturist.

José seemed pleased to show off his little patch of plants and, as he did, Trevor crouched down and started crushing and rubbing various bits of them between his palms before holding them up to his nose; nodding and making approving murmurings. Well, this was obviously the thing to do and so I decided to follow suit with all the: rubbing, crushing, sniffing and murmuring. I hadn't a clue what I was doing or nodding approval for, of course, but well, it did smell quite nice I suppose. Trevor meanwhile, had his connoisseur's face on and so, not wanting to interfere, I wandered off into the surrounding forest for a bit and when I came back Trevor had already struck up a deal. Then, when the two 'businessmen' had shaken hands, from somewhere behind the hut, Trevor's two sacks magically appeared ready stuffed full of grass - presumably, some they'd prepared earlier! We then said our thanks and goodbyes and headed off back to the road, me with my rucksack and Trevor merrily bouncing along behind with a large sack of grass slung over each shoulder; a rather drab but extremely happy looking Santa.

The bus schedule back to Kumiley appeared to be a little erratic in that there clearly wasn't one! We stood by the roadside for an age, but there was nothing. Then, all of a sudden around the bend...absolutely nothing appeared. All around was silent; even the odd strutting chicken or occasional wisp of a breeze strangely muted. "Perhaps this road up in the hills had been built merely as a fire-break", I thought, "Or as a rather unusual folly by some bored local government official who was sick to death of the colour green". Who knows! Still, it was a nice place to be stuck. After all, how could we possibly complain; the temperature was perfect and it appeared we had the whole

300

mountain to ourselves.

Another hour passed by and in all that time, only the high-pitched shrill of a solitary bird broke the silence. Then, a not so short while later, just when I was beginning to think I might end my days up here; the distant sound of an engine cut through the still air and within minutes, an old Landrover had broken through the trees just up the road. Having waited so long for a bus, truck, car...anything, this seemed too good an opportunity to miss and so, as the vehicle approached, we demonstrated our desire for a lift by totally blocking off the road on both sides. The driver looked a little startled at first but this seemed to do the trick. The Landrover slowed up, jerked to a halt and, though he didn't seem overly keen, after a brief conversation -mostly about not being highwaymen- we piled in; adding our bags to a motley assortment of other bags already piled up higgledy-piggledy in the back. (I daresay the driver had already worked out for himself that he was perfectly safe with us, as Trevor's 'swag bags' were already full to overflowing.)

Unfortunately, though this lift may have been very much appreciated, it really was, as they say, 'just too good to last'. For we'd hardly got settled in when, not five minutes later, we squeaked to a halt and had to pile back out again. The Landrover had only gone as far as the next blessed village. What a complete and utter waste of time -all three minutes of it. This, of course, may account for the driver's slight reluctance to give us a lift in the first place. Why, it wasn't so much a case of the driver being 'anti-vagabond' or highwayman-ist at all, just that his destination was about the same distance away as Trevor could have thrown his sacks. Quite frankly, it had hardly been worth loading up; especially as we could still see the point where we boarded. Strange really! Perhaps the Landrover spent its entire existence simply doing short shuttles back and forth between highland villages, I don't know. Still, at least we were taken in the right direction...just! And eventually, around nightfall, a bus did actually make an appearance and we managed at long last, to hop on and get back down to Kumiley.

It had been an interesting cultural experience going to Double Cutting. We'd spent a long and gruelling day of doing bugger all but sniffing plants and waiting for buses, and now, all I wanted to do was hit the sack -though hopefully a rather more comfortable and less expensive one than Trevor's! We checked back into the same hotel as we'd stayed at before, and went straight to bed.

CHAPTER 19

- ELEPHANTS, TERRAPINS AND MILK AND SARI SALES -

South to Rameswaram

The following morning I woke to find Trevor already gone and so spent the rest of the day doing well, not a great deal actually. Now, I don't want to give the impression that I'd become accustomed to this way of life for, unlike many of the travellers whom I'd met, I'd never quite mastered the art of doing 'sod-all'. But anyway, today, I'd decided I was certainly going to give it my damnedest. To start with it was a rather leisurely rise, and then I sauntered off and managed to find a place where I could get a pretty decent scrambled egg on toast for breakfast. Even better, I also discovered that they did the same for lunch. This was a really unexpected bonus because I didn't actually get up until lunchtime.

Now, normally of course, I enjoyed sampling all the local food but, just occasionally, there was something deliciously comforting about having scrambled eggs on toast. Granted, it may have something to do with rekindling memories of growing up, but you know, it was also such a tremendous treat to be served anything at all which didn't come with at least a hint of chillies. And in any case, eggs -protected as they are in their very own little hermetically sealed containers- surely have to be the ultimate in safe foods...don't they? Well 'no', is the answer, not exactly; but at the time I think salmonella had yet to be 'invented'!

Ironically -or not- a few hours after eating my scrambled eggs, I retired to bed early with a particularly nasty dose of diarrhoea. What a pain in the...yes, well, you know what I mean. I lay on my bed in the coma position feeling decidedly fragile; wondering if, like the pigs in Goa, the chickens here are partial to the odd 'hot meal'!

I was up extra early the next day feeling slightly dishevelled but relieved that I'd at last stopped shuttling portions of reconstituted scrambled egg between bed and bathroom. It would've been all too easy to spend another day doing sod-all, especially feeling a bit on the weak side, but however willowy, I felt that I just couldn't quite manage two whole lazy days on the trot -so to speak- and so, I decided to hire a pushbike and go to the Periyar Wildlife Park.

NB Whilst on the subject of bikes; you know I'm always accused of being a little old fashioned in calling a bicycle a 'pushbike', which I suppose I am really. But in any case, it does strike me as a bit of an odd name, as the only time I ever push a bike is when it doesn't work; and even then only until I can get it home. Then, of course, what normally happens is I threaten to mend it sometime; store it in the back garden until it's nice and rusty; and then take it up the local dump. I suppose really I should eh, 'recycle' it...but no, that's just being silly!

Although I only had the one day at Periyar, it was both a memorable experience and a good first insight into some of India's wonderful wildlife. Mind you, because I hadn't done any reading-up on the subject, I didn't really know what to expect. So rather than wander aimlessly about, I opted to go on a three hour guided walk in the morning; then this was followed by a two hour boat trip on the lake during the afternoon.

Now, this was the first ever time I'd seen elephants in the wild, and do you know, to come this close to fifty or sixty of them was such a tremendous thrill. Sure, they certainly weren't the only animals around the park but they were undoubtedly the biggest stars in every sense of the word; and to witness, at close quarters, the interactions between the mothers and young was something quite special. You know, they're remarkably caring creatures elephants, and, like so many other animals, though not perhaps possessing the so called, 'intelligence' of humans, neither do they possess a lot of our faults either. Anyway, away with the soapbox; as I've said, in Periyar elephants certainly weren't the only draw; I was also able to watch langurs, giant squirrels and a multitude of birds, and all of these animals in quite beautiful and natural surroundings. In fact, I have to say, it was so wonderful that had there been no wildlife in the park at all, it would still have been worth the trip for the countryside alone. "What a marvellously calming tonic for a city slicker this is," I thought, "or a traveller perhaps, who's stood in one too many railway station queues".

But it was the wildlife, of course, that I'd come to Periyar to see, and I found that every living creature there whether big, small, fat, thin, bald or hairy had its own individual appeal. Yes, even the lowly terrapins down by the lake, stretching their stripy little necks out; blinking and sunbathing on half submerged branches. Though, when I say 'lowly' terrapins, these actually were especially

305

interesting on a personal level because, as it happens, I once kept them with my girlfriend. Well...I didn't actually keep them 'with' my girlfriend as such, rather...we both kept terrapins. (Mind you, in this particular relationship I often found myself in the dog house, so I don't see any reason why she shouldn't have been in the terrapin tank!)

Actually, whilst on this subject, you know I may be one of the few people alive today who has ever given the kiss of life to a terrapin. An unusual occurrence perhaps, but one which came about because, when I came home from work one night, I was aghast to find Terry -yes, Terry Pin-floating motionless in his tank, seemingly trapped underwater by the aeration hose. Well, I was horrified of course. I quickly lifted him from the tank and, as I did, his head just flopped to one side as limp as a hairdresser's handshake. Then, although all seemed lost I thought, "Well, there's nothing to lose by trying is there!" And so I gave him a bit of a squeeze; but...nothing; dead as a Dodo! Now, I hadn't the foggiest how to find a pulse on a turtle and trying to kick-start a heart through a shell seemed unlikely so, I opted for the only other option...mouth-to-mouth -or rather mouth to nose in Terry's case, as his little mouth was very firmly shut. Well, anyway, I lifted the poor thing up to my lips and started blowing rhythmically up his nostrils before waiting; looking for a sign of life...There was nothing. I tried again; still nothing. Finally, on the fourth attempt, against all odds, Terry took a deep gasp, opened his bleary little eyes and stretched out his neck. He was okay; he was alive! Terry, I'm pleased to say, survived and went on to reach a ripe old age, eventually ending his days in Brighton Aquarium after a family bust-up. (His, not mine.)

From Periyar, I cycled on my 'pushbike' through the dappled light of huge deciduous trees. The afternoon sun was drawing ever lengthening shadows across the road and so, by the time I'd made it back to Kumiley, the light had all but gone. Then later, that very same evening, I left and took a particularly bumpy four hour bus ride to Madurai.

Of course, a bumpy ride was about all I needed for an already sensitive stomach and, at one time, I seriously had my doubts as to whether or not I'd make it to Madurai without having to resort to the bicycle clips. I didn't quite know why but somewhere down in the bowel region it felt like somebody was gently simmering a cauldron of Stroganoff, and so when we pulled in at the bus station shortly before midnight, it was with great relief. I then quickly grabbed my bag and made straight for the first hotel I could find; tearing along the road with tiny steps and tightly clenched buttocks, like a Chinaman who's just sat on a red hot poker.

By this time my insides sounded uncannily like your typical Indian plumbing and so, when a couple of Danish lads at the hotel asked me if I'd share a room with them in order to save money, I must admit, I did have slight reservations. I'd have liked the company of course, but my condition wasn't really one that I wanted to share. The trouble is, how could I possibly tell them the truth? "Yes of course, I'd love to share a room with you; don't mind me, I'll be the one in the corner cooking cabbage and blowing raspberries all night". I couldn't really think of an excuse 'not' to share though and so, well...I did. Thankfully though, the night turned out to be a remarkably quiet and uneventful one. In fact I actually slept quite soundly. And the Danes, well; they were mercifully spared the all-night rancid, scrambled egg shuttle. Yes, for the moment at least, my internal plumbing remained even more Indian...non-functioning!

I spent most of the following morning looking round the famous temple of Madurai. It was I suppose, justifiably famous; but the trouble is that when you're in a country littered with a zillion other temples, it's all too easy to get a bit blasé. Madurai's temple would certainly have been a bit special had it been built in Milton Keynes say, but here, well! It's a bit like some of the manic birdwatchers I've met. They'll travel the whole length of England to see a yellow crested, black-bottomed, hob knobbler that's accidentally been blown off its migratory course from Twitchistan, when actually, they're two a penny in say, Scandinavia. I guess that occasionally, it's not always only about the subject, but also the location in which you see it. In any case, where was I? Oh yes...By lunchtime it had become unbearably hot in Madurai and so I hopped on a train bound for Rameswaram.

Now, ever since leaving Goa, I'd been dying to reach Rameswaram as, for me, it was yet another major milestone. This was just about as far south as I could possibly go on the Indian sub-continent and, although a significant religious centre in its own right, it was, more importantly for me, the place where I could take a ferry across the straits to Sri Lanka.

The ferries from Rameswaram didn't run every day and so, as a considerable amount of people filtered through here en route to Sri Lanka, there were a fair number of waiting passengers -both Western and local- milling about the place. Naturally, this meant that, because of the human traffic jam awaiting boats, it was going to be a lot more difficult to find a bed for the night. Still, I had to stay somewhere and so I quickly grabbed hold of a waiting bicycle rickshaw and did a brisk reconnaissance of several of the cheap hotels in the area. Rather worryingly, after nearly an hour of being peddled around, there still wasn't a spare bed to be had. Eventually though, with a little more persistence, I did manage to find a vacant room which was surprisingly near the town centre.

By this time it was already too late to try for a ferry ticket and so I decided to take it easy and to flake out on my bed, quietly smug and satisfied with my day's progress; or satisfied, that is, until I realised exactly why this room was still available. Why, I'd hardly kicked off my shoes and put my feet up for a well earned slice of R. and R., when all of a sudden someone -clearly in excruciating pain and armed with a megaphone- began screaming at me through the open window. God; I nearly leapt out of my hot 'n' leaky skin. I jumped to my feet and ran to the window clasping my hands over my ears; and there, just there not a short camel's spit from where I stood, was the almighty, massive, mammoth silhouette of a mosque; and from it blared the loudest, most chronic, glass-shattering din you've ever heard in your life! Why, oh why, oh why, on this very day, did they have to choose a tone-deaf octogenarian to do the calling to prayer? And why on earth did this particular old muezzin have to be issued with rock-concert type speakers that come with that extra special, super-duper, built-in sound distortion button. Well, I'd heard many of these 'callings to prayer' before which were evocative, stirring, pleasurable even; but this just wasn't one of them. Perhaps the fat wailing woman in

309

the Hindi movie in Cochin wasn't so bad after all; it was simply horrendous!

Well, having absolutely no chance of sleep there was nothing for it but to lie on my bed praying; praying that the bloody awful racket would be over as soon as possible. It was, without a shadow of a doubt, quite the worst din I'd experienced in my life. Mercifully though, it didn't actually last that long. After just a couple of rousing verses, interspersed with short silences where he appeared to fight for breath, the muezzin finally let out one last, long, milk-curdling note before dropping the mike and clearing half a pint of phlegm from his throat. He then, realising that the whole of Rameswaram could still hear him, recovered his composure to round off his final note and...it was over.

I slept surprisingly well after that. Well, that is, until the whole thing was repeated at the 'ungodly' hour of five o'clock the next morning. Now, how is it that, back in England, the neighbours come round banging on the door just because you're getting carried away with a bit of Strauss on the stereo; but over here, you can 'publicly' broadcast what sounds like a hypochondriac giving birth to quads in an echo chamber, and nobody even bats an eyelid. I don't know, it beats me...perhaps this is what they call 'religious tolerance'! (I would like to point out here that this was very much an isolated incident and I find most aspects of humanity and most religions absolutely fascinating. It's just that when one man is calling to thousands -and this one in particular- you may well wish to stand up and be counted but...you really don't want to be first in line geographically.)

There seemed little point to staying in bed after my rude awakening. In any case I wanted to get down to the port and see about the ferries going to Sri Lanka. It was only a short walk to the port but, by the time I got there, I was slightly dismayed to see that half the town were already queuing for tickets. This was particularly annoying as I'd been awake since 5am. But though I freely admit that waiting in queues isn't on my list of favourite hobbies, I'd still far sooner have been standing here than have my ears sand-blasted by guttural Gupta; and anyway, I had little option if I wanted to go south from here. And so I joined the throng and hoped that the time would pass quickly.

Surprisingly, whilst waiting not so patiently in the long queue, I again came across the friendly faces of Julie and Katie, my old pals from Goa; so although it took a full two hours to reach the end, the wait was made ever so slightly more bearable by the presence of the two girls.

Most of the people here who wanted to cross the water were going straight on to the capital of Colombo and so, rather than buy separate tickets, they tended to opt for the combined ferry/train ticket that would take them all the way to their final destination. I decided that I would also follow suit; I hadn't the foggiest idea of what Sri Lanka had to offer -other than an incredible amount of tea- but at least when I reached Colombo I'd have mail to collect, and that was a big enough carrot for me to make my mind up. Unfortunately, on finally reaching the ticket counter, I discovered that the next ferry wasn't actually leaving until Monday -three whole days later- but well, as it happened I didn't have any pressing engagements, so I wasn't unduly worried.

It wasn't long after leaving the ferry terminal clutching my precious ticket that I bumped into yet another familiar face from the past. I'd last seen John wandering round the caves of Ajanta and it turned out that, not only had he a ferry ticket for the same day as I did, he also had the misfortune to be staying in the very same hotel with me alongside Gupta, the tone-deaf karaoke singer. By this time though, I'd ceased to be amazed by coincidences as just about everyone who passed through India appeared to be on exactly the same route as one another. And like sand in an egg-timer, eventually we'd all find ourselves piled up in the bottom of India.

It was incredibly hot in Rameswaram and anyone with an ounce of sense spent the middle part of the day -from about ten am until two pm- languishing in what little shade they could find. In fact, the temperature at this time was such that every single mad dog -of which there were plenty- and Englishman, were left panting in the shadows. In this, I was certainly no exception. I always enjoyed looking round the various towns I came across whenever I got the opportunity, but this sort of heat was something else. There was absolutely nothing that could tempt me into the sun, not even a visit to one of the rich and gaudy temples that always brightened the place; the ones seemingly painted by passing fairground people. But, you know, my biggest and most favourite discovery in Rameswaram, wasn't of any large or famous monument at all, but that of a lowly milk shack. This 'building' was nothing more than a square wooden shed about half the size of an ice-cream van; but, you know, I ended up spending more time there than I did at the Taj Mahal. Well, not actually in it as such, but pretty damned close;

for, just to the side of this shed were two stools which, because of their location, I was instantly drawn to.

It was a bit like being back at infant school, sitting there; for whilst these two pieces of furniture may well have started life as quite normal stools, they were now the height of a couple of kneeling down sausage dogs. I don't really know why, they just were. Perhaps the shack owner fancied himself as a carpenter and had got a bit carried away; always trying to saw down the one slightly long and wonky leg. Whatever the case, during my stay in Rameswaram, one of these two pygmy stools very nearly became my second home. Okay, so I didn't sit there the whole day -of course not- but, after day one of my discovery, and because of the incredibly intense heat here, my score at the milk shack was thus: one plain milk, one rose-milk and nine rather splendid chocolate milks.

These flavoured milks all came in handy little half-pint plastic bottles which were somehow miraculously kept slightly chilled by the friendly milk-shack owner, and so this place was a little slice of heaven. In fact by the end of the first afternoon, I was already well on my way to becoming like a pub regular; I'd simply walk up to the little opening in the side of the hut, and before you could say the Hindi for, "I'll 'ave the usual please guvnor," another chocolate flavoured milk would appear on the counter. Wonderful!

Now, as the milk shack could only accommodate two sitting customers, it would've been all too easy to be selfish and keep quiet about my fantastic discovery, but well, I'm afraid I just couldn't help myself. The very next day a number of faces from the previous evening's socialising began turning up in their dribs and drabs and, horror of horrors, there were times when I couldn't even sit at 'my own' kitchen stool. Still, it was certainly good business for the milkman and, anyway, I did enjoy the extra company, even if it did mean standing room only.

One interesting chap who happened along the way was a young Italian who told me he'd been travelling the world, without a break, for the past three years. This, as it turned out, was all on the proceeds of a simple currency scam which he'd pulled off in Zimbabwe. Now apparently, at this time, there were a number of countries which didn't allow their own local currencies to be taken either in or out of their boundaries. Well, this alone would have meant that you could be stuck in say, Zimbabwe, with local currency which somehow had to be disposed of before leaving. However, several governments soon realised that this was hardly likely to attract tourists, and so in order to counteract this slightly negative policy, when you were ready to leave the country you were able, quite legally, to go to any bank and change all your remaining Zimbabwe dollars back into a hard currency -in this case US dollars. And so, this is how the scam worked:

This Italian chap had entered the country; changed half of his hard currency into Zimbabwe dollars at the bank and the other half -at several times the bank rate, of course- on the black market. Then, he'd go to another bank; tell them he was about to leave the country, and they'd change 'all' of his local currency back into US dollars for him; thus giving him a rather handsome profit. This process was then, quite simply, repeated over and over and over again; easy! And apparently, over a two week period, this Italian had raced all over the country, nipping in and out of every bank he could find, continually replicating the same idea, and in the process amassing a small fortune. Now, naturally, I'm not condoning such an act, in fact, in all honesty, I think it extremely immoral; but I have to confess, it is all rather entrepreneurial and one heck of a story to boot.

As I've said, not all of my three days waiting for the ferry were spent sitting outside the milk-shack of course. A good deal of it, yes; as apart from wonderfully refreshing milkshakes, it was also a great place to sit and people-watch. But what a terrific pastime that is, isn't it! For whilst I just love to talk to people from all over the world, isn't it also nice to be able to observe them as they go about their daily routines. You know, it always seems funny to me how, even as a 'stand out like a sore thumb' foreigner, you can become almost invisible simply by sitting in one spot and observing; lives seemingly carrying on around you as if you weren't there. But walk around trying to capture local life on film, and you immediately intrude into the very thing which you're trying so hard to capture. In much the same way, you can spend a whole day out walking and trying to observe birds or other wildlife with little result but, take a little time to sit still…and very often the animals will come to you.

One oven-hot day, between glugs of cool chocolate milkshake, I happened to notice that the same little Indian chap kept passing me by. He was easy to pick out in his floral shirt and Daz-white trousers but, even more, he drew my attention because every time he passed, he'd look across and give me that same coy smile. In fact, rather worryingly, it was that very same smile I'd seen so many times before, when an Indian boy is trying to attract a mate but has yet to pluck up the courage to do anything about it! This particular boy though, would always walk on past the shack and then glance back over his shoulder -still with that same look on his face- before continuing on his way again. Now, on these occasions, I always liked to give the benefit of any doubt I had. Okay, so I realise that in all likelihood he was almost certainly after one of three things: my friendship, my money or...my body -or perhaps a combination of at least two of these- and so the odds of us 'both' enjoying any encounter with one another weren't terribly good. As a consequence, I decided that for the moment, I'd stay exactly where I was; and in any case, I wasn't about to leave my precious stool for odds like that. But, as things turned out, I didn't have to; for one day he came over to me. Well, although heavily accented, he actually spoke pretty good English but, sad to say, our little chat had hardly lasted a milkshake long before the subject of conversation was dexterously manipulated round to that of business.

Now apparently, my shy little Indian mate had a friend up the road who just happened to own a silk shop (well, I'm blowed!) Yes, okay, I know what you're thinking; but as he rightly said, "There was nothing to be lost by looking", was there! In any case, I quite fancied having a closer look at some of the beautiful saris I'd seen being worn around the place. Mind you, however beautiful the saris may have been, they were as nothing compared to some of the contents I'd seen so exquisitely wrapped within them. Simply stunning! Anyway, fantasy thoughts aside; I figured I'd been around a bit by now and had grown both rather older and wiser than when I'd first left England. I was now a seasoned traveller and certainly wasn't going to be duped into buying something I didn't even want by some shy but smarmy silk salesman was I! I left the silk shop after two long hours; three silk saris heavier...but £45 lighter. Well, they were rather nice and besides, how could I possibly lose. After all, I'd been absolutely assured, re-assured and re-reassured by my coy middleman that I could easily sell them at his 'uncle's' shop in Sri Lanka for a humungous profit. (You'll be surprised to learn that the address he gave me for his uncle didn't actually exist.)

In my defence though, it had already occurred to me that this just might not be the deal of the century; but I reckoned that with such a sizeable Indian population back in England, I could feel quite confident, if it came to it, of at least making a profit from the saris back home. In the event, having lugged the three saris around in my rucksack all over Sri Lanka for a whole month, I got home and never did quite get around to taking them up to London, as intended. I ended up selling them to my local Pakistani corner shop -the one selling fruit, dusty tins and hand-stapled plastic packets of smelly spices- all three for a £5 profit.

The funny thing is, at the time I thought I had the whole thing worked out. When I first bought the saris I'd actually taken the precaution of snapping a photograph of the overfriendly silk salesman outside the very shop from whence he came, and assured him that, "If things didn't turn out as promised, then...I'd be back!" Mind you, with hindsight, he probably didn't believe a word I said; he just kept right on reassuring me that the deal was indeed a fantastic one, and then saw me off out of the shop with a confident wave and that same 'sickly' smile. Not that I bear any malice mind...the slimy, conniving, wobbly-headed silk-worm.

On my second day in Rameswaram, I moved into the town's official youth hostel, which happened to overlook the bay. It was a great relief to get away from the screeching mosque of course, but also a real bonus to be down by the sea; not only for the views but for the breeze it afforded. The building itself, though hardly oozing charm and character, was remarkably clean and well cared for -for a youth hostel- and comprised two single sex dorms of eleven beds each. And though it wasn't terribly big on home comforts, it did have the one big plus in that it was situated right next door to the Mail Nadu Hotel, which served both excellent and cheap-ish breakfasts. In fact, this alone, was such a draw, and it was such a nice change to be offered anything other than chapattis or rice for breakfast, that for my very first meal there, I ordered absolutely everything on the menu. And, do you know what?...I may have walked out of there looking porkier than a plump and pregnant, pot-bellied pig but, I have to confess, I've never felt quite so marvellously full and satisfied. "How odd" I thought, "how very odd that you can look and feel so round from eating a good square meal, or rather...several of them!"

Later that same day, whilst still unashamedly thinking about my troughful of breakfast, I waddled contentedly down to the beach. A slight breeze coming off the ocean made the heat just bearable and so I wandered round the bay to see who or what was about. The sea here wasn't the turquoise or azure of the glossy holiday brochures but a deep blue-green; the sand a sort of um…sandy colour. It was only midmorning now, but already the beach shimmered and simmered beneath a faint haze, its soft undulations of sandy sand broken by quivering horizontal lines of imaginary water. The sand itself was so hot, it seemed the soles of my shoes would simply melt away to nothing were I to stop walking for even a moment. As I strolled along, a clutch of colourful little boats bobbed happily about in the shallows, shackled to their anchors somewhere on the sea bed. Others lay on the beach awaiting restoration, pale and jaded looking, helplessly tilting to their sides as vulnerable and forlorn as beached whales.

Up ahead I could hear singing. I followed the happy sound and watched as seven or eight young men -in their twenties perhaps- ran around a large winch pushing on a cross of six foot wooden handles; slowing easing one of the brightly coloured fishing boats into shore. They spotted me and beamed with delight as I began photographing them. Then they all started to sing louder, laughing more and more, running faster and faster round and round in circles egged on by the attention I was giving them. Next, without so much as breaking a single stride, one of them excitedly beckoned for me to join them. I put down my stuff on a lump of driftwood, grabbed hold of an empty two foot of handle and ran alongside them, all of us laughing out loud and kicking up sand as we went. I hadn't a clue what it was they were singing, but I joined in anyway; their brown sinewy bodies shone in the sunlight, glistening with rivulets of shiny sweat. As we ran around, the chain clanked rhythmically away and the boat slowly eased its way up towards us. It was hot, hot work but there was no let up in their pace; and the more they ran, the more they sang. By now it was so unbelievably hot and dry that, no matter how happy I felt, I couldn't even raise a smile without my upper lip becoming Superglued to my teeth. Any attempt at singing now soon reduced me to heavy panting and, within a mere three minutes, I'd had enough. I gave up breathless and left them to their work. Then I gathered up my stuff from the log and, without ever stopping, they waved me off down the sand. And, as I disappeared along the beach, I could still hear their songs and laughter ringing out in the distance. I thought, "Sometimes life can be so simple and yet so wonderful…yes, simply wonderful!"

A little further on, two boys of no more than eight and ten were rowing a small wooden boat close to shore. I waved to them and, just as the winchers had done before, they beckoned for me to join them. So I waded out to thigh height, jumped aboard and both boys giggled excitedly. They didn't have a word of English between them or I a single word that they could understand, but still the three of us laughed and played together as happy as 'sand boys'. We spent the next hour rowing around the bay and at no time was there even a hint that they would want any money for their efforts. They were just two young boys having a good time, and sharing that time with a total stranger. Certainly, there was little in the way of verbal communication but, just like my encounter with the merry bunch of boat winchers, this moment was well, special.

Soon though we'd pulled back into the shallows, I jumped back into the warm water again and, still with the broadest of beams across their little faces, they enthusiastically waved me off. I then started wading into shore, but when I looked back over my shoulder, the waving had stopped and instead, the elder of the two boys was holding aloft a silvery flat- fish the size of a deflated rugby ball. He asked me -in eye-brow speak- if I might be interested and so, in less than an hour, the boys had gathered some driftwood together and made a camp fire. Then they simply gutted the fish, rolled it up neatly in a handy banana leaf and threw it on the fire. Shortly the three of us were sat on the beach in the sun, eating large chunks of beautifully fresh and delicate white fish -cooked to perfection. Quite superb!

Of course, after finishing our Indian style picnic, I could hardly go without paying the boys something, if not for the boat ride, then at least for the fish. This I felt all the stronger for the very fact that no payment was expected. All the same, when I did give them a little money, the boys seemed happy to receive it; and then, when we parted company, they just carried on playing about and splashing in the water. It occurred to me, what a lovely, carefree mentality you have at that age; and what a great shame that we all have to lose it...albeit some of us more slowly than others.

It was mid-afternoon now and a chap along the beach had just climbed down from harvesting coconuts from their lofty palms. I bought a couple from him which he deftly decapitated with a machete, and then spent the rest of the daylight hours sitting in the shoal, slowly sipping fresh coconut milk from their husks. The sea here was, beyond doubt, the warmest I've ever known. And as I sat there in the water with my two coconuts and the late afternoon sun on my face I thought to myself, "What a wonderful and fitting final memory of India this is"; for whilst I'd certainly had my share of hassles over the past couple of months, they now seemed to ooze away in a single magical moment, and I knew that I really must come back. Then, I once more gathered my stuff together; put my decidedly rose-tinted specs firmly in my shorts pocket and strolled off back to the hostel.

Vic, the slightly built and shy atypical Aussie, arrived in Rameswaram that same evening. We'd shared a lot of Goan memories together, from sunset mullings and football matches to numerous wacky-backy parties. And, in fact, he'd also been Doug's 'second' in the great Sunset Café, bread roll eating contest. But now like the rest of us, he'd been sifted down to the foot of India to await the crossing to Sri Lanka; yet another piece of fluff in the toe of this giant, hot and humid woollen sock.

Of course, it was almost inevitable that we'd meet again somewhere down the line, but I was surprised it was so soon. But then, when later both Julie and Katie also showed up, well, it felt like we were re-enacting a scene from 'The Great Escape'; once again inadvertently thrown together; a motley assortment of disguised British prisoners waiting on the platform for the same train out of Germany. But, if there was one thing even more inevitable than meeting up again, it was that when we did meet, there was going to be an awful lot of catching up to be done. So, that night, along with a handful of new found friends, a small coach party of us hit the poor old Tamil Nadu Hotel for what turned out to be a particularly liquid dinner, accompanied by a great deal of raucous reminiscing.

My final day in India was spent, once again, barefoot; paddling ponderously round the bay, cooling my feet in the shallow water and watching the gentle rocking of the tethered fishing boats. Then, when the sun became just too hot, I went and found Vic -who'd at last recovered from the previous night's revelries- and he accompanied me, for one last time, to sit in the shade of the old milk-shack.

Later in the afternoon, we were sitting outside the youth hostel with the two girls singing old show tunes and sixties songs, and before we knew it, the sun had dipped below the horizon. The four of us were well lubricated by now and Katie and I did a bit of alcohol-induced jiving before collapsing on the sand in heaps of laughter. The moon was little more than a slither that night but it left a wonderful glossy trace across the calm sea. As we lay there on the sand, breathless, the mood suddenly changed. It was a stunningly beautiful evening and here was I lying on the sand panting breathlessly next to a young girl. I don't know why but, it was only now that I truly became aware of Katie's sexuality. Up till then she'd merely been a friend, another traveller; but at that precise moment in time, her skin looked just that much softer, her eyes brighter, her lips more smooth and rounded. Our eyes met...was she thinking what I was? Had we both been duped into romance, temporarily hypnotised by the magic of the moment, or was it simply pure unadulterated drunken lust on my part? We looked at each other and I desperately needed to know what was going through her mind. We dusted ourselves down and with hardly a word, went inside. Then, both of us quietly climbed into bed; her into hers and...me into mine!

Do you know, I never did find out what she was thinking

and well, I never asked. I lay on my single-sex dorm bed wondering: how damned frustrating! How bloody, bloody stupid I was! Why, on earth didn't I at least ask her? How could I be so soft in the head and yet so hard*...well, you know what I mean. Still, the moment had gone. There was hardly time for regrets before I'd closed my eyes and drifted off into a deep, deep sleep. Tomorrow I'd be up early to catch the ferry to Sri Lanka.

(*I really must apologise for turning a 'Mills and Boon' moment into, 'Confessions of a carpenter', but I can only say what I truly felt at the time.)

CHAPTER 20

-HOMESICK DAYS AND SWEATY NIGHTS-

Into Sri Lanka

It was only a three hour crossing from India to Sri Lanka but an all day journey nonetheless. This was largely because, as usual, half the population of the planet were gathered at the port, with the other half close behind ready to wish them all a 'Bon Voyage'. And of course, it was quite impossible to see where you had to go because everybody had formed themselves into a thousand orderly queues of one. Nobody seemed to be in any sort of a hurry though, so I joined the throng and hoped that, eventually, I'd be squeezed in roughly the right direction. In the event, it took me nearly five hours to reach the point on the dock where everyone was being filtered between two khaki-clad customs officials.

Now, by the amount of time this operation was taking, you'd have thought that every passenger was being given a strip search and every single item of luggage logged in triplicate. As it turned out though, neither of these things was true. The process wasn't a tediously bureaucratic one at all but simply, extremely leisurely. Why, if the passengers had seemed relaxed about the whole protracted affair, then these officials were positively comatose. Strangely, they seemed to show little interest in the vast assortment of objects that passed before them, but when it came to passport checks, the reason for the delay became rather more apparent.

Now obviously, most of the prospective passengers here

were either Indian or Sri Lankan, but that didn't stop every single passport from being so gawked at, so scrutinised, you'd have thought that some joker had shuffled all the photos and then gaily stuck them back into different passports. And as for European passports, well, I can honestly say that I've never in my life seen such fascination in something so dull and ordinary. Granted, the various foreign visa stamps may have looked just a tad interesting to some officials, and I can even understand why the hideous borstal-type photos might provoke a second glance; but what I will never understand is how on earth every single, totally blank page held these officers' stare as if it were hiding a secretly coded message, or a 3D nude photo of Pamela Anderson perhaps. This wasn't bureaucracy at all, it was umm, well…I don't really know; whatever the word is for abject curiosity in the mundane, I suppose.

Still, eventually we did all make it through customs and then we were shuttled out to an already heavily laden ferry by a couple of small and smoky, putt-putting motor boats. Then, once the ferry was packed to way, way beyond the gunnels, we turned away from India and chugged out to sea; bound for the beautiful tropical island of Sri Lanka.

Having crossed to the other side of the channel, I discovered that the proceedings there were no less slick, and we had to endure the same old rigmarole that we'd already gone through just a few hours earlier. Here though, thankfully, it took a mere three hours to pass through customs. But it was then, and only then, that I was at last able to board my carriage for the 10.30 night train to Colombo.

It had been a long and tiring day, this ferry crossing, and

I was more than ready now for a good sleep. For a handful of passengers though, the day would be an even longer one. You see, a small group of Indians were prevented from boarding the train; held back by the local police. I didn't know why of course. It seemed extremely unlikely, but perhaps the Sri Lankan officials had found something that had been missed at Indian customs; a stash of hash perhaps; a secret stowage of silk saris; who knows! Maybe some of the Indians' passport photos really had been shuffled. Whatever the reason, there would be no night train to Colombo for these men. I sat there pondering; "What had these men done? Were they really all guilty or, for them, was this to be...a 'missed carriage of justice'."

It was a twelve hour journey down the coast to Colombo, but the seats were mercifully soft and even 'intentionally' reclinable, so I slept well. My excitement at being in a new country was tempered by tiredness for the time being but, come morning, I awoke newly refreshed and with the superb lushness of old Ceylon filling my carriage window. Shortly, I was chatting away to a Sri Lankan who spoke considerably better English than most English people I know. He informed me, quite matter-of-factly, that on the previous day a local farmer had been hit and killed on the track by this very train. It made me think about how tenuous and cheap life can be. To these passengers and others who rode the train every day, the farmer was merely the subject of idle chatter; to the poor farmer's family though, it would've been the absolute deepest of tragedies.

When we reached Colombo, I quickly checked into a dorm' at the Ex-servicemen's Hostel. Then I took a quick shower before going out and embarking on a wild goose chase around every little alleyway in the city, trying to find the phantom uncle who was going to buy my silk saris and give me a handsome profit. As mentioned previously, neither the address nor the uncle existed. Of course, it would have been nice had the sari saga been a more fruitful one, but at least it had given me an excuse to explore rather lesser known parts of the capital. Well, lesser known that is, to all bar the equally gullible clients of the silk sari salesmen of Rameswaram.

And so it was, after I'd trawled every street in Colombo, I eventually crawled back to the shade of my room with all the vitality of an over-dunked Rich Tea finger. But then, just as I was about to collapse onto my sheet-sleeping bag in a tired and sweaty heap, I suddenly remembered that I was awaiting mail at the GPO. So, with renewed -or rather, slightly plumped up- vigour, I hurried along to the post office and, just as before, excitedly sifted through the 'M' pile. Well, what a lovely surprise; not one, not two but no fewer than 'nine' letters awaited me. Fantastic! I skipped back to the dorm, jumped onto my ever-so-creaky bed and proceeded to slowly read through every one of the letters; all the while, my faced fixed with the soppiest of grins and my eyes filling pathetically like miniature reservoirs. (For some inexplicable reason I was always blubbering away at happy things -like watching Chitty-chitty-bang-bang for example- still, we all have our little idiosyncrasies, don't we!)

Most of the letters were from family back home, of course. But it was always lovely to hear about what had been going on back in England, however mundane that news might be. And in any case, these day to day goings on were always likely to be a rather dull contrast to the excitement of travel. But it wasn't the content of the letters that was terribly important; just as long as it involved those I loved, I wouldn't have cared less if it was about which new magazines the hairdresser had in, or what everyone thought of the various soap operas' latest deaths and datings -which it frequently was- the letters would invariably pluck away at the old heart strings and, like sipping hot chocolate in front of an open fire on a cold winter's day, they'd never fail to give me that sort of...warm feeling.

My first proper meal in Colombo was that good old Sri Lankan standard of fish and chips. I was out at a restaurant called, 'The Pagoda Tea Rooms' and I'm sorry but, when I spotted, 'fish and chip supper' on the menu, there was nothing for it; I just simply couldn't resist! And you know, it wasn't at all bad. Though, in truth, I hadn't realised the menu was being quite so literal until I received in front of me: my fish, and my one chip! (Actually, that's not strictly true, as shortly I found another four small specimens cowering under the fish.) Still, it was a nice bit of home-comfort food all the same and just the thing having read all of my letters from back in Blighty. Then, just for a bit of local flavour, I quickly washed it all down with a half glass of good old Sri Lankan whisky. A somewhat odd accompaniment to 'fish and chip' perhaps, but about the only drink -bar tea of course- which was truly local. Mind you, we're not talking whisky here as in Scotch, but something called Arrack; the local firewater made from coconuts: an unusual and potent spirit -somewhere midway between coconut flavoured tequila and white spirit- but actually, quite bearable...if you're partial to the odd shot of paint stripper.

Colombo was unbearably hot and sticky at this time. I'd thought that Rameswaram was hot, but at least there'd been a sea breeze and milk-shack. In Colombo the humidity was such that, if you hit the streets whilst the sun was still up, your body just became one huge pink percolator (though, thankfully not in the 'aural' sense since my bowel problem had cleared up). Even at night, sleep was only made remotely possible by the huge Casablanca-type fans whirring away above the beds. These were an absolute God-send for, without them, the air was so oppressive, so exceedingly heavy, it seemed an effort even to blink.

Determined not to be confined to a hostel bed though, I decided to make an outing to the local supermarket to see what they had to offer. Now I'd taken the precaution of venturing out that day in a super-ultra-lightweight cotton shirt but, nonetheless, within thirty seconds of leaving the room, felt compelled to walk the streets with both elbows held akimbo in a futile attempt to prevent over-leaky armpits. Now there's no denying I must have looked pretty daft -like a carpet salesman carrying two very large but invisible rolls of lino, or a Bollywood gun-slinger perhaps, minus the guns- but well, that's about the only way I could possibly handle the complete and utter, almost sauna-esque humidity.

When I got there, the air-conditioning in the supermarket was worth the walk alone. Though paradoxically, of course, had I not made the walk there, then I wouldn't have needed the air-conditioning in the first place. But, you know, the air-conditioning wasn't the only reason to come here -just the best one. No, this supermarket was surprisingly well stocked, not only with local produce, but with tins and packets which had seemingly come from all over the world. Why, it was surprising enough to find Heinz baked beans here in Sri Lanka, and I was even more taken aback when I came to the Marmite; but, beyond doubt, what really did it for me was when I moved down the aisle and came to a neat little row of -wait for it- yes...Sugar Puffs; good old British 'Tell 'em about the honey mummy' Sugar Puffs.

Now, I suppose that my mild addiction to these things, having eaten them by the washing-up bowl full for many years, made Sugar Puffs my ultimate reminder of home; but you know what, I'd never, until that moment, quite realised to what extent. I slid a family sized pack off the shelf; clasped it in both hands; lent back on the chilled goods section, and my eyes welled up to such an extent that I couldn't even read the writing. I laughed out loud at myself for being so bloody daft but knew that, not so deep down, I was really missing those back home. I slid the Sugar Puffs back in line, dashed back to the hostel -with my two invisible rolls of lino- and then laid out on the bed under a furiously whirring fan, writing letters to my family.

In the morning I did some clothes washing in the communal bathroom. This was always a real chore for me and so didn't get done quite as often as it should have. Still, at least here the drying wasn't a problem. In fact, what little laundry did get done was nigh on crisp before I could even get it from the basin to the washing line. And whilst on the subject...do you know, it's always amazed me how some people can look so annoyingly well turned out when backpacking. I've never quite discovered their secret; in fact, as you now know, the one and only time I'd tried to wash my jeans on a rock in Goa, they'd virtually fallen apart. And if ever I've worn clothes that I've cleaned and rung out myself, they invariably take on the appearance of that spirally type pasta.

Girls, on the other hand, always seem to have the knack of getting the washing and drying thing about right. God knows how, they just do! This isn't a sexist remark, simply a statement based on a good deal of observation. In any case this certainly isn't an insult, and I've never in my life been accused of sexism unless it's been deemed 'derogatory', such as…don't know left from right and can't park a car to save their lives…that sort of thing. Anyway, whether it be wrung, hung or left to rest in peace, whatever I choose to wear when travelling, you can bet your haute couture wardrobe that come morning, it'll end up looking like it's been the material of choice in an all night origami competition. Not something I'm proud of, just the sad truth.

After the mild disappointment with the sari selling saga, I thought I'd look into the possibility of making some money out of precious stones. You see, Sri Lanka was supposedly 'the' place to buy both sapphires and -the not so precious- moonstones. This much I'd managed to glean from the Swiss chap whom I'd met in Pakistan; and the fact that the address he'd given me back then had led me to a remote marijuana farm in Southern India, was neither here nor there. But whatever the case, I thought, what was there to lose! So off I set and did a bit of wandering around town -periodically diving for cover in the nearest air-conditioned supermarket- and went to see what I could find. Not that I knew what I was looking for really; I knew as much about precious gems as your average American knows about world geography, or world history or...world anything really. But anyway, I thought, "Why not, I'll give it a go!"

And so it was, I found myself on a slow circuit of the gem shops of Colombo; and in each shop that I entered, I'd express my interest to buy, be offered a seat, and then duly be presented with several trays of brightly coloured gems. I'd then try my level best to peer knowledgeably at each little gem through the magnifier, turning each one around between thumb and index finger, occasionally holding my chin and nodding -as us experts tend to do. (I'd also invested in a note book and Bic biro, by the way, just to make sure they knew I was for real.) Then, having studied each stone methodically, I made a note of their size, colour and shape -and of course their price- before poking them all back into their neat little velvet display cases.

Now, I dare say there may have been the odd gem trader who wasn't fooled by my antics for one second but, as a matter of fact, I wasn't particularly bothered. They may well have been merely waiting for me to leave the shop before collapsing in heaps of laughter -having witnessed my approving nods at their 'coloured glass' collections- but so what. I didn't actually buy any so what's the worst that could have happened; a bunch of gem salesmen having a laugh. Okay, so it might have been at my expense but I can live with that. In fact the whole experience was far from being a waste of time because, at one particular shop, I was even invited to go downstairs and see a gem cutter in action, and this alone was worth the visit.

Now, this gem cutter was a rather fat but amiable little man; probably in his late fifties. Unusually, he somehow managed to possess both piggy and puffy eyes - presumably from years of fine work under a not so fine lamp- and this gave him the unfortunate appearance of a toad with conjunctivitis. He spent his life sitting at a small rectangular desk with a bendy light peering over one shoulder, and was permanently crouched and hunched over a teeny-weeny bit of shiny rock, like a myopic dwarf trying to remove a splinter. When I was introduced to him, he very kindly took time to tell me a few crucial facts about gems; facts that would hopefully prevent me, in the future, from buying nice but very expensive pieces of glass. It was good of him to do this of course, but though I listened intently, I knew that the chances of my making a small fortune from something of which I knew so little, was as likely as snow drifts in downtown Colombo. Still, at least I left there with a little more knowledge than when I'd entered, and so the experience was a worthwhile one. (Subsequently, I have indeed gone on to use this knowledge and now have an enviable collection of rather beautiful but expensive...glass!)

The following day I posted off my small, freshly penned wad of letters to England; the one to my mother requesting even more money, as, yet again, I was beginning to get a little low on the financial front. I hated the thought of having to write another begging letter, but at least it felt a little better this time; not because I'd become accustomed to begging, but because the money would enable me to get back home. Then, that done, Vic and I hopped on a bus going up to Kandy.

CHAPTER 21

- CANOODLING COUPLES, TEA LEAVES AND TOY TOWNS -

The Sri Lankan hills

Kandy was a beautiful three hour bus ride inland from the west coast and is largely recognised as being the capital of the Sri Lankan highlands. However, though reasonably close geographically, in every other way it's a far, far cry from the baked and busy streets of Colombo. From the very moment you leave the coast, you start climbing into a much cooler and greener country; the traffic chaos then quickly evaporates and the whole atmosphere soon becomes more calming, more charming. Odd then, to learn that Kandy actually retains one of the largest urban communities on the island. But this certainly isn't obvious; for with its central lake, its beautiful botanical gardens and luxuriant surrounding vegetation, it still manages to convey a wonderful air of tranquillity. Either that or it was half day closing!

After a bit of scouting around, Vic and I found a vacant room that was being let within one of the family houses up near the lake. We were greeted by our plump little landlady -complete with obligatory voluminous, floral dress- and once we'd settled in, there was just enough time for an early evening saunter around the water to walk off our dinner. (Not that we'd had any yet, but it seemed a good idea whilst it was still light.) Then, after just one lap of the lake, we went to a nearby restaurant to sample yet another typical Ceylonese meal: a nice plate of number 37, 16 and two egg fried rice. (Yes, okay, so it wasn't exactly a 'local' dish as such but, as I still had stomach problems, I was hankering for something bland but not completely boring, and Chinese seemed to be the answer.) That night I was woken yet again with chronic cramps around the kidney and intestine region and spent most of the night trying to massage them. This was, without doubt, the longest night-time session I'd ever had massaging one of my organs…and most certainly the least fun (Oops, sorry; there goes another extract from, 'Confessions of a Carpenter'!)

Now mentally, I'd long since grown tired of just about everything in this part of the world being laced with 'a hint of chilli'; physically however, despite the visit to the Goan doctor, I suspected that the damage had already been done. Strangely though, as had happened before, I awoke in the morning to discover the pains had completely gone. I never did quite understand that. Why, I even felt up to breakfast, though this was somewhat limited in the, 'absolutely no bloody spices at all' section of the menu. So when asked want I'd like, I eventually settled on the blissfully bland but none-to-exotic 'boiled eggs' option; though I did hold back from requesting soldiers of course, for fear of being misunderstood. Consequently, my breakfast that morning consisted of: two plain boiled eggs, a 'whole' slice of toast and a deft bit of DIY with the supplied knife.

Later, Simon, the photographer from London, also showed up in Kandy. The last I'd seen of him, like so many others before, was in Colva. He seemed extraordinarily pleased to see me, though this may have had something to do with the fact that I could now pay him back the £50 I owed. But because there were also another couple of old faces around, by now I'd just about caught up with everyone who'd passed through Goa during my stay there. This meant that financially I could very nearly wipe my slate clean, an event worthy of celebration. And so, a small group of us retired to a bar and passed a long evening filling the table with empty brown bottles. Not, you'd think, the recommended diet for a man with gastric problems but, at that precise moment, copious amounts of both beer and laughter seemed to be the absolute ideal tonic. I slept well that night and, though in the morning I thought I might pay dearly for my over-indulgences, when I awoke it was to nothing but brilliant sunshine and birdsong. Mercifully, for Vic anyway, the only wind was that which rustled the tops of the trees outside my window.

Later that morning, I found a beautiful old tree down by the lake and spent a very lazy time reading under the dappled light of its huge leafy canopy. As relaxing as this was though, I still found it difficult to be totally absorbed in a book with so many new things about, and so my progress, as always, was slow. Not that there was much happening around here, but even the slightest of things was pleasantly distracting. Everybody seemed so very relaxed as they went about their business; everyone from the chattering, brightly uniformed school-children to shuffling grandparents; box laden deliverers to bag laden shoppers. Even the street sweepers found time to acknowledge me, if only with a nod and a smile. Later, I braved the heat of the day (yes, Kandy was cool compared to the coast but only relatively so) and wandered off to find the botanical gardens.

The gardens, when I arrived, were quite wonderful; a natural haven of peace and tranquillity. In fact, so much so that at first it seemed I had the whole place to myself. But after a short time I began to notice that there was rather more blossoming here than flowers. It transpired that the shrubs and trees of Kandy's botanical gardens weren't only a wonderful retreat for travel weary tourists, but were also the secret haunts of numerous young courting couples. Unable to display too much affection publicly, it seemed that teenagers from all over the town habitually sought sanctuary amongst the beautiful and lush vegetation here. Of course, I tried not to pry, honest; but what was I to do when every time I rounded a bush I bumped into an amorously canoodling couple! But it wasn't that I wanted to invade such a very private moment, it was their reaction to being caught in the act that would always make me smile; for it was invariably the same. The couple would suddenly spot me and, almost immediately, the girl would turn her head away shyly whilst I exchanged a knowing but approving look with her partner. Then, she would try to bury her face in his chest whilst he put a comforting arm around her. It was just so lovely to see, and virtually all the girls were so incredibly beautiful. They had that wonderful combination of long, glossy dark hair, dark smouldering eyes, unblemished brown skin and dazzlingly white teeth. This combination I found tantalising enough, but coupled with the absolute coyest of smiles well, it just made me melt away like an exceedingly large and warm pat of butter...well at least ninety five percent of me anyway!

"How extraordinarily lucky those boys are," I thought. How I wished, at that very moment, that I too could be canoodling in the bushes. It made me think of what incredible power girls can have over us men. And what a lure it is; such raw and natural beauty coupled with that look of sweet innocence. Though sadly, I do recognise of course, that maybe it's me who's the innocent or naïve one here in thinking such a thing still exists; but well, I like to think it does.

That same evening, I joined a German chap for a few beers over a game of chess and afterwards, for a change, managed to get to bed at a reasonable time. In the morning the crowd from Goa were once more splitting up and going their separate ways; some to the north of the island and others back down to the coast to await flights to various far flung places. Others still, had come to the end of their travels -their liberating wanderings- and were re-stuffing their backpacks for the very last time before returning to the real world; a world dictated by routine and heaps of gratuitous paperwork; where the need to actually earn a living would, once again, put out of reach this marvellous fantasy life-style.

Katie and her new found French beau joined me on the bus to Nuwara Eliya and Aussie Vic was there to see us all off. I was sad to be leaving him after our time together and it was plain to see that both of us felt it unlikely we'd ever meet again; and so, we never did the 'swapping addresses' thing, as is the norm'. On reflection, of course, I wish I had. At the time I was probably as guilty as anyone - particularly us males of the species- of enthusiastically jotting down addresses and never bothering to make contact with that person ever again. More latterly, however, I've often envied the relationships struck up whilst away, particularly between girls, and so have made much more of a conscious effort to keep in touch with far flung friends: as my mother constantly reminds me, "If you don't send out any boats…you don't get any back"!

Climbing up to Nuwara Eliya the scenery was simply spectacular; though strangely, not actually very natural. You see, at one time, virtually all the central area of this island would have been thick, thick jungle, but it has long since been turned over to huge tea plantations. Nevertheless, even in its present guise, it's still an undeniably beautiful place. Of course, all this dramatic change in vegetation was largely the fault, or at least 'the doing', of the British who, during their colonial period here, seemed to be willing to move heaven and earth for 'a nice cup of tea'. And this, they very nearly did -well, the earth part anyway.

But it wasn't just the topography, the natural scenery that they changed beyond recognition; they also very much left their mark on the small towns in the area, such as here in Nuwara Eliya. So whilst I may have been slap bang in the middle of Sri Lanka; what with all its neatly clipped hedgerows and orderly flowering front gardens, this little town seemed far more 'Home Counties' than on a lush tropical island. And as for the post office well, if there's anything more quintessentially English, even in England, then you'd be hard pushed to find it. With its bright red brick walls, little boxy windows and perfect paintwork, it just looks fresh out of Trumpton. It even sported the same steep pitched tiled roof and large clock.

Why, I half expected a fire engine to come 'clanging' around the corner manned by, 'Hugh, Pugh, Barney Mcgrew, Cuthbert, Dibble and Grub!'

Alain, the Frenchman, and I passed an afternoon playing snooker at the Grand Hotel. We were both dressed more for the beach than for a smart Country Club, but they let us in all the same. It would've been all too easy for the impeccably turned out staff to turn their noses up at such a couple of ragamuffins but, much to their credit, we were treated like we owned the place. Whether or not this was because the club was totally abandoned I don't know, but in any case, they appeared genuinely pleased to have somebody to serve drinks to, even if it did mean serving the cheapest thing on the menu. (I can't actually recall what it was we had but, having spent a night's accommodation worth of rupees on a game of snooker, it certainly wasn't much!) Still, the setting and ambience of 'The Grand' was quite superb and, for me, this alone justified the outlay.

I daresay, to some, it may have seemed mildly ridiculous pushing little coloured balls around a table with a stick in the middle of the tropics, an audience of ever watchful trophy heads gazing down glassy-eyed from the oak panelled walls; but it was a nice way to spend an afternoon. In any case, it's probably about as close as I'll ever get to sampling life as one of the colonial gentry. Showing up there fifty years too late does have its advantages though; for had we arrived dressed as we were back then, we most certainly would have been shown the door, if not, flung through it.

Nuwara Eliya wasn't big on activities and entertainment

but it was a beautiful place in which to relax. "How nice", I thought, "that however meagre your budget, you can still be surrounded by five star scenery." This, in stark contrast to the places I slept in, of course. By now though, I never really expected much in the way of accommodation for the price I was willing to pay, so I could hardly be disappointed with what I got. It was a little annoying though when, one day, for some inexplicable reason there was a water shortage in town. Particularly annoying, in fact, because this seemed the most unlikely place on the planet to suffer a shortage of water. The lush surroundings and numerous waterfalls were an obvious indication that the place certainly had more than its fair share of rain; it's just that none of it appeared to be reaching the taps. I could have taken a bus to go and wash at one of these waterfalls of course, but nobody seemed to know just how 'temporary' the water stoppage would be, and so I decided to stay put for the time being and hope that I'd be able to wash before my foot and armpit odours joined forces...somewhere, mid trunk. Mind you, at least everyone in town was in the same boat; just unfortunate that it was a boat in dry dock.

Thankfully, the water shortage -or should I say 'stoppage', for there was none- did only last a mere two days before normal service was once more resumed. Now this was fine and heartily welcomed, but it would have been even finer had there been some way of heating the blasted water once it did start running. The thing is, having to choose between two cold taps down on the coast wasn't such a problem but here, up in the hills, the water temperature - when it was running- was rather a shock to say the least. In fact, it seemed the only way to avoid all over frostbite when washing, was to shower well after midday, when the sun had got to the pipes a bit and at least allowed the shower to run in a slightly less solid form. You know, I can never understand people who swear by cold showers - swear 'in' them, yes. Are they trying to prove something or are they all just totally stark raving bonkers masochistic? The only single advantage I can possibly see of standing under bloody freezing cold water by choice, is that if you're a male...it gives you just a little less to wash!

Do you know, if having a shower without water wasn't frustrating enough, I also made an excursion to the local brewery to discover that they didn't have any beer. Now I'm not one to moan but, how frustrating is that! I've known plenty of people who, 'couldn't organise a p*** up in a brewery' but...in your own brewery? Well, actually that's not strictly true about them having no beer; but whilst they claimed to have tons of the stuff, there certainly wasn't any that they were willing to part with. Not that I had any ulterior motive other than to sample the local produce you understand; it just would have been nice to try a drop or two; you know, from a sort of cultural and cuisine-y point of view. Mind you, with hindsight, perhaps they were wise; the last time I did any sampling of this nature was with a girlfriend at a liqueur brewery back in Corfu. They'd very kindly lined up all fifteen of their varieties which I'd duly felt obliged to sample for fear of appearing rude. We'd then returned to our tent on the other side of the island -by motorbike- via a rather more scenic route than I first remembered.

Anyway; back in Sri Lanka...there was clearly no danger

of being one over the 'fourteen' here, so I left the brewery and went and played football with the boys at a local school.

The following day Katie and the sickeningly good-looking Alain, went off walking somewhere -probably to canoodle in the botanical gardens…if there was room! I, meanwhile, sat outside my room listening to Joni Mitchell on Alain's walk-man, and then joined the family -with whom I was staying- to watch a documentary on TV about Prince Charles and Lady Di. None of this family had a particularly good command of English but I tried anyway to explain that I'd actually been there at the royal wedding myself. (I wasn't in St. Pauls of course; I'd just slept on the pavement outside the Cathedral all night -alongside several hundred others- and the following day, had watched the wedding from the top of my carpenter's trestle.) But, as I told this story, the whole family seemed both extremely surprised and delighted by this; to such an extent, in fact, I'm not totally sure that they quite understood the bit about 'sleeping on the pavement' or indeed, 'watching from a trestle'. In any case, they were all so chuffed, I really hadn't the heart to try and make them understand that I wasn't actually invited; it would have been such an anticlimax. So I left them in near 'blissful' ignorance.

In the afternoon I left my family still in their confused excitement and returned to the school to watch the local sports day. It was a lovely way to pass the time; all the children neatly turned out and dressed in white, like they are at sports days the world over -an idea, presumably originating during a convention for washing-powder manufacturers! It was a well ordered and sportsmanlike affair, with every participant gleefully encouraging every other. I sat there on the grass watching the various races and, as my thoughts drifted back to my own old sports days at junior school, so the excited chatter of the children before me gradually faded away, melting somewhere into a hazy background.

Soon my head became filled with distant memories; of sprinting in narrow lanes of strong smelling creosoted grass; of huffing and puffing the three laps round my old playing field; up past the grazing horse, down by the swings and roundabout and back alongside the little stream. Memories of egg and spoon races, sack races, wheelbarrow races in which over-zealous fathers ran with their offspring held rigid by the thighs two feet above the ground, their sons' arms flaying about wildly in mid-air; races where you had to dress in oversized clothes at one end and run to the other to excited cheers from mums; races involving balls, hoops, benches and tyres and, of course, girls in navy-blue knickers. Then my mind drifted back further to the time when Miss Sauter made me spend all afternoon standing in the girls' toilets because I'd chased a girl in there during playtime. It had been an embarrassing episode for a ten year old, and besides, I'd only gone in there chasing some girl during a game of kiss-chase; ironically, I hadn't even wanted to catch her - it's just that I couldn't resist the devilment. Anyway, why should I care; I did my 'time' in the girls' loos and, though occasionally that mixed odour of dust and bleach still permeates my nostrils, I think I came through it all relatively unscathed. And, what's more, they can never ever take away the fact that I still held the playground record for kissing Linda Birchmore for just over three minutes. Ah yes, those were the days!

But, my infantile and halcyon memories were all too short. I was suddenly jolted from my reminiscences by an excited cry as somebody ran across the finishing line. I slowly got to my feet and headed back to the hostel.

That night the two young love-birds, sexy Katie and Alain the bastard -to give him his full title- decided that they'd climb Adams Peak. I was feeling in far too mellow a mood to join them and, in any case, would have felt decidedly gooseberry-like.

Now, Adam's Peak is the highest point on Sri Lanka and, I imagine -because I still haven't climbed it myself- affords terrific views over the whole island. The idea, apparently, is to climb to the peak overnight and reach the summit just before dawn breaks in order to see the sun come up. Then, I'm told, as the sun slowly climbs higher and higher in the sky, you're able to watch the spectacular pyramidal shadow of the peak race across the island until it disappears into the sea on the far side of the island. Quite something...I'd imagine!

Anyway, though I'd made my decision not to go, no sooner had the others left than I lay awake full of envy; not something I'm proud of but...I just was. It occurred to me that, whatever I felt about Katie and Alains' relationship, perhaps, on this occasion, I really had cut off my nose to spite my face. After all I thought, it's surely preferable to be a reluctant gooseberry with company than to lie there alone, 'green' with envy! Not that this was typical behaviour mind; gooseberry or not, normally I absolutely hated to miss out on anything but well, I'd made my bed and now I was just going to have to lie on it!

Katie and Alain returned at 4am the next morning; damp, cold and forlorn. For some reason the train they needed to take wasn't running and they'd spent half the night just trying to get there and the other half trying to get back again, without ever having got anywhere near the peak. They crashed onto their beds next-door to mine, exhausted. I couldn't help but feel a little sorry for them both of course, especially Katie; but, that night, my little bed seemed somehow…just that teensy bit more snug.

Sri Lanka has, without doubt, both wonderfully dramatic scenery and some lovely little towns dotted amongst it. But in my view, the only place which truly combines the two is Haputale. This place just has to be one of the most superb locations of any town I've ever set eyes on; for it's not only reached via a beautiful train journey up through lush tropical forests but, perched as it is, high up on a razor-like ridge, it affords unbelievable views in two directions.

When I first arrived in Haputale, I managed to find a family who were letting out a couple of rooms to supplement their incomes. These rooms were about as near to the crest of the ridge as you could possibly get; and so, location-wise were pretty hard to beat. I quickly moved in and then excitedly went off to explore around town. There were very few places to eat and drink in Haputale and, of the restaurants that did exist, strangely not one of them seemed to have taken advantage of the superb views. So I bought myself a bottle of beer, a small bag of potatoes, carrots and tomatoes, and returned to my room to boil myself up a stew (my host family had very kindly lent me an old blackened pan which doubled nicely as a plate.)

I then sat down just outside the room, alone with my home-cooked supper, watching one of the most magnificent sunsets imaginable; and all in total silence. Sheer bliss!

Up here in the hills it was so much cooler than the coast and therefore, far, far easier to sleep at night; so in the morning, I awoke completely refreshed (from what, I don't know) and went to sit on the other side of the ridge. How strange and wonderful it was to see the sun come up from that spot; a spot not a hundred yards from where I'd seen it sink below the horizon hours earlier. "What a unique and privileged position" I thought. And as the light gathered itself together, I took out my pen and paper and wrote some letters.

Later, when the last of the morning colours had leached from the sky, I returned to the house to do a bit of well overdue clothes washing and to grab some breakfast. Then, feeling decidedly perky and chuffed with myself, I caught a local bus out to the Diyaluma waterfall, down in the valley below. Well, what a place! Look, I don't want to go on again 'but'…here was I at one of Sri Lanka's biggest falls, one of its very best beauty spots, and not a single other person in sight; not a tourist or local, not a fence nor turnstile; nothing but gloriously unblemished nature.

I, once again, passed the whole day doing very little. This was because frankly, it seemed about the best way I could spend my time here. And yet, as I've said previously, this wasn't something which came naturally, it had taken quite some time to acquire the art of doing bugger all, but now that I had the knack, I really quite liked it.

On this particular day, most of the time I just sat about in the sun on a large, smooth rock surrounded by my own little piece of tropical utopia. Then, just occasionally, I'd go and cool off in one of the shallow pools below the falls, languishing in crystal clear heaven. Meanwhile, birds flew about me flitting from perch to perch in total silence, their shrill calls drowned out by the rushing of water. Butterflies everywhere performed synchronised semaphore, opening and closing their fragile, technicolour wings in perfect unison whilst contentedly sucking salts from the warm stones at the water's edge with their long, spirally, liquorice tongues. Then, at my approach, they'd take flight, flying up past the falls; tumbling over and over one another in the air like multi-coloured confetti caught in a thermal updraught, before disappearing somewhere up in the canopy.

I returned to Haputale that evening, relaxed and happy, and went to sit on my ridge again with yet another sunset stew. The scene before me was just so indescribably beautiful; so absolutely perfect that it somehow didn't seem enough just to gaze at it. I wanted so much to be a part of it, to swallow it up. Yes, I realise of course, that this sounds stark raving bonkers but, at that very moment, I felt an incredible urge to jump into it, to be really there, to become one with this miracle of nature. "Christ" I thought, "With scenery like this, who the hell needs drugs!" Maybe it's just as well I didn't have both or who knows what would have happened!

Come morning, in the cold light of day, I felt rather relieved that I hadn't jumped into the scenery. After all, I had to catch the 7am train to 'World's End' -an appropriate destination perhaps for someone who, only hours earlier, had nearly flung himself off a mountain top.

The station I was due to get off at was totally deserted when I arrived; an almost forgotten terminus hacked out of the forest eons before by the British. I had a quick look around and then took a path that led seven and a half miles up through the jungle to a place called Horton's Plain and then, finally, on to World's End.

When I'd seen the name on the map it sounded so intriguing I just had to go. I'm not sure quite what I expected though; the walk there was certainly worthwhile, punctuated as it was with numerous little troops of monkeys chattering and clattering through the branches above; exotic looking birds darting to and fro before a curtain of vivid green. But on arrival at World's End, it seemed the only thing that was intriguing was indeed its name. Why, there didn't actually appear to be anything there save for a solitary old building selling soft drinks to lost souls. Though to be fair, I suppose there could well have been other buildings around, or indeed a whole village for all I know; but the mist up there was so blessed thick it was like wearing glasses made of tracing paper. Granted, it was a beautiful walk to get there alright, but if the station had looked forgotten, then the building I found at World's End well...I can hardly remember if it was memorable enough to look forgotten! No, I'd had quite enough for one day. I walked down the hill a few miles to a place called Farr's Inn and managed to hitch a lift in an old army jeep back to the station. Then, with all the birds and monkeys presumably tucked up in their respective beds, I caught the last train home.

Word on the dirt street here was that the High Cliff Hotel was 'the' place to eat at in Haputale, so the following evening I put my stew on the backburner and went to eat there. Now, The High Cliff, despite its name, didn't quite have the same stunning panorama that my own ridge offered -even though it was sort of high and sort of on a cliff; it did, nonetheless, have very nice food (even nicer, I have to say, than my very own sunset stew.) So, on this occasion, 'the word' on this particular street, was quite right! What's more, it also had other guests of course, and as I'd spent the last few days with nobody to talk to bar myself, I now felt just about ready for some company. This came, yet again, in the form of a rather familiar face for, whilst enjoying my meal there, who should walk in but Aussie Vic. Apparently, he'd just reached town that very day and had moved into the dorm' here at the High Cliff. And so, after a little chat, I decided I'd join him. Here, whilst the views weren't quite perfect, I would at least still be able to have my sunrises and sunsets; but then, once the sun had sunk, how much nicer, I thought, to be able to chat round a table with an old mate, and especially over a few products from the local brewery - assuming they were available!

Talking of which...the brewery down in Nuwaya Elya may have been a tad frugal when it came to dishing out samples, but when it came to Sri Lanka's more famous export, I did at least manage to squeeze a cuppa out of the local plantation, courtesy of Mr. Lipton. You see, Thomas Lipton had been growing tea in Sri Lanka for donkey's years (in fact several donkeys' years -as a donkey's years are normally around say, 30-35 each) and so, I'd decided to do the standard tea factory tour. This was all very interesting of course, and it was nice to see, first hand, the various processes that the leaves have to go through before they arrive in your cup. But what was most revealing was the reason why it's near impossible to get a half decent 'cuppa' here in Sri Lanka. This had always seemed a little intriguing and bizarre to me; a bit like saying to an Inuit, "Shall we build a snowman?" "Oh, sorry, we're fresh out of material!" Anyway, when you actually watch the tea processing, the reason for the lack of quality tea for domestic use soon becomes transparently clear because - and this is a rather basic description of the process- once the leaves are picked, dried and cut up, they then go through a variety of giant sieves and are graded so as to eventually leave nothing but dust. And it's this dust, of course, which is especially reserved for domestic consumption. Well, no wonder the locals drink their tea with mountains of milk and sugar, I thought. These other ingredients aren't added merely as accompaniments to enhance the taste, they're there to provide at least some sort of flavour to what would otherwise be...a cup of hot water. As for the tea dust; it seems it's there purely to add a hint of colour.

What's really much nicer to see than the factories though, are the tea pickers themselves who actually work in the plantations. I found it quite extraordinary how all those women can toil away in the fields for hours and hours on end, and still manage to look so colourful, cheerful and glamorous even. I, for one, have every admiration for them. In fact these particular women made me feel, once again, just how much we have to learn from people in this part of the world, or indeed many parts of the so called 'developing' world. The difference in mentality is nothing less than striking. For these are people whose attitudes to life have still yet to be tainted; whose aspirations are so much more basic, more real. Whose existences have far more meaning than to the majority of those who live in Western society; where lives are dictated almost, by the constant desire to possess more and more material things. Okay, so I'm not so naïve as to suggest that, for these women, theirs is anything but a tough life, and that given half the chance most of them would instantly choose a Western life-style over their own; but then, sometimes, it can be difficult to see the good in what you have without experiencing what you haven't. In any case, there is surely great virtue in harbouring few aspirations whilst still retaining a sense of pride and happiness in what little you do possess. So maybe those 'possessions' aren't always material ones; but, then maybe, just maybe, they're all the richer for that!

(I apologise once again for this outburst. I'll now get off my soapbox and put it up in the loft alongside just about all the possessions I've ever owned...and still do - hypocrite that I am.)

There was supposed to be a wildlife sanctuary of some sort in this area, but every enquiry I made was met by a familiar blank look and an indecipherable, waggling head. So, after roaming the countryside for the best part of a day, I returned to the hostel rather hot, sticky and slightly dejected. In fact, I began to have serious doubts about my chances of ever spotting much animal life in the wild when I couldn't even find them in captivity. But anyway, I never found the sanctuary so that was that.

Back at the hostel meanwhile, I consoled myself by

listening to the birdsong coming from the nearby canopy. I'd made myself a well-salted boiled egg sandwich -to counteract the saline solution which was cascading from my armpits- and then washed it down with a most satisfying cup of tea-coloured milk, with sugar. A lone German traveller called Stephan had just moved in next door and he joined me for lunch. He was an odd looking character really; all thin and wiry, with unruly, straggly blonde hair which, with his pointy features, made him look remarkably like a young weight-conscious Catweasel. It turned out that he came from Berlin, and although he spoke excellent English, he spoke it through a gap between two rather large front teeth, as if trying to whistle at the same time. The outcome of this was that every word he said appeared to have several S's in it; and so, whilst I could understand him okay-ish, a certain amount of concentration was required as if trying to pick out the vocals on an old '78' record.

Like most people though, Stephan had his own particular hidden talent (I firmly believe that most people do possess some sort of hidden talent; it's just that some never get to find out what that talent is, whilst others simply don't recognise it as such.) Anyway, Stephan, it became clear, was a first class classical guitarist -or at least first class to my ears, which of course, from a personal point of view, is all that matters. He'd studied guitar at a variety of different places around Europe -apparently even playing for two years in somebody's conservatory- and, although he only dared travel with a rather cheaper instrument than he was used to, I could have quite happily listened to him for days on end; it was simply wonderful. However, I freely admit that, along with all the adulation, there was also a certain amount of envy on my part as, even as we speak, I have yet to master any tune on the guitar with an 'F' in (yep, I just can't play no 'F'in song!) Still, and this certainly isn't sour grapes, I was extremely pleased that Stephan's forte was 'classical' guitar and not rock or pop. A great guitarist he may have been, but I don't think I could've suffered rock vocals with those teeth. "And she'ssss buying a sssstairway to heaven". No thanks.

By this time I'd become more used to, or even slightly blasé about, my stunningly beautiful surroundings; and the bus ride to Ratnapura was again, no exception. I got off the bus and walked a mile down the road to go and stay with a family whom I'd heard about. I was now in the heart of gem country and so, of course, there was a gem museum nearby and a small store selling overpriced sapphires. I had hoped that the sapphires up here in the hills would be a lot cheaper, being as they were closer to the source where they were mined. Unfortunately this didn't appear to be the case, and so any ideas of reviving my new business as a gem trader -which hadn't actually started anyway- were once again shelved.

Like a lot of people in this area, the father of my host family had spent all of his post-education life in the local mine. I asked him if he'd ever come across anything of real value. He replied that in all the years that he'd worked at the mine, he'd only ever once personally found a sapphire of significant value. Apparently, the stone which he'd discovered -and subsequently handed in to the mine owners- had turned out to have a market value of over US$13,000. He, as merely the finder, had received rather less...such is life!

355

Do you know, one of the real benefits of staying with a family over say, at a hotel or hostel, is that not only are all meals provided, but that they are usually typical of the region -though I did have a quiet word about the chillies. The downside is -in this particular case- that, though the miner's wife provided a very nice home-cooked dinner, it was only of a size meant for an Asian body. My problem was, how could I possibly say anything about it? It wasn't as if I could sneak off to my bedroom and fill up on an emergency supply of peanuts and biscuits. One: because it would seem incredibly rude to my hosts; and two: because...I didn't have any. So, that first night, I spent a quiet evening in around the television with all the family; quiet that is, apart from an irritatingly raucous TV programme and a most ungrateful stomach!

It was a little difficult to explain to them all that I would much sooner talk than to watch a second rate American soap on TV. I did make a few attempts at conversation, of course, but I always got the impression that I was interrupting something. To me the programme was mind-numbingly boring, but I could see that to every member of the family, this was something quite special; still, each to his own. I suppose there were odd times when their eyes did leave the screen briefly, but -as in Lahore- only ever to satisfy themselves that I was equally entranced in what they were watching. Well, what could I do! I sat there with my eyes on the TV screen and my mind anywhere but; just occasionally, giggling or exclaiming...and hoping that I was doing it all in the right places. They were a nice, kind and homely family though, and I couldn't bring myself to be too honest. But in the morning, I thanked them for their hospitality and hopped on a bus down to the south coast and Tangalle.

CHAPTER 22

- SCORPIONS, QUICKSAND AND THE RELUCTANT FISHERMAN -

The Sri Lankan beaches

Tangalle was my first brochuresque type palm-fringed beach since Goa. I plumped for staying at the Sunflower Guest House, right down on the beach, checked my stuff in and then went off to change the last of my money. (There must be something about being near destitute and being on a palm-fringed beach!) I then bought a few provisions from a local store and spent over two hours there playing 'caram' with the boys who ran it. Now, caram is a popular board game normally played with draughts, or 'coins', as they're called -if you can afford the real thing- but in this part of the world, is invariably played with specially serrated metal counters of the type supplied free with beer bottles. (There's a certain irony perhaps lost on non-beer drinkers, about using bottle tops as 'draughts'.) It was interesting to note that this game seemed to take precedence over everything, including serving customers. To be fair, this may have been because there weren't any, but I somehow doubt it. It's just that, compared to back home, they happen to have a slightly different set of priorities here.

It was nice to while away the time playing with these boys; and then, after a few games, in which I was soundly thrashed, I went for a stroll along the beach. It wasn't long though before I was enticed by the sound of the waves and decided to go for a quick dip in the sea. I'd been warned of the heavy undertow in this area but, unaccustomed to such things in Worthing, I thought, "Well, how bad can it be?" Not five minutes later, I found out. I'd only intended wading out to waist height, but no sooner had I got that far than I turned and started back up the beach. Well, within seconds the ground had completely disappeared from beneath me. It was simply incredible; unbelievable! Like the Main Man upstairs was playing a cruel joke; like he'd suddenly, on a whim, magic-ed a trapdoor in his vast and watery stage. I tried hard to find a footing; I managed a couple of toe-holds in the roaring shingle and tried to claw my way back up the beach, but it was hopeless; it was like trying to climb a turbo-charged escalator in the wrong direction. I was losing ground quickly and began to panic. Then, just as I was getting seriously out of my depth, suddenly I was propelled forward by a massive, explosive surge of water from behind. I desperately grasped at the gritty sand on all fours, but the hand and foot-holds quickly disappeared between my fingers and toes. Again I was buffeted from behind. I took in a mouthful of salt water then, gasping for air, again desperately plunged both arms into the sand, this time holding just a little more ground before being dragged back. Then, just one more massive surge from behind and at last I was clear of the steep slope. I coughed and spluttered exhaustedly at the water's edge. There was no-one on the beach; absolutely no-one to see or hear me. I'd made it this time but...only just. Next time perhaps, I would take a little more notice of what I was told.

That evening I chatted to Ely -a girl from Anglesey- over a beachside curry. The surf looked beautiful in the fading light, but all the same, I was happy to be viewing it from a distance. I lay on my bed that night with the sea breeze tap-tap-tapping a palm frond against my roof; the roar of the surf still scouring the beach, ushering a warning to heedless strays. Then, I drifted off to sleep.

It took all day getting from Tangalle to Hickadawa. Hardly a great distance, but a journey involving no less than two local buses and a train; so by the time I'd arrived it was already 6.30 in the evening. The main street was completely lifeless at this time and so I made for the only bright light that shone out of the darkness, a solitary beckoning beacon. Its source was a small and typical corner shop -except that it wasn't on a corner- and outside stood a man-sized cut-out of a tube of Colgate toothpaste; above it, a sign saying, 'The Pharmacy'. I went in and sidled past a couple of hunched up old women who were there examining the small print on a remedy for piles or the suchlike, and strode up to the counter,
"How can I be helping you?" said the proprietor.
"I'd like a bed for the night please," I said jokingly. He smiled a Colgate smile, waggled his head from side to side and led me out the back to a small dark room, leaving his two customers still out front studying his wares. You know, I hadn't really expected to be offered a room at a chemist, but after a whole day on road and track, I didn't much care where I lay my head for the night which, as it happens, was just as well. For, although I was glad of the room, it was absolutely miniscule; as dark and depressing as a Munchkin's coal-hole, with nothing but a postcard-sized window hidden behind a filthy net curtain for light. I pulled back the curtain to reveal a pane of equally filthy and exceedingly frosted glass which appeared to have been coated in dust and curry. "That's useful" I thought,

"wonder if I'll ever know when it's morning?" But it seemed there was no choice; I quickly moved in, dumped my pack down and went out of the pharmacy to see if there was any life in Hickadawa after dark.

Out on the street, there were faint sounds coming from somewhere just up the road, and so I followed them to a hostel called, 'The Pink House'. As I got nearer, it seemed the only nightlife around was being provided by a lone TV in its communal lobby. But what came from this television sounded strangely but intriguingly familiar, so I went in to investigate. I didn't really have very high expectations about what I'd find there of course but well, some two hours later, I was back in my dark, dank shoebox of a room as pleased as punch. For however tiny and squalid my little hutch was, right now I couldn't have cared less; I'd just watched good old Spurs beat West Bromwich Albion 2-1, and right here in the middle of a tropical ghost town. How very satisfying; what an absolute treat! But alas, my buoyant mood was short lived; for later that same night -whilst asleep in The Pharmacy- God knows why, but I had a horrendous bout of diarrhoea; the mother of all Delhi bellies; a cataclysmic case of the Calcutta quickstep. The Pharmacy, somewhat ironically, remained very much closed; and in the morning when it opened…I'd recovered.

The following day I was up bright and early, though due to my ultra-frosty window, hadn't actually discovered that it was either bright or early until I'd left the room. I thanked Mister Colgate for his kindness -but not for his room- and went over the road to stay at The Pink House.

Later that morning, I found somewhere where I could hire a mask and snorkel and went snorkelling just off the beach. It was the first time in my life I'd ever snorkelled over a coral reef and well, what a fantastic thing it is to do, isn't it! You know, I'd go as far as to say, it has to be about the nearest you'll ever get to watching a natural history television programme...but in reality. Okay, so I agree that real life is a hundred times better than watching a screen, but given that wildlife photographers spend days, weeks or even months bringing us the sort of shots we are used to seeing on TV, trying to watch wildlife in the flesh can often be somewhat frustrating and disappointing. Coral reefs, however, are most definitely a rare exception to this. The colours, shapes, sizes and sheer abundance of both fish and coral are just indescribable; so, so beautiful in fact, that they are beyond, well, beyond...clichés. It's almost as if you've been shrunk down to the size of a tadpole and thrown into a great big watery kaleidoscope; the privileged guest of myriad fascinating creatures, all of them very much in their own strange but beautiful element. It was hard to believe all this was real. In fact, I spent so much time suspended over that reef, slowly treading water and gawping in sheer wonderment that, by the time I'd decided to call it a day, I looked like I myself was something from the deep. The whole of my body looked like a giant, well pickled albino walnut, I had severe salt sores around the crutch and a bright red ring round my face from the snorkel mask; the ring so incredibly defined, it looked like I'd just been snogged by an extremely large and passionate gospel singer.

That same evening I walked along -still with my red ring- through the black night from The Pink House to The Blue Fox...for a slap-up seafood meal with a couple from Enfield. They too had been snorkelling that day and so we talked and ate fish; and then finished off a long evening with banana fritters, ice-cream and far too much beer. I then returned to The Pink House in the small, 'wee' hours of the morning and spent most of what was left of the night, in the small 'wee' room just outside.

Given my excesses of the previous night, when I eventually surfaced later in the morning, I decided to give breakfast a miss. I washed what few clothes I had left and then caught a bus to Weligama. Now, Weligama is one of those places that few foreigners are likely to have heard of but, on seeing an advertising poster of Sri Lanka, would almost certainly let out a knowing, "Aaaahhh, that place!" You see, it may be only a teeny-weeny village on the south coast of the island, but it is home to one of Sri Lanka's most famous and iconic images; that of the 'stilt fishermen.'

Well, ho-hum…It was a beautiful day yet again and so I decided to stop off at Weligama and try to get some shots of the fishermen in action. I walked down to the beach and could plainly see the tall stilts -with all their cross pieces tied on as standing platforms- sticking up above the waves. It was an unusual spectacle really, more like a small coppice of rustic crucifixes than fishing platforms. The only trouble was that whilst I found the stilts alright, there wasn't a single fisherman in sight. I hung around for a while, all seemed just perfect: cool breeze, sun, beautiful backdrop, everything; just no blessed fishermen. After a couple of hours and still waiting, it was beginning to look as though nothing much was going to happen and so I wandered off through the trees and knocked on the door of one of the thatched huts sprinkled amongst the palms. A tall lean chap -I'd guess in his forties- came to the door and stepped out into the sun, so I asked him what was going on,

"Why aren't there any fishermen out on the stilts today?" I queried.

"Too rough" he replied, squinting heavily against the sunlight.

"Well yes, I suppose", I replied disappointedly. In reality though, I thought, "Yes, admittedly there's a bit of a breeze, but doesn't it make the sea so wonderfully frothy for my photos!" Still, I sort of understood his predicament; he was, after all, a fisherman rather than a photographic model, there for the whim of a passing tourist. I nodded a slightly dejected nod and turned to go. "Blast" I thought, "I've come all this way and missed out on capturing one of the greatest and most iconic images of Sri Lanka." I started to walk away, silently cursing my luck, but then swivelled to face him.

"I don't suppose...?" But I didn't get to finish. Already, I could see the answer written across his broadly grinning face. He disappeared into his little hut and reappeared two minutes later clasping a rod and tackle. Then, after brief negotiations, we settled on a sum of ten rupees (or about 13 pence) for him to become my 'model' ephemeral fisherman.

Now, I have to say, it's normally a little against my principles to pay people simply to pose for photographs, but as I'd had to manipulate the whole situation in the first place, today seemed an excellent time to make an exception. Anyway, if I needed to justify lowering my principles at all, well, he did seem an exceedingly likeable chap -both convivial and extremely un-pushy- and besides, I felt quite sure he could use the money.

And so, as far as I could see, we were now all set; me with my camera and him with his rod and tackle. So off I started toward the beach again. But, before I'd walked two or three steps, to my surprise, I was immediately beckoned back by the fisherman. He then indicated for 'me' to follow 'him', but in totally the opposite direction. Perhaps he had other fishing gear to fetch, I thought; maybe he wanted to show me a more scenic route down to the beach? We hadn't gone more than twenty paces when we came across another small cluster of near identical huts; and that's when the shouting started. Well, before you could say Tom Sawyer, at least a dozen other men had popped out from their little doorways, and all of them happily brandishing fishing rods and tackle. Do you know, I could have talked 'til I was blue in the face but it was absolutely hopeless trying to explain to them that I'd never actually intended paying the whole village to turn out. So off we all strode back toward the beach, me and my small army of fishermen, all laughing happily as we went; their laughs rather heartier than my own.

When we reached the water's edge, I readied myself on the beach whilst my one bona fide hired fisherman waded into the water, closely watched -on dry land- by all the others. It was only now that it became clear why this had been deemed a 'rest day'. Why, the beach cut away so steeply here that, only a little way out, the waves were already lapping purposefully at his chest. Then, just a few very slow and tentative steps more and, by the time he'd reached his stilt, he was up on his toes and desperately fighting to keep his head above the surf. He then began to clamber up onto the stilt, all the while being buffeted by wave after wave after wave, and yet still trying to hang onto his precious rod. Well, there just didn't appear to be any easy way of doing this; it looked so pitiful a sight; and by the time he'd even got the one leg hooked over the cross-piece he looked absolutely worn out. The poor chap clung onto both pole and rod like a bedraggled five-legged spider trying desperately to avoid yet another wash down the plughole; he was completely and utterly spent, pooped, done in! Now, naturally this did make me feel just a tad guilty at being responsible for such a stunt, but all the other fishermen around me well, they seemed to neither share my concern for their mate nor indeed did they seem terribly bothered about whether or not they joined in. In fact they appeared to find the whole spectacle highly amusing.

Eventually of course, my one brave and gangly fisherman did manage to scramble up onto his cross. He then gingerly stood up, wrapped a sinewy brown leg around the upright for balance and got himself into a semi-comfortable position before dutifully sticking out his rod to do a spot of mock-fishing. I then smiled, gave him the thumbs up and quickly took a couple of snaps before beckoning him back to safety. Well, by now his fisher-mates were all laughing out loudly and, as he gasped and scrambled back up the beach, it became quite clear that this was nothing but pure entertainment to them. I gave him a friendly slap on the back; he spluttered and smiled, and then I handed him his money and we shook hands. Of course, no sooner had I produced the money than, within seconds, almost simultaneously a dozen other hands were thrust out toward me. I looked up from the circle of hands to the faces above them...not one wore a smile! Slightly nervously, I again tried to explain that "I'd only ever wanted one fisherman", and besides, regardless of whether they'd turned up or not, there was only the one of them who'd actually done anything. I awaited their reaction, realising only too well that my own ideas of 'fair play' didn't alter the fact that this could be a rather delicate situation. I just didn't quite know how these men would react; I felt alone and vulnerable. With no money forthcoming, they withdrew their hands; there were looks of disappointment all around. But then, before I could even think of having second thoughts....every single one of the fishermen's faces immediately broke into the broadest of grins. It was all okay; just a game; they'd simply been playing with me: a merry bunch of mischievous fishermen 'baiting' a gullible tourist. Well next, they did nothing more than turn and walk back to the village, but all the while smiling at me over their shoulders, still laughing away well into the distance. I stood and watched them go until they disappeared amongst the palm trees; then I picked up my pack and headed off to the main road.

Sometime during the afternoon I managed to catch a bus back along the coast to Galle. I then bought another nice warm film for my camera and sat on top of the fort wall, alone there, watching the sunset in blissful silence. The big walled fort seemed totally deserted at this time; the sunset, one of the most beautiful and glowing I'd ever seen. The light was dimming fast now and, as the sun sank into the ocean, so it tinted the huge stone fort rhubarb red; filling every crack, crevice, joint and pockmark with deep dark shadows; lending the rough stonework the appearance of a deep pink but natural sponge; a surreal sort of lunar texture; an exaggerated third dimension. Then, just as the sun disappeared below the horizon, I left my wall and ambled off through the half light, back toward the road.

A few minutes later, just as I rounded a corner within the fort, a small slim figure stepped out from the dark shadows,
"You want jiggy-jiggy?" the voice said. A small girl sidled toward me and took hold of my hand. "Odd time and place for a dance", I thought? She was a young and pretty little thing, from what features I could make out, no older than fifteen or sixteen maybe. How very sad then that she was 'willing' to rent out her body to a total stranger. I strongly suspect though that she had little choice; who knows! I felt so sad and sorry for her, but shook my head before slowly, sympathetically removing my hand from hers. Then, before I knew it, she'd disappeared back into the shadows. I left the fort in contemplative silence.

Once again back at The Pink House, I passed what was left of the evening chatting to Colin and Ali, from Enfield, over a few beers. Although nearly all my days seemed to be amazingly rich and varied, in truth, most diary entries for the evenings could have been photocopied thus: "Chatted over a few beers". This was never intentional mind, but almost invariably how the days would finish up. Of course, most of these conversations were with like-minded travellers, often with people representing countries from all over the globe. But, though I came across just about every conceivable language, almost all of the conversations were conducted in the near global one of English -apart from with the French of course! So, although the majority of evenings were pretty similar, because of the incredible diversity of races involved, I found the topics of conversation both fascinating and varied. That is to say, once you've got over the initial ten minutes of conversation, in which just about every living soul I met could simply have exchanged personal travel cards with me with the answers to: name; country you come from; countries you've been to; countries you're going to: cheapest place you've stayed at; longest and most uncomfortable bus ride you've taken; where your worst bout of diarrhoea was. And when the answers to all these have been satisfied, it is then, and only then, that you are free to partake in a perfectly nice evening's conversation, freely exchanging ideas and views.

You know, if you happen to be an English speaker, one of the biggest advantages of travel in a country like India or Sri Lanka, is that it's not only possible to converse with most travellers but -for those of us who choose to- with many of the local people also. This for me is an incredible advantage; for what better way can there be to get to know a country than to talk to the people who actually live there. Personally, I enjoy these impromptu encounters immensely, and it's surely one of the best reasons to travel, even though, invariably, the conversations with the majority of local people will fall into one of three categories - and often, all three. That is to say: Religion, money or…sex! Now, all of these three topics seem to have a profound influence on the lives of every population in every place I've ever come across. But if the topics of conversation remain the same, the influences they have on life could hardly be more different. For, in this part of the world, it's almost invariably the pursuit of the first which helps people to forget about the lack of the second; unlike in the West where; the pursuit of the second 'makes' people forget about the first. And all the time -in my experience anyway- the most talked about subject by both parties, is actually......the pursuit of the third! (I make no judgement about any of these things...merely observations. I'd also like to add though, that 'the pursuit of the third' conversations were almost invariably...with men.)

For me though, most of the really, really interesting places to travel to in the world, are also, rather conveniently, the cheapest; or at least they have the potential to be -depending on the individual's needs for 'home comforts' like electricity and running water...that sort of thing. Do you know what though; no matter how frugal I am when it comes to transport and accommodation, somehow, half my travel budget -rightly or wrongly- seems to go on beer. Not that I have a particular weakness in that direction; it's just that beer, to me, happens to be the perfect accompaniment to an evening's conversation, when an evening's conversation is often the only form of entertainment available...especially when you don't have the luxury of electricity and running water.

The other reason why the beer tab usually makes up a significant proportion of my total budget is that, even where it's available cheaply, it's never going to be cheap compared to say, local food; and quite rightly too. Though, by 'local' food, I am of course, referring to the likes of rice and chapattis rather than the normal travellers' fare such as banana pancakes, muesli, porridge and ginormous tropical fresh fruit salads. Mind you, beer drinking does have its advantages -apart from the bleedin' obvious. One: that it's almost always safe to drink anywhere in the world, and two: after just a few nights out on the razzle, you'll have just about acquired enough counters for your own caram set!

The next night, still pondering the fact that I'd turned down the chance of a 'jiggy-jiggy', I retired to my room in The Pink House reasonably early. But just before performing my pre-bedtime ablutions, I spied a rather large scorpion at my bedside. Now, I know that this is purely a personal view -not necessarily shared by all- but well, it was a rather beautiful animal. So anyway, I got down on all fours and studied it up close for a while under the one candle power light bulb and, as it had decided to remain totally motionless, I gave it a gentle prod with a piece of paper. It still seemed terribly reluctant to move though, however indignant at being prodded, and so I left it alone a while and ran out to the communal room, excitedly beckoning a couple of locals to share in my discovery.

Shortly, I returned with the two local boys following behind me, and when I showed them my new pet scorpion, they quickly crouched down as if to study it. But then, before I could even think about reaching out a protective arm, "Noooo!"..........Thwack! It was too late! The poor wretched creature was splattered into the lino floor by a giant brown sandal. It was terrible; horrific; I stood there aghast! But, you know, it was quite pointless ranting. Neither of the boys could understand a word of English and even less, my obvious frustration and annoyance with them. They looked at one another and then at me, clearly perplexed. Then, they both shrugged and left the room, the second of them casually scuffing his foot into a scorpion-juice stained sandal. I went to bed that night feeling decidedly sad and guilty.

The following morning I'd intended making an early start

back to Colombo, but as a young French girl had just checked into The Pink House, I was easily persuaded to stay on for breakfast. As I sat there, it didn't seem all that important what we talked about; in fact, personally, I wasn't really bothered about talking at all. Just to sit there and listen to a French girl speaking English was enough for me -and especially a beautiful one. God; why does that always sound so damned sexy! But, you know, I decided at that very moment, it isn't French that's the 'language of love' at all; it's simply the accent. Why, a Frenchman speaking French merely sounds as if he's trying to dislodge a particularly large snail from his throat, but get him -or in my case, her- to speak English, and I, for one, just totally go to pieces. In fact, "I um, ow you zay…like putty in zer 'and!" Too bad then that the French girl in question didn't feel the same about my English accent or, I don't know, perhaps she did and it was the 'words' I used which were wrong? Either way, her answer was a definitive "Non!"

It was lunchtime by the time I'd left Hichadawa, but by mid-afternoon I'd already checked back into the old Ex-Servicemen's Hostel in Colombo. Outside, the capital -as usual- was full of the daily hum-drum of people and traffic, and the air lay draped over the city like a hot and heavy blanket. I decided to brave the afternoon heat for a visit to the post office again and received yet another letter from my mother, which I eagerly read over steak and chips at the Metropolitan Hotel. This wasn't normal, of course; the steak, I mean. It was supposed to be a sort of, 'welcome back to civilisation' treat; but frankly, I should have stuck to the chapattis. You know, I don't think I've ever eaten a piece of beef which tasted so much like a lightly charred flip-flop; and the chips were little better. How on earth can somewhere with such a grand name serve up such utter garbage! And to make matters worse, my 'special' meal hardly lay inside my stomach long enough for me to pay the extremely overpriced bill. Yes, okay I know; I won't go into detail but suffice to say that, since Goa, my body didn't always seem terribly keen on what was being put into it. Of course, had the effects of the problem been on a more regular basis i.e. every time I ate something, I'd undoubtedly have bitten the bullet and abstained from all food for at least twenty-four hours -as this seems to me the best cure for any form of Calcutta Quickstep. The trouble was that my bowels just weren't sending me consistent messages, and some days I felt quite healthy even; so well, I just kept right on stoking them up. Also, you have to remember, I still didn't know about the rather longer term problems to come; that this wasn't simply a case of Delhi belly, Calcutta quickstep or Bombay bowel but…'Revenge of the crunchy-coated prawn!'

By this time I'd learnt just a little more about how to, and how not to, obtain money whilst in Asia; and so, in this aspect at least, I was a tiny bit wiser than a few weeks earlier. Granted, I was once again edging precariously close to the banana and bread line, but at least this time round, I'd had the forethought to write home for more money 'before' I'd actually needed it.

That morning I received a telex from home saying that there'd be £300 deposited in a bank in England and that I could pick it up at a local bank in Colombo. Well, to my great relief and surprise, that's exactly what happened. I went to the bank and received the money over the counter without having to endure so much as a single bus ride, ferry ride, excruciatingly futile and frustrating queue; nor even a single ear-steaming, gasket blowing, pull-your-hair-out-by-the-roots phone-call. Why, I didn't even have to sell off any of my remaining clothing. Absolutely brilliant! In fact I felt that, if ever there was a cause for celebration then this was surely it. And where better to celebrate than at my very next discovery; yes, not for me one of Colombo's pubs, clubs or restaurants, but, hurrah…another milk-shack -uncannily like the one back in Rameswaram. In fact, my new discovery even carried the very same stock of plain, strawberry and chocolate flavoured milk, and so I celebrated my being rather flush by going for 'a few pints' at the local. And well, what can I say; I was in seventh heaven. Within ten minutes of arriving, I felt like a joyously happy but colour-blind snooker-player; quickly sinking a white, a pink and…a nice long brown.

A short while later -halfway through downing another pink, in fact- then who should happen along but Stephan, the Catweasel-esque German guitar-player whom I'd met back up in the hills. What a nice surprise! I offered to buy him a pint, which he eagerly accepted; though he seemed to find it hard to hide his disappointment when I gestured to the stool beside me. Nevertheless, we had a good old chat, mostly about the ssstrange sssightsss we'd both ssseen; or else I'd tell him sssome ssstupid jokesss. And then he'd laugh as one laughs when not quite understanding the punch line -starting off quite boldly and heartily for a second or two, but then coming to an abrupt halt mid-cackle. Not that Stephan was at all dense in any way; he just didn't seem to share the same sense of humour as me -though this may have been to his credit. Anyway, after a while, he put his half finished pint down beside his stool, got up, said he'd "ssssee me later". Then he disappeared into the crowd. It was the last I ever saw of him.

I was quite happy sitting there on my own though, and stayed on to sink a plain milk chaser (four point penalty of course). Then, I waited for the sting to vanish from the afternoon sun before returning to the hostel for a refreshingly cold shower.

Over the next couple of days it was far too hot and humid to move from my room -apart from the odd shuttle to and from the milk shack. Life outside though, carried on as usual; (no such choice for the vast, vast majority.) This was without doubt the most uncomfortable and oppressive atmosphere I'd ever experienced; and it seemed, every single non-native around was of the exact same opinion. Consequently, anytime I was back at the hostel during the daytime, my dorm would be full to the brim with semi-naked bodies spread-eagled atop their sheets like extras in a scene from M.A.S.H. Just occasionally a couple of us would exert ourselves enough to get through a whole game of chess, but others simply stared blankly at the ceiling all day long, like rows of half baked gingerbread men on a baking tray: all expressionless and immobile, listlessly listening to overplayed tapes of Dire Straits. All the time though, amongst this 'orgy' of lethargy, there was the constant flow of people plodding back and forth between dorm' and shower block, all plodding and dripping...in both directions.

One day in February -February 4th in fact- as I lay on my bed mesmerised by the rigorously whirring ceiling fan and vaguely listening to a neighbour's radio, I heard the tragic news that Karen Carpenter had died! The most crystal clear female singing voice in history -in my humble opinion- had gone. It wasn't terribly obvious what she'd died of at the time, though subsequently somebody said that it may have been anorexia (though, as yet, this disease didn't seem to have been 'invented'.) You know, people often say that they can always remember where they were when JF Kennedy was shot, or when Elvis died; well, for me, it was Karen Carpenter. To me she would be a great loss. Not in any sordid or carnal way; it's just that she had the most beautiful singing voice imaginable. (The sordid and carnal stuff I normally reserved for Natalie Wood. Mmmm, now she really 'was' sexy. Ah well...time for another cold shower!)

Of course, I didn't spend the whole two days lying on my bed or downing pints at my local. No, that only accounted for 90% of my waking hours. But then, just occasionally, I'd nip -or rather drag myself- out to buy the odd bit of food; just enough to survive on -which wasn't a great deal really. I suppose though, it would be fair to say that my food shopping wasn't always terribly imaginative at these times. In fact the full extent of my groceries normally consisted of nothing but canned mackerel and a bit of bread; which, like a hamster, I would smuggle back to my dorm' and eat in the privacy of my own little space -not so much, cordon bleu, as 'cordoned off'! But this sudden penchant for eating in wasn't because I'd suddenly contracted a severe bout of agoraphobia, it was simply because the fan above my bed afforded such rare relief from the giant al fresco sauna outside the door. I could have eaten at one of the many restaurants in town of course, but for two reasons: one -my body was still having severe objections to anything even remotely spicy, hence the bread and mackerel: and two - even if I could have stomached a 'proper' meal, unless I was willing to dip into my new flight fund, the only restaurants within my normal budget, most definitely wouldn't have had ceiling fans.

Downstairs at the hostel meanwhile, there was a large communal room reserved for the 'real' ex-servicemen. Shuttling past this room every day, I often looked in to see what was going on. In the daytime this usually wasn't a whole lot, but during the evenings there would sometimes be quite a sizeable gathering. Naturally, all the ex-servicemen there were of normal retirement age and so, as they were around when the British were still in Sri Lanka, they could all speak fairly good English. Somewhat surprisingly though, most of these men appeared to have nothing but good memories of the British occupation and they seemed only too happy to tell me their stories about 'the good old days'. Whether this was because I myself was an Englishman and that it was partly for my benefit it's hard to know; but, all the same, they were an exceptionally nice and amiable old bunch. In fact, I enjoyed our couple of evenings together immensely; chatting away and drinking more than our fair share of Arrack and sodas; singing old English songs until it was time for us all to be chucked out. Then, we'd give each other over-amorous, alcohol fuelled hugs and they'd all toddle off back to their homes and wives somewhere in the city, and I'd return to my M.A.S.H. bed and fan upstairs. Actually, in truth, I wasn't terribly fond of Arrack, but it was virtually impossible to sleep without having consumed substantial amounts of the stuff. Why, even after a hearty, well lubricated singing session I'd still sometimes find myself standing upright, bleary-eyed and woolly headed under a cold shower at 4am. A couple of times I even resorted to creeping downstairs to pass the time reading one of the complimentary newspapers at reception. Mostly though, I'd just lie on my bed bored out of my tiny mind; not knowing quite what to do with myself. God, it was boring! Hour after hour after hour, lying there in the half light, spread-eagled under a miniature helicopter. It was like, well like...watching paint peel; which is quite ironic really, given that this was one of the few places I'd stayed in where... it didn't!

Katie, Julie and Alain had also moved into the ex-servicemen's hostel and so, as this particular day was Katie's birthday, we managed to track down a place where we could both eat and dance the night away in order to celebrate the occasion. This wasn't just a birthday party though, for sadly, it was also to be my very last night in Sri Lanka before flying back home to England.

The venue we chose for our big night out was in Mount Lavinia, just outside the city. But before going out for the evening, we decided that, as it was considerably cheaper, we'd have a few drinks at our hostel bar first. Now, I don't doubt that, with hindsight, downing two bottles of Arrack between the four of us, before even arriving at Mount Lavinia, wasn't one of our better ideas. Apparently though, we all had a fantastic time -as we later discovered from other sources. And, whilst I can't precisely vouch for the other restaurant guests and courting couples around us,

I'm sure they would have shared in our euphoria. I mean, who could fail not to be moved by such melodic singing at one in the morning; and especially as this particular 'gig' came from such a wonderful venue -namely, from within the centre of the fountain outside the restaurant.

Anyway, though thoroughly soaked on the outside and pickled on the inside, we did all eventually manage to hitch a lift back to Colombo. Not that I actually recall this very well but, all I can say is, we obviously found ourselves an extremely charitable truck driver, who saw to it that we all arrived back at the hostel, sodden but in one piece. Mind you, it did strike me as rather fitting that I should leave a puddle on the cab floor of both the very first and last lifts of my journey from England to Sri Lanka. At least this time the driver had the none-too-small compensation of being squashed up alongside Katie in her ultra-wet T-shirt. We slept well that night; as I'm sure did one…slightly damp but happy truck driver.

In the morning it was difficult to say whether my sheet sleeping-bag was wringing with sweat or with the contents of the previous night's fountain. Katie and Alain had yet to surface and so Julie and I went for breakfast at a small street café somewhere. We sat there with our thick heads and thin teas; the conversation decidedly intermittent. Then I went off to a local travel agent to pick up the flight ticket which would take me back to London.

When we returned to the hostel the others were already downstairs and so we joined them at the bar for a very last drink. Not that I felt in the mood for alcohol of any description, but the others were nothing if not persuasive. The thing is you see, I don't normally believe all that 'hair of the dog' stuff; and in any case, it seems to me there's always the danger you can end up staying on for the whole dog. On this occasion though, we all felt pretty much the same as one another, and so it really was, 'just the one'; yes, just the one for our long, long and various roads. We then said our goodbyes and parted company for the very last time on this trip; the three of them going on to Negombo, and me off to the airport.

At Colombo airport the two customs officials were pleased to see that I'd somehow mislaid my money declaration card. Pleased, that is, because this meant that they didn't have to make up any sort of excuse in order to extract a bribe. (Incidentally, this declaration card is a bit of paper that you fill in on entering the country, and on which you're supposed to record what you're bringing 'in' so that, when you leave, they can check that it doesn't differ greatly from what you are taking 'out'.) Anyway, after a thorough searching session - by me on myself- the upshot was...that I'd clearly lost the thing. I knew, of course, that there was likely to be an on-the-spot fine of some kind the moment I saw the two officers' eyes light up. I also knew though, that I had a few US dollars in cash that I'd been sent, cunningly tucked away for just such an occasion should it ever arise.

Now apparently -according to the customs officials- the normal fine for losing your declaration card is US$10 in 'cash'. Well, naturally, my initial reaction to their demand was to plead poverty, but under the circumstances, I could hardly act the poor traveller any more than I already looked the part. Still, I did my very best to look pitiful and helpless, and even went through a great charade of desperately searching about my person for money...And all the time the busy queue of people behind kept right on going; shuffling past me through customs; annoyingly, every single one of them passing without incident.

"Umm, how about US$2?" I said, a little thin and pathetically. The first officer looked at me briefly, unimpressed, and waved more passengers through. A few more minutes passed; I did some more mock rummaging.

"Look, it's the end of my holiday and that's all I have left" I said, trying to look even more desperate. Still he was unmoved. Another handful of passengers filed through.

"Look, pleeeease," I begged, indicating my T-shirt, shorts and well aerated baseball boots, "I don't even have any more clothes!" -well at least this was true. Yet more people passed by, several of them pausing just long enough for a scowl; that, "Oh yes, I wonder what he's done?" sort of look; eyeing me up and down and curling their lips in that accusatory fashion.

Another few minutes; and then…the very last passenger. Time was running out. It was metaphorically, 'the eleventh hour' of our uneasy stalemate (in reality, pretty damned near the twelfth hour.) I hung it out for as long as I possibly dared, continuing to look as dejected and desperate as was physically and mentally possible. There was a long, long pause and then…one of the officials beckoned me forward. With hardly a cursory glance in my direction, he held out a hand. I tried to stifle a smile, feeling rather pleased and smug with myself that I'd actually pulled it off; that I'd beaten 'the system'; hoodwinked the officials. I then fished around in my wallet for a US$2 note. Well, it was, let's say…a tad disappointing when all I could find there was…a 'US$10' note. I looked up a little sheepishly at the customs officer, who continued to sit there totally unmoved, expressionless. Then I handed him the US$10 note, shrugged my shoulders and walked on through to the departure lounge...It seemed a touch optimistic to ask for change!

CHAPTER 23

- HOMEWARD BOUND -

Colombo to London

In Colombo the temperature had been over 100f with well over 90% humidity, and for my going home outfit I'd opted for: yellow T-shirt, white shorts and open-toe bumper boots; though, as I've said, this was mainly due to the fact that these were the only clothes I had left. It was therefore, rather a shock to arrive in England and step down from the plane at Gatwick Airport into torrential rain and a temperature barely hovering above freezing. Outside the airport building meanwhile, hundreds of stooped Lowry figures ran about in grey hats and grey Macs and scarves, barely pausing to frown at my summer apparel before leaping into an assortment of waiting vehicles.

I'd rung my mum as soon as I'd landed and so, by the time I'd collected my rucksack from the carousel and reached the pick-up point outside the airport, there was barely time for even a mild bout of hypothermia before a familiar car pulled up in front of me. Then, there were hugs and kisses, and kisses and hugs all round. It was so lovely to see my mum again and an even bigger bonus that my younger sister Candice was there to greet me too. (She'd been living away from the family house for several years but had now moved back in my absence due to severe marital problems.) We then sped off through the drizzly English winter and in less than an hour I was back in the warmth and familiarity of home

Back in Horsham, the package which I'd spent so long preparing to send whilst in Delhi had arrived. Somebody made the obligatory cup of tea and then I excitedly opened my estranged parcel and went through the contents of the package, whilst my family patiently endured the stories attached to each and every item. It had been a long time since I'd seen my Pakistani prayer mats and, as for all the colourful posters of various Hindu Gods, well, I could hardly wait to look at them again...before rolling them back up and putting them up in the loft, never to be seen again! Then, I pulled out the large handful of beautiful peacock feathers that I'd bought somewhere in Northern India. I carefully arranged them in a vase before putting them in pride of place on a shelf in the corner of the sitting room.

"You know they're supposed to be bad luck don't you?" my mum said.

I laughed. After all, like most mums, she believed in things like that: star signs, touching wood, not walking under ladders; that sort of thing. Just four weeks later, my little sister Candice was driving home late one night, fell asleep at the wheel and hit a tree. She was killed outright! The next day...I threw the peacock feathers away.

EPILOGUE

Do you know, I still don't believe in any of that old hocus-pocus, luck or fate stuff. In fact, rightly or wrongly, I've probably become even more of a sceptic, if that's possible. Well, it's hard not to be when, as you go through life, you begin to learn that much of what you read in newspapers is at best, educated guess-work and at worst, utter twaddle.

Anyway, if I'd been bitten by the travel bug before, then I was positively consumed by it now. When I'd first left on this adventure I had no idea what would happen, where I'd end up or for how long I'd be away. By the end of the journey though, I'd decided that this was most definitely the life for me. And so, my plan had been simply to return to England for three or four months, in order to earn a bit of cash, before continuing my fantastic journey around the world. However, Candice's death stopped me in my tracks; it would be a life changing experience and one which would force me to take stock. Obviously, for myself and my other two sisters Dawn and Sandra, our loss was an absolute tragedy; but for my mother well…it was very nearly unbearable! There was no way that I could even think of leaving her right now. She needed me like no time in our lives before.

If there was anything remotely good to come out of all this, then on a personal level, I did at least decide that whilst I was in England, I'd try to get a foot on the property ladder; and this, when it would've been all too easy to become a full-time travel-bum. And so, I shortly settled down, bought myself a house and got stuck back into work. Why, I even managed to convince my old girlfriend that it was a good idea to come back to me. In short, I was in grave danger of becoming half sensible; of leading a 'normal' existence. But, do you know, it was already too late…the seed had been sown and I knew it wouldn't be long before the pangs for travel returned; that constantly nagging, all consuming and addictive wanderlust; that newly acquired and chronic case of 'itchy feet'. Oh, I was reasonably happy at home alright, but there was something missing; something always tearing away at my insides; building, burning, raging within me. Was it that deep, deep passionate longing to see more of the world, or just a bout of flatulence? Well, after India…maybe it was a little of both!

THE END